# My ARSENAL Life

**Doubles, Invincibles, Glory and Despair**

LIVED AND REMEMBERED BY
## MARTIN WENGROW
WRITTEN BY DAVID FENSOME
Foreword by David O'Leary

First published by Pitch Publishing, 2025
1

Pitch Publishing
9 Donnington Park,
85 Birdham Road,
Chichester, West Sussex,
PO20 7AJ
www.pitchpublishing.co.uk
info@pitchpublishing.co.uk

© 2025, David Fensome

Every effort has been made to trace the copyright.
Any oversight will be rectified in future editions at the
earliest opportunity by the publisher.

All rights reserved. No part of this book may be reproduced,
sold or utilised in any form or transmitted in any form or by
any means, electronic or mechanical, including photocopying,
recording or by any information storage and retrieval system,
without prior permission in writing from the publisher.

A CIP catalogue record is available for this book
from the British Library.

ISBN 978 1 80150 938 1

Typesetting and origination by Pitch Publishing

Printed and bound on FSC® certified paper in line with
our continuing commitment to ethical business practices,
sustainability and the environment.

Printed and bound in India by Thomson Press

# Contents

Acknowledgements . . . . . . . . . . . . . . . . . . . . . . . . 8
Foreword . . . . . . . . . . . . . . . . . . . . . . . . . . . . . . . . 9
Prologue: . . . . . . . . . . . . . . . . . . . . . . . . . . . . . . . 12

**Part One:** Beginnings . . . . . . . . . . . . . . . . . . . . 15
1945–1952 . . . . . . . . . . . . . . . . . . . . . . . . . . . . . . 16
1953–1962 . . . . . . . . . . . . . . . . . . . . . . . . . . . . . . 21
1963–1966 . . . . . . . . . . . . . . . . . . . . . . . . . . . . . . 32

**Part Two:** Bertie Mee . . . . . . . . . . . . . . . . . . . . 43
1966/67 . . . . . . . . . . . . . . . . . . . . . . . . . . . . . . . . 44
1967/68 . . . . . . . . . . . . . . . . . . . . . . . . . . . . . . . . 51
1968/69 . . . . . . . . . . . . . . . . . . . . . . . . . . . . . . . . 54
1969/70 . . . . . . . . . . . . . . . . . . . . . . . . . . . . . . . . 59
1970/71 . . . . . . . . . . . . . . . . . . . . . . . . . . . . . . . . 64
1971/72 . . . . . . . . . . . . . . . . . . . . . . . . . . . . . . . . 76
1972–1975 . . . . . . . . . . . . . . . . . . . . . . . . . . . . . . 84
1975/76 . . . . . . . . . . . . . . . . . . . . . . . . . . . . . . . . 92

**Part Three:** Terry Neill & Don Howe . . . . . . . . 95
1976/77 . . . . . . . . . . . . . . . . . . . . . . . . . . . . . . . . 96
1977/78 . . . . . . . . . . . . . . . . . . . . . . . . . . . . . . . 103
1978/79 . . . . . . . . . . . . . . . . . . . . . . . . . . . . . . . 106
1979/80 . . . . . . . . . . . . . . . . . . . . . . . . . . . . . . . 114
1981–1986 . . . . . . . . . . . . . . . . . . . . . . . . . . . . . 122

**Part Four:** George Graham . . . . . . . . . . . . . . 133
1986/87 . . . . . . . . . . . . . . . . . . . . . . . . . . . . . . . 134
1987/88 . . . . . . . . . . . . . . . . . . . . . . . . . . . . . . . 139
1988/89: Part One . . . . . . . . . . . . . . . . . . . . . . . 143
1988/89: Part Two . . . . . . . . . . . . . . . . . . . . . . . 149
1989/90 . . . . . . . . . . . . . . . . . . . . . . . . . . . . . . . 157
1990/91 . . . . . . . . . . . . . . . . . . . . . . . . . . . . . . . 162

1991/92 . . . . . . . . . . . . . . . . . . . . . . . . . . . .168
1992/93 . . . . . . . . . . . . . . . . . . . . . . . . . . . .174
1993/94 . . . . . . . . . . . . . . . . . . . . . . . . . . . .185
1994/95 . . . . . . . . . . . . . . . . . . . . . . . . . . . .193

**Part Five:** Bruce Rioch . . . . . . . . . . . . . . . . . . .201
1995/96 . . . . . . . . . . . . . . . . . . . . . . . . . . . .202

**Part Six:** Arsène Wenger . . . . . . . . . . . . . . . . . . 209
1996/97 . . . . . . . . . . . . . . . . . . . . . . . . . . . .210
1997/98 . . . . . . . . . . . . . . . . . . . . . . . . . . . .216
1998–2001 . . . . . . . . . . . . . . . . . . . . . . . . . . .223
2001/02 . . . . . . . . . . . . . . . . . . . . . . . . . . . .236
2002/03 . . . . . . . . . . . . . . . . . . . . . . . . . . . .242
2003/04 . . . . . . . . . . . . . . . . . . . . . . . . . . . .245
2004/05 . . . . . . . . . . . . . . . . . . . . . . . . . . . .252
2005/06 . . . . . . . . . . . . . . . . . . . . . . . . . . . .259
2006–2009 . . . . . . . . . . . . . . . . . . . . . . . . . . .267
2009–2012 . . . . . . . . . . . . . . . . . . . . . . . . . . .273
2012–2014 . . . . . . . . . . . . . . . . . . . . . . . . . . .283
2014/15 . . . . . . . . . . . . . . . . . . . . . . . . . . . .290
2015–2017 . . . . . . . . . . . . . . . . . . . . . . . . . . .294
2017/18 . . . . . . . . . . . . . . . . . . . . . . . . . . . .302

**Part Seven:** Unai Emery . . . . . . . . . . . . . . . . . . .307
2018–2019 . . . . . . . . . . . . . . . . . . . . . . . . . . . 308

**Part Eight:** Mikel Arteta . . . . . . . . . . . . . . . . . .311
2019–2024 . . . . . . . . . . . . . . . . . . . . . . . . . . .312

Epilogue . . . . . . . . . . . . . . . . . . . . . . . . . . . .318

This book is dedicated to the memory of my late son

Danny Wengrow

23 September 1969 – 14 March 1975

What might have been?

# Acknowledgements

I WOULD like to thank Jane Camillin and everyone at Pitch Publishing for their support, enthusiasm and guidance from day one of this project. I would also like to give a special mention to Alex Daley and Duncan Olner.

It was an absolute thrill to be able to speak with Liam Brady and David O'Leary when I was researching Martin's story. Both gave me so much of their time and dealt with me with absolute courtesy and I cannot thank them enough – their hero status in my eyes was only enhanced by the time spent talking with them.

I would like to acknowledge the support and guidance I have received from my brother and sister, Matthew and Jane, over the years. They have always been positive and honest in their feedback on my writing. Thank you also to Asela Premachandra (Prem), Dave Day and Michael Cohen for their support, good humour and feedback in connection with this book – three wise football people.

Finally, thank you to Sarah for facilitating in so many ways the writing of this book. I genuinely couldn't have completed a project of this magnitude without your unending patience, love, encouragement and support.

**DF**

# Foreword

I FIRST came to know Martin when I saw him after games in the mid-70s in the players' lounge, where he had been a familiar face for some time. In those days, he was a big friend of men like Peter Storey and John Radford, plus a number of the other lads. I could see that the senior players were all happy to discuss the game with him and they clearly valued his opinions. I was just breaking into the first team and Martin quickly became a trusted friend to turn to as I encountered the usual hurdles of an aspiring young pro in the game.

When Pat Jennings joined us at Highbury, we immediately hit it off and, along with Martin, they are two of the friendships from back then which have most endured. The fact Martin was accepted and clearly trusted by older, established players meant I felt confident that I could talk freely with him with no fear of it going any further. Martin was clearly obsessed with the Gunners and you quickly learnt he had only Arsenal's best interests at heart.

As my career progressed, I shared many great moments in the club's history with him – Wembley finals, especially the 1979 and 1993 FA Cup Finals; and, of course, the greatest night in our history, Anfield 1989. I saw Martin in the crowd on our lap of honour; there we were, two old blokes crying like children, both completely understanding what the moment meant to the other.

Away from football, Martin became very close to my family and the two of us remain in constant touch. When I had a testimonial in 1993, I was grateful to Martin for his help and suggestions as a member of my testimonial committee.

Martin has witnessed at first hand for decades the Arsenal story on and off the pitch and it's important that all that knowledge and all those memories are captured, for he has seen Arsenal's highs and lows and followed the club while the game has been completely revolutionised since he first went to Highbury back in the 1950s.

I am very proud to hold the record for appearances in an Arsenal shirt and I think Martin must have come close to seeing very nearly all of them. We shared Arsenal's good times and bad times and we still share something else – a great love for this iconic old football club.

**David O'Leary**
**November 2024**

'The football fan is not just a watcher. His sweat and his nerves

work on football, and his spirit can be made rich or destitute by it.'

– **The Football Man**, *Arthur Hopcraft*

# Prologue:

SOME THINGS are with you for your entire life: memories and dreams which you carry around with you, deep in your pockets, like dust from the streets where you were born. If I look back far enough in time, there is just one thing: a small boy, staring back at me across the years, who set out in life to follow his dreams. Not, perhaps, that different to a thousand other small boys and, yet, these dreams all came true. He dreamt of Arsenal and Highbury and Saturday afternoons; of glory and of belonging to something bigger than himself. That small boy is me and this is the story of *my* Arsenal life.

If I go back to the start, then each year is remembered through the prism of Arsenal Football Club; through players, games, trophies and defeats – where the passing years are measured out in football matches. I've seen it all, lived it all, from the great European nights and domestic glories to some of the bleakest lows that tested friendships and, indeed, sometimes ended friendships. There are some things it has taken me a lifetime to understand.

I have been lucky enough to have known many of the great players who have worn the famous red and white shirt – and have been able to count some as close friends – but my love for the club is greater than for any individual. Through it all, my support for Arsenal has remained unyielding; it has always been Arsenal first and foremost, at times even above family. My love for this great football club bends before nothing and no one. For this is my club. It is a passion that follows only the bloodbuzz of my heart. It is a total obsession.

I first found Arsenal in the early 50s when almost everything was beginning to change. It was when we were being told we'd never had it so good and, when the brave new world began for Britain, there was still one reference point which remained largely steadfast against this backdrop of modernisation … Highbury! That beautiful corner of Islington where dreams were woven on a Saturday afternoon, a stadium which gave the club a mystique it has never really lost.

Back then, Highbury was still dressed in a livery of oak-panelled dignity, marble, mahogany and old leather; where the scent of fine malts and cigars still drifted down corridors of potted aspidistras, where power and authority were still worn lightly, assumed with an easy, nonchalant air by aristocrats of the realm and aristocrats of football. Arsenal were still the standard bearers for the game back then, albeit a game renewing itself tactically, financially and culturally. By the late 60s and early 70s, footballers were fast becoming superstars, the equivalent of contemporary showbusiness icons and pop idols; the club blazers, starched white collars and club ties were now worn with longer hair and lamb chop sideburns. Footballers were becoming part of the 'in crowd'. Even at Highbury, the winds of change were slowly, almost imperceptibly airing the deepest and darkest corners of the institution that is Arsenal, then the world's most famous and most successful football club.

I was just approaching adulthood when Bertie Mee took over from Billy Wright in the manager's hotseat at Highbury and before long I was rubbing shoulders with two generations of Arsenal footballers and some of them – like Frank McLintock, Peter Storey, John Radford and, later, David O'Leary – became very close friends. Those friendships have endured to this day. They took me to the heart of the club I love and gave me a very privileged insight into the life of Arsenal behind the scenes while I grew from being just another wide-eyed supporter to becoming perhaps one of Arsenal's best connected and most influential supporters.

In the late 60s, I watched my friends becoming Arsenal legends while the club became a powerhouse in English football once more. Beyond the inner circle of players, there were others who added different shades of colour and interest to this football world – the 'King of the Ticket Touts', Stan Flashman, football writers Harry Miller and Jeff Powell, the softly spoken and implausibly polite enforcer supreme from London's gangster underworld, Frankie Frazer, the football agent Jerome Anderson and, from the world of entertainment, Pete Murray and Bernie Winters, amongst others; and, from the authentic working class football culture, there was the great Arsenal 'rogue' Johnny Hoy, leader of Arsenal's 'firm', the top football terrace boys in London in the late 60s and early 70s.

It's been a long life and now is the time to empty my pockets of the dust that has collected there, of memories and recollections, of pictures of a world that has now largely disappeared, for this is partly a chronicle of a lost football landscape and a story that could never happen again for one simple reason – no ordinary supporter such as I could ever again get as close to their heroes as I got to mine.

This is Arsenal, inside and out – my Arsenal, the club I have loved all my life – from the wilderness years to now, via Doubles, 'Invincibles', glory and despair, with friendships which have lasted a lifetime; and, yet, Arsenal will outlive us all, it is a name that will endure as long as football is played – proud, defiant and certain of its worth.

# Part One: Beginnings

## Chapter One

# 1945–1952

I WAS brought up in London's East End; Hackney and then, later, Stoke Newington. I lived in a loving home where I enjoyed a complete sense of belonging but also in a home where an all-pervading sadness lingered. This sadness belonged mainly to my parents, who were Polish, Jewish refugees who had managed to flee the evil unfolding across Europe in the years leading up to the Second World War. They had found, in Britain, a welcome and a home where they could live a normal life of work, family and the uneventful hours of a wonderfully ordinary life. My parents had started to read and hear about the concentration camps and, when letters from family members left behind in Europe began gradually to dry up, inevitably a sinister implication began slowly to dawn on them.

I recall that some years later, when I was a young man, I was told by a cousin that, one day after the war, some people from the Red Cross had called and had imparted the information my parents had, perhaps almost daily, expected to hear; that all the members of their families, every single one, had perished in the Nazi concentration camps. That day, a wave of sadness descended and never really left our home. Perhaps the pursuit of glory with Arsenal has been a lifelong attempt to fill the void and the emptiness this unimaginable loss left in our home.

Consequently, we never talked about the war; nor did I ever hear mentioned the names of friends or relatives who were lost. My mum was especially sensitive to the concentration camps; if ever they were mentioned, she would just break down in tears. My parents mostly kept their feelings hidden; people did back then. After Mum had passed away, my dad opened up to me, but not about the war or the specifics of what preceded it, only about his own life growing up and the anti-Semitism they and other Jews encountered in Poland.

Like most children back then, my time was spent mostly out on the street, playing football and cricket with mates. On Sunday afternoons, my brother and I would always be the only ones left out kicking a ball around. I later realised that the simple explanation for this was that the other children were all going on Sunday afternoon visits to see grandparents or relatives – extended family my brother and I didn't have.

After the Second World War, Oswald Mosley and a ragtag of groups, all of them racist and anti-Semitic but now, perhaps, less publicly so, with the word 'alien' becoming the catch-all word used, began to concentrate their provocative efforts in the areas of London that I was brought up in. Mosley's provocations were beginning once again to precipitate trouble on the streets of London. There were rallies I recall on Ridley Road in Dalston, which would get broken up by groups of anti-fascists. By then black people were the main target; a message of 'anti-black' was thought more likely by Mosley's mob to gain some traction than a purely anti-Semitic message. It wasn't unusual to see messages like 'blacks out' daubed on the side of houses. It seems inconceivable to think this was happening while we kids still played amongst the bomb-damaged streets and houses, which were a very visible symbol of the recent fight against fascism. What my parents must have thought of Mosley's posters and boots while they were still psychologically laying their loved ones to rest can't even be imagined.

A vivid feature of winter life back then were the sulphurous fogs which shrouded the daylight hours, unhealthy weather which famously culminated in the Great Smog of 1952. Out of this veil of acrid, misty dampness we could hear the cries of the rag and bone man doing his rounds, the sound of his horse-drawn cart; and the daily milk cart, too, echoing down streets and through yards, drawing us momentarily away from our games of marbles, of conkers, the swapping of cigarette cards and the endless games of street football. In many ways, it was a wholly typical childhood for the time: but what made it untypical was how Arsenal loomed over it so totally, so comprehensively. As I look back, it feels strange that, of all the memories I can capture, almost every single one of them has Arsenal at the centre of it.

In 1951, I would have been five or six years old and by then I knew I was an Arsenal supporter. I recall that nearly all the boys in the street, including my brother, Jack, who was four years older than me, followed Arsenal and I suppose I must have initially simply followed suit. Arsenal had won the FA Cup in 1950, beating Liverpool 2-0. The cup final back then was such a huge deal; the FA Cup meant everything. To supporters, lifting the cup at Wembley was more important than winning the league title. I suspect that most players would have said the same; winning the league bestowed pride but winning the cup dressed you in glory.

On my first day at school, I can remember sitting and looking through a copy of *Charles Buchan's Football Annual*. In it, there was a photo of Arsenal's captain, Joe Mercer, holding aloft the FA Cup. That photo mesmerised me like a holy relic and every day, when I got the chance, I would go and take the same book down from the shelf and stare at that photo; it was like a proof that there was something special about Arsenal.

Northwold Road Primary School in Clapton was where I began my education, in 1951, and it was here that I would later prepare for my scholarship examination (later the 11-plus) for Grocer's Company Grammar School (later Hackney Downs School), by far and away the most prestigious school in the whole of the East End at the time. It was my parents' dream that I would get into the school. I was surrounded at Northwold by fellow students who would go on to leave a mark in a variety of spheres when they grew up: the entrepreneur Alan Sugar; the pop and jazz singer and actress Helen Shapiro; the psychedelic singer/songwriter Mark Bolan (Mark Feld in those days); and the businessman and, later politician, Michael Levy (The Lord Levy). I recall once having a fight with the latter, although I have no recollection of what it was about.

By the age of seven, I had read so much about Arsenal that I knew every bit of information on every single player at the club; I don't think there was anything I didn't know. By this time, I was going to Highbury to see Arsenal play. This was all accomplished on pocket money of half a crown. I recall that the bus fare to Finsbury Park was tuppence either way and admission to the ground was one shilling and nine pence. Programmes in those days cost six pence, which meant that my outing to see Arsenal cost the sum of one penny more than the value of my pocket money! As a consequence, I had to forego the programme and try to get one on the way home from an adult who, by then, might have finished reading it. It never crossed my mind to ask my dad for that extra penny, something I have no doubt he would have given me.

By the mid-1950s, I was a nine-year-old at Northwold Road Primary School. One day, the sports tutor, a Scottish gentleman by the name of Mr Burns, called me to one side and said: 'I've been watching you play football in the playground. Will you play for the school team tonight?' My first practical thought was that I had no boots but that was brushed aside with: 'Play in your school shoes.' So, I played and gave a good account of myself against Craven Park. I turned out at centre-forward and up against me that day was a young lad who already had a reputation in school football and developed into one of the toughest defenders of the 60s and 70s – Ronnie 'Chopper' Harris! I sometimes wonder what he must have thought of me, in my smart shoes!

Nineteen-fifty-two saw Arsenal back at Wembley for another FA Cup final, this time against Newcastle United. Although the 1952 FA Cup Final ended in defeat, it stands out as an illustration of what 'Arsenal' means and captures that wonderful, slightly mysterious quality that runs through this club, always has, and always will. A group of us listened to the match at a friend's house, huddled around their radio. Arsenal lost and by the end of the game, I think we only had two or three players still able to run and we had just tried to hang on. I was so hugely disappointed but proud of the never-say-die attitude of the team that day.

I have since learned that there is an honour and a glory to be found even in defeat. Nineteen-fifty-two reminds me of 1980 in a way, the heartbreak of having nothing tangible to show for the team's wonderful efforts; at one stage in 52, we were looking good for a Double but ended up empty handed.

Twelve months later, however, when I was aged seven, we claimed the league title by the smallest of statistical margins: 0.09 of a goal, with goal average being the slightly arcane manner in which things were settled back then. Arsenal's final game of the season, which we needed to win to finish top, was versus Burnley at Highbury on Friday, 1 May and, thankfully, we won 3-2. The next day was cup final day and not just any old cup final day; this was the year of the 'Stanley Matthews final' and the whole country wanted Stan to finally get his winner's medal.

That year saw my first visit to Highbury; 4 October 1952 was the day. Everyone remembers their first game: the approach to the ground as it emerges out of the streets of residential housing, the click of the turnstiles, the eager climb to the top of the stairs with a growing expectation and then that almost heart stopping moment when the pitch appears, revealing itself for the first time, spread out before you with two goals standing at either end, the teams confronting each other like opposing armies in that moment before they are given the order to charge. The smell is uniquely of a football ground. After that moment, you are never quite the same person again; you have crossed a threshold and entered a new and different world.

We were playing Blackpool, which meant Stanley Matthews, and the crowd was 67,000 – Matthews would put 10,000 on the gate at every ground he played. It was the noise which I remember most vividly; no 'Highbury library' about it in those days. The atmosphere was electric! I was instantly caught up in it, this vast cauldron of noise; the 'Highbury roar' it was known as. I recall the flat caps, rosettes and rattles. Wonderful! We won 3-1 and from that moment on, I simply couldn't get enough of it. I was completely hooked; nothing and no one would ever draw me away from Highbury. This was where I belonged.

There were further visits to Highbury that season: a 4-0 victory against Spurs – in front of a crowd of 70,000; 5-3 versus Liverpool; and a 4-1 success towards the end of the season against Bolton. Before the match with Bolton, I can remember hanging around on Avenell Road and I was approached by a very nice couple who, it turned out, had a spare season ticket and offered to take me in to watch the game with them. I must have been only seven or possibly eight and my first thought was 'I can save the admission money and have an extra two shillings to spend in the supporters' club shop after the game!' We all sat in the East Stand and the height of it made me feel quite giddy. I'd never been so high up. It was very kind of them; perhaps they often did that? I never thought to ask, just accepted my stroke of luck.

So, my first season of attending games had finished with us crowned as champions. It would be 17 years before Arsenal lifted another trophy and I would be a man when we won the Inter-Cities' Fairs Cup in 1970 on that emotional night at Highbury. By then, the Gunners had become so central in my life that they would push everything else – family and work – to the edges. A club later famously troubled by addictions, Arsenal would become my own all-consuming obsession.

## Chapter Two

# 1953–1962

IN 1953, when I was seven, we had a national celebration, one of the first non-Arsenal events to capture my imagination: the coronation of Queen Elizabeth II. Things were still pretty bleak in '53; the material side of life felt very much the same as the war years. Meat rationing was still in place and only in 1953 did things like children's sweets become non-rationed. The coronation was a welcome splash of colour in an otherwise monochrome world – well, at least it would have been if it hadn't rained all day, with the pageantry muted beneath leaden grey skies. The street parties were washed out, so the celebrations moved inside and centred round the television. People all over the country were saving to buy their first set, so events like the coronation really helped sell the idea of family TV to countless households.

At the age of eight or nine, I learnt one of those valuable, but uncomfortable lessons that life can teach us every once in a while. During the school holidays, I helped out Bill, our local milkman, to deliver bottles. Bill was a nice chap and I got the grand sum of six pence for a couple of hours work a day. One day, after running up the stairs to deliver some bottles to a flat, I noticed that there, on the front doorstep, was a shiny half-crown piece. As soon as I noticed it, something within me didn't feel right. I picked it up and popped it into my pocket. I knew it wasn't the right thing to do, so I have no defence. I was probably a bit sheepish when I got back to the cart and I certainly didn't mention it to Bill. It was on my mind for the days that followed and, of course, in the end, Bill tackled me about it. I was walking home from school for my dinner one day a week later and Bill was waiting for me on the corner of Osbaldeston Road, where I lived. As soon as I saw him, I knew. He asked me if I had taken it, a customer's money left for him to collect. I was totally ashamed of myself, humiliated and that was it for my job. I felt awful about it and I've never lost the taste of that experience. Bill did me a bit of a favour by tackling me and it became a lesson I didn't need to learn twice. I've never done anything like it again. Bill was a decent man and I let him down.

By the end of the 1953/54 season, I had become a regular at Highbury. It was also the season of my first away game. We made a poor start; in fact, we didn't even manage a goal until the fourth game and after ten games we stood at the foot of the table. On 10 October, I made the shortest of journeys for my first away game, travelling to White Hart Lane to take my place in a crowd just short of 70,000. That afternoon, Arsenal hit Spurs early and hard and by half-time were leading 4-0 through two goals from Logie, one from Milton and one from Joe Mercer's swashbuckling wing-half partner, Alex Forbes. Arsenal claimed the points with a 4-1 win.

There is a vivid football memory from that season, too; a sad affair involving one of football's gentlemen, Joe Mercer, who captained Arsenal to two league titles and an FA Cup during his time with us. On 10 April 1954, Liverpool journeyed down to Highbury for a match Arsenal won 3-0 as the season drifted towards the sort of benign conclusion that would soon become commonplace at Highbury. I think everyone in the 33,178 crowd would swear they heard the crack of the bone when Joe broke his leg; it rang out across Highbury like a death knell. There had been talk of Joe's retirement for years; he had his grocer's shop back in Wallasey. Colliding with a team-mate, Mercer sustained a double fracture of his leg. I can still picture him being stretchered off and before he left the field of play, he still managed, despite being in absolute agony, to raise his arm and quite clearly wave to all four sides of the ground in response to the standing ovation ringing around Highbury. He was 39 and must have known instantly that he'd never play again; we all realised that was the end. Joe had been a wonderful player, a decent man and a really fitting symbol of what Arsenal meant back then.

Despite a downturn in results and a growing sense of the end of an era, Arsenal remained a massive club; its reputation preceded it wherever football was played. It is interesting to note that as attendances at Highbury began to fall, Arsenal still attracted enormous crowds whenever they travelled; every year, some club would set a new record for their home attendance when the Gunners visited. Everyone still wanted to see Arsenal. Everything goes in cycles and, deep down, I feared that this was the end of the years when Arsenal dominated. Not only were Arsenal in decline, by the mid to late-50s, Wolverhampton Wanderers and Manchester United's 'Busby Babes' were just two of the teams moving upwards and away from Arsenal.

In the years after the war, there was a national sense of decline; Arsenal probably just illustrated that in microcosm. The country had the Suez Crisis, when perhaps a bloated idea of our national importance and power skewed our thinking. In lots of ways, Arsenal mimicked that. You could see it in how we viewed ourselves as a club; the board thought it didn't need to try too hard when we wanted to sign players and having Highbury as our home probably helped sustain this presumption of unending superiority. Players still wanted to come to Arsenal, certainly; the facilities and the history of the club helped to impress them but perhaps the board overplayed it and thought they really didn't need to offer any perks to get top players to sign. For a long time, the idea that it was a privilege to pull on the famous Arsenal shirt was thought to be enough. It certainly didn't do Arsenal any favours and to the players we were courting, we must have seemed arrogant; 'look, we are doing you a favour by signing you', had had its day as a recruiting slogan.

Arsenal's manager at the time, Tom Whittaker, in some ways illustrates the problems that confronted Arsenal, as the world changed into a different, modern place. Tom had been at Arsenal since 1919, first as a utility wing-half, then as a physiotherapist and then as manager. He had a vast array of abilities. He served in both world wars and was a man known to be loved by the players; he was a very popular figure. But, looking back, I think he had struggled with problems at Arsenal since the mid-1950s and this had taken its toll on his health. In the end, as results declined, I don't think the board knew what to do with this great servant of the club. One can't underestimate what he achieved as a manager – two league titles and an FA Cup – but, towards the end, he made some unquestionably poor signings and I think his judgment was starting to go. He cut a sorry figure and one who seemed to lack confidence; odd in a man who had achieved so much inside and outside football.

I was given a small insight into poor old Tom Whittaker once. My brother, some friends and I were outside the main entrance on Avenell

Road to collect some autographs when Tom came out of the car park in his big black car and promptly drove straight over the wheels of my brother's bicycle, which was lying on the ground. Tom stopped and got out of his car and seemed very upset about it. He wasn't cross or annoyed; in fact, he went the other way and was very apologetic. Almost immediately, he pulled out his wallet and offered my brother a crisp £5 note and said: 'I hope this will pay for the repairs.' The average weekly wage was £10 in those days! What I noticed about this little scene was just how shaky Whittaker seemed. He really didn't look well. He died fairly soon after, of a heart attack, in 1956. He was only 58 but that day, when I saw him close up, he looked much older. Towards the end of his reign, the club seemed in complete disarray. The board did try to address the football side of things but that was badly handled, too, and only resulted in Whittaker's nose being put out of joint. A dapper young coach called Alec Stock was appointed as first-team coach; he only lasted 53 days but Whittaker must have felt publicly undermined. If you were trying to be fair to the board, then you could say they were motivated to do the right thing with the appointment of Stock but just went about it the wrong way.

In 1954, both Arsenal and Tottenham were keen on signing Danny Blanchflower. Tottenham had tabled a bid and Arsenal let it be known that whatever Spurs bid, Arsenal would beat it. Blanchflower, in any event, had his heart set on joining Arsenal but began to worry when their bid didn't materialise. Time and again, Whittaker assured Blanchflower not to worry, that he would be joining the Gunners. But when nothing happened, Blanchflower started to lose confidence in what he was hearing from Whittaker. Eventually, he would sign at White Hart Lane for £30,000 and Arsenal would miss out on one of the shining lights in the British game.

A few years later, in March 1959, and with the now deceased Tom Whittaker replaced by Jack Crayston and then George Swindin, Arsenal were again chasing the sort of transfer target who might reignite the club's fortunes. Chelsea, Tottenham and Arsenal were all after the strapping Welsh international Mel Charles, brother of the legendary John Charles. Swindin, in the end, managed to convince Charles that Arsenal were the club for him. When Arsenal signed him from Swansea for £42,750, it was for a record fee between two British clubs. The fact that Charles's stint at Highbury fell so flat, plagued as he was by injuries, is only part of the story; the other part is probably one of the best illustrations of the law of unintended consequences. Once Spurs got wind of Charles's decision to sign for Arsenal, they immediately withdrew their bid and, as an alternative, went out and signed Dave Mackay from Hearts, who, along with Blanchflower, set in train the development of perhaps Tottenham's most successful ever team; two deals which so comprehensively changed the immediate futures of both clubs.

Towards the end of the 1955/56 season, Arsenal started to look a reasonable young team, with Groves, Herd and Bloomfield all beginning to flourish. We progressed to the quarter-finals of the cup after beating Charlton 2-0 at The Valley in front of 71,758 spectators. However, Birmingham City, the eventual losing finalists that year, beat us 3-1 at Highbury. After that, we went on a run of eight wins in the remaining 11 games and finished the season strongly in fifth place. There was a bit of optimism that summer and the following season, too, when we again finished fifth.

My parents weren't into sport and had no real interest in football but tolerated my obsession with all things Arsenal. Although we were Jewish, I suppose we might now be called 'cultural Jews', we certainly didn't practice the faith but we observed Jewish High Holidays and the intention, I am sure, was to be respectful of our roots. Given the experiences of my parents, that feeling of a rootedness in a culture and identifying with it perhaps took on a special significance to them. Inevitably, Arsenal and my Jewish upbringing had eventually to collide. On 15 September 1956, the Jewish Day of Atonement, or Yom Kippur, coincided with Arsenal versus Newcastle United at Highbury. My father made it clear where he expected my priorities, and my brother Jack's, to fall and, by way of emphasising this, he wouldn't give me my pocket money until after the game, knowing full well, given the chance, I would have headed to Highbury, N5. Jack didn't go to the game but I did. I don't think I ever really considered not going to Highbury that afternoon. I slipped out of home and when I got to the ground, I hung about at the Clock End, where I received the kind of providential benefit that, on reflection, my behaviour didn't really deserve; a gentleman in a flat cap offered to pay for me to get in. Once inside Highbury, I remember standing with him to watch the game and I got on with enjoying the match as best I could, given what I knew awaited me upon my return home. Arsenal lost 1-0, Bloomfield just failing to rescue a point at the death when he hit a post. With the game concluded, I had no choice but to return home and face the music. My mother was the first to see me and she said simply: 'You have behaved very badly and your dad has punished you.' And the punishment? At the side of my bed, in a group of shoe boxes, I kept a hoard of Arsenal programmes, home and away, and copies of *Gunflash*, the supporters' club publication. These had been lovingly collected over a long period of time and were taken out each evening by me and pored over; they represented the spoils of every last penny of pocket money. I was taken to the dustbin by my father and made to look at them, every single one of them ripped to pieces. I was only a boy and I cried for hours afterwards. It still feels, to this day, a very severe punishment; it remains a moment from my young life that I have carried with me through the years and I can vividly recall the sensation of cold emptiness that spread through me as I stood there looking at the torn pages. My parents' lives were hard ones and perhaps my actions were interpreted as a small desertion or belittlement of a culture and way of life they sought to defend and which brought them some comfort.

It wasn't until I was much older that I began to reflect and to see why it might have been that Arsenal meant so much to me. I am sure it goes back to the almost wholesale loss of my extended family. At a stroke, my history had been wiped out; a yawning chasm remained where all those people should have been and perhaps Arsenal filled that loss. Perhaps, too, as a young boy, my own sense of Jewishness simply hadn't taken hold of me. Needing something to belong to, something that bestowed upon me an identity and the membership of a community, I turned to Arsenal and Highbury and, luckily, found a place for myself there.

During the 1956/57 season, my brother, Jack, joined a youth club, the Victoria Club, and one week it was announced that Arsenal star Jimmy Bloomfield was going to begin a series of coaching sessions. Jimmy probably would only have picked up a couple of quid for his time but players back then were always on the lookout for a few extra quid. I wasn't old enough to join in the coaching sessions but I went to watch and the chance to see Bloomfield was enough for me. After the sessions, I would bend his ear with questions. I literally bombarded him and wouldn't shut up. Jimmy took it all with a wonderfully kind heart. I must have tested his patience – he certainly earnt his couple of quid.

To cap it all, Jack and I were invited by Jimmy to a game at Highbury – against Manchester City on 6 October. We turned up at 2pm sharp to collect the tickets from Jimmy himself. The seats we had been given were in an area of the ground known as The Paddock, located in the lower East Stand on the halfway line and the game turned out to be a ten-goal extravaganza, with Arsenal winning 7-3; Holton playing at centre-forward scored four and Bloomfield got one, too.

That season, I completed another Arsenal rite of passage – I joined the supporters' club, with a membership number of 22351. Another bond with my destiny secured.

The progress of the two previous seasons felt like it stalled in 1957/58 and there was another humiliating third-round cup exit, too, this time at the hands of Northampton Town of the old Third Division (South), 3-1.

Only a few weeks after that cup defeat, Arsenal entertained Manchester United. A huge crowd that day of nearly 64,000 caused the gates to be closed by 2pm and they witnessed a fantastic and memorable game of football. United, the reigning champions, swept into a commanding three-goal lead but early in the second half, Arsenal struck back with a magnificent passage of play when they drew level with United at 3-3 in the space of four frenetic minutes. Although United would go on to win the game 5-4, Arsenal took much encouragement from their performance. It was a fantastic game and for years after it was referred to as 'the greatest-ever game'.

The events which followed a few days after the match have immortalised that afternoon: the Munich air disaster. The game at Highbury remains a very fitting epitaph for the 'Busby Babes'. One newspaper report stated that there had been a whiff of the good old days about it; it had been such a tremendous occasion and I remember the sides leaving the pitch arm in arm – it had just been one of those matches. While the disaster was very much Manchester United's private grief, it was also the wider game's loss – to a degree, we all felt it. The 'Babes' were a brilliant team. At least that afternoon at Highbury can stand as a very fitting memorial to the lives lost in Munich.

I generally had the happy knack of making my parents proud. After the Grocer's scholarship, and a sudden and unexpected move to Ilford,

I put in a very sound performance in 1958 during my bar mitzvah, the traditional Jewish coming of age for a boy on their 13th birthday. It requires an aptitude for Hebrew and I found this aspect of the process quite difficult but, after much perseverance, I got there and gave a good account of myself at the Beehive Lane Synagogue, much to my parents' obvious pride. Perhaps this was one small payback to my father for disobeying him when I chose Highbury over joining him in our family observance of Yom Kippur! These sorts of rites of passage in Jewish culture are usually accompanied by a big and happy family gathering but, because of our family circumstances, there was no large family to help me celebrate. I was the only boy in my Hebrew classes who didn't have a party. If I am honest, this didn't overly bother me but I confess to being a bit sore at missing out on the presents!

I settled at my new school and I really began to enjoy my developing social life in Ilford. Through my older brother, Jack, I began to meet a lot of boys and girls of a similar age. Around this time, Jack became friendly with a lad called Michael Tabor, who, after a classic rags to riches story, went on to be become the famous and successful racehorse owner, whose successes included The Derby, the 2,000 Guineas and the Prix de l'Arc de Triomphe amongst many other victories as a part owner. Michael was a West Ham United fanatic; in fact, he tried to buy the Hammers in 1996. Michael invited Jack and me to accompany him to the Boleyn Ground over the Christmas period of 1957. West Ham were fighting for promotion from the old Second Division and were, in fact, promoted as champions that season. The Boleyn Ground had a very different feel to Highbury; more compact, more enclosed, with a more immediately partisan atmosphere to it, which, if I am honest, made a real impression on me – I was quite in awe of it. The whole crowd joined in with 'I'm Forever Blowing Bubbles' and the supporters on the terraces would sway in unison. It was the first time I had witnessed the famous Chicken Run terrace, from which visiting wingers were prone to copping some good old East End abuse. I used to love how different grounds had their own little traditions, something which was lost over the years as grounds were redeveloped and, later, some were replaced altogether by new, largely out-of-town, edifices of metal and concrete – the rush to modernity seemed to wipe the slate clean of some aspects of the game's history and culture. West Ham won that day 6-1 against Bristol Rovers and it felt like the crowd just never stood still all afternoon!

There was a massive upswing the following season, 1958/59, and it's not going too far to say we could have won the league; in fact, if it hadn't been for a run of injuries to key players, we probably would have done. One of those injuries was to Scottish international Jackie Henderson, who we signed from Wolves. Tommy Docherty joined us, too. We were starting to look a decent team at last; everyone had settled in and things were looking good as we went top in mid-September after winning a north London derby at Highbury. We remained top or thereabouts up until the end of February but, when the injuries hit, things began to fall away. Some of the football we played that season was the best for years. Bloomfield was really hitting his stride by then but I think a lot of it can be put down to a young coach we had: Ron Greenwood.

We had style and a bit of panache to our football that I am sure Ron was responsible for. The players obviously bought into it and there were some great results and performances that season. Greenwood, who combined his Arsenal duties with coaching the England under-23s, was one of a small group of young coaches who were revolutionising the approach to tactics in English football. He had studied continental coaching methods and managed to introduce many of the ideas he discovered into the English game. He was well liked by the Football Association from these early days and, after a successful spell at West Ham as manager and then general manager, he succeeded Don Revie as England's permanent boss.

Greenwood, though, was a central player in another bad mess-up by the club in the 1959/60 season, although in no way could the blame be laid at his feet. That season saw us fall back into mid-table obscurity, while another massive misjudgment by the club resulted in us missing out on the most keenly sought-after young footballer in Britain. After all the messing around which eventually undermined the attempted signing of Blanchflower, you would have thought the club would have been careful not to make the same mistake again but perhaps that old, 'it's a privilege to play for Arsenal' sentiment still lingered.

Everyone agreed that Huddersfield Town, managed by Bill Shankly, had a prodigy on their hands. Denis Law had had four successful years with the Terriers and I remember seeing a headline in the papers: 'Denis Law: I want to join Arsenal.' Arsenal boss George Swindin had effectively sealed the deal, helped by skipper Tommy Docherty, who had privately brought the young Law to Highbury and shown him round, allowing him to experience the atmosphere and the aura of the place. Law was smitten and all it needed was for him to sign on the dotted line. I went to bed that night very excited at the arrival of one of the game's genuine rising stars, someone who, at a stroke, was going to put 10,000 on each gate and raise the club's spirits again. I came down the following morning to find that Law had signed for Manchester City for a new record transfer fee between British clubs of around £55,000. What I later learned had transpired was this: Swindin, believing the hard work had been done and that Law had, in effect, been secured, sent his coach, Greenwood, to conclude the formalities. Law was perhaps put out – annoyed even – by what he might have interpreted as him being taken for granted. He promptly turned down Arsenal and signed for Manchester City instead – perhaps with some additional incentives? I do think Swindin should have gone to complete the deal in person. It would have been a really significant signing; it would have certainly helped lift the gloom over the next couple of seasons, especially as Tottenham were soon to do the Double.

One day, out of the blue, my parents told me that, because they hadn't really settled in Ilford, we were moving again, this time to Whetstone in north London. 'Great,' I thought; I'd not even heard of Whetstone. This was in 1960, we had only been in Ilford for three years and, at the formative age of 14, I found it all pretty unsettling. However, Whetstone offered a leafier lifestyle than I had been used to and one even bigger bonus: my new school, Tollington Grammar, in Muswell Hill was co-educational! This was definitely an improvement. My first day there turned out to be a good one. Walking into the classroom as a new boy, there right in front of me was a group of lads exchanging Arsenal programmes – it was an absolute blessing, as the lads, every one of them, welcomed me as a fellow Arsenal supporter. I immediately felt at home.

My first P.E. lesson was an eye-opener – the goals had nets! I really enjoyed my football at Tollington. We had a pretty strong side and while I was there, I represented Middlesex Schools a couple of times – perhaps the pinnacle of my own football career.

In late 1961, Arsenal hit some great form, beating title challengers Burnley away 2-0 and they followed that up with a thrilling 2-1 victory over the Spurs side that had recently won the Double and which now had Jimmy Greaves in its ranks. So, when we drew Manchester United away in the fourth round of the FA Cup at Old Trafford, we travelled up full of confidence. I arranged to go to the game with my very good friend at Tollington Grammar, David Stubbles, and we were to travel up with the Arsenal supporters' club. I was 15 years old and this was my first visit to Manchester; I was incredibly excited.

We gathered at Highbury Corner at around seven on the Friday evening and the coach travelled overnight up the A1 (this was before the M1 was opened). When we arrived early on the Saturday morning, it was like arriving on a different planet. Rows of little terraced houses and narrow streets; the locals with their strong Mancunian accents with that strange nasal resonance. *Coronation Street* was just becoming the most popular programme on TV and, for us, it felt like we were in the Rovers Return.

The Arsenal fans gathered in their thousands behind the away goal and were raucously awaiting the kick-off. Then, half an hour before the start, and out of nowhere, we watched in horror as a fog descended from the Old Trafford Station and completely enveloped the ground. The kick-off was delayed for an hour but the fog only grew thicker before the match was called off. Talk about disappointment! I was absolutely convinced that we were going to win this tie and my disappointment was compounded when we lost the rearranged midweek fixture which, of course, I couldn't attend, by one goal to nil.

## Chapter Three

# 1963–1966

THE SOCIAL life around Muswell Hill at this time was amazing; this was the 'Swinging 60s'. I rubbed shoulders with some famous faces of the future in the coffee bars on The Broadway, such as Rod Stewart and the band The Kinks. Raymond and Dave Davies were both big Arsenal supporters but it was their bass player, Peter Quaife, who had absolutely no interest in football, who became my biggest friend of the three.

In 1963, at the age of 17, I began to mature politically. The hard-right was beginning to make itself felt again across London, with cries of hatred which echoed down streets where Jewish families, my friends and neighbours, lived. This was seen in singular acts of hatred perpetrated against my Jewish community, in persistent attacks upon synagogues and Jewish houses, in public rallies, which were becoming more outspoken and more daring, and in the widespread dissemination of anti-Semitic rhetoric, literature and propaganda. I was a young man and I felt it was right to stand against this hatred directed towards me and my community.

Coming home from the Second World War, Jewish servicemen – soldiers decorated for their public bravery in defence of a freedom from tyranny, oppression and hatred – soon once again found themselves, as Jews, the target of the hard-right in Britain, a political 'perspective' which had survived the war but which had done so by enduring underground. Within months of the end of the war, British fascists were again openly meeting in rallies and three pro-fascist book shops had opened in London alone. The situation gave rise to the forming of the 43 Committee, which represented the number of people who had attended the first meeting. Men such as Julius Konopinski, an ex-commando who, so ironically, had fought for a peaceful future for the people now abusing and attacking him and the community he came from, were typical of the kind of person getting involved. Their courage and bravery prevailed once again and the scourge of anti-Semitism began to dissipate and retreat.

The re-emergence of the far-right in the 60s prompted the rekindling of this spirit of resistance, which became manifest in the new 62 Committee, which emerged out of the ashes of the 43 Committee. There was a rally at Trafalgar Square in the summer of 1962, organised by the National Socialist Movement, under the banner of 'Free Britain from Jewish Control', which perhaps turned out to be a good recruiting exercise for the 62 Group – the need for resistance was made clear and put out there, in the open.

Most of the founder members were Jewish ex-servicemen, although there was also a sizeable group of non-Jewish members, too. The new force became known as the 62 Group and, as a 17-year-old, well-built and fit, I was asked if I would think about joining this clandestine organisation. My friend, David Sharr, got a job working for a bookmaker called Cyril Paskin, who by 1963 was a leading figure in this new resistance group; it would be more accurate to describe him as a 'field leader'. With my family history, a background riddled with suffering at the hands of hateful ideologies, I was known for my feelings towards fascists and neo-Nazis. David asked if I would like to be introduced to Cyril and a meeting went ahead. During it, my age was referenced in the context of what would be expected of me should I join their ranks; I would have to be prepared for violent encounters if I wanted to join.

Our main task was to break up public meetings and heckle. Initially, this was aimed at the likes of Mosley, who by then was getting on a bit in years. Then, a new wave of emerging neo-Nazis began to make itself felt. These new agitators were even more hard line than Mosley, who they disparaged as the 'Kosher Fascist' for not being rigorous and tough enough in his attacks on Jewish people. We also tried to drive the people peddling their publications off the streets.

Over the years, there were numerous incidents but, thankfully, I never got badly hurt. I gave eight years of loyal service to this cause and I made lifelong friendships along the way. Until he recently passed away, I used to see Julius and his partner, Valerie, regularly, latterly in his care home, and to this day I remain fiercely loyal to all the people who stood up to be counted back then.

Arsenal were in danger of becoming something of an anomaly, a gentleman's club in an altogether more meritocratic age. In our dealings with the outside world, we were perhaps too cocksure of ourselves, still too proud of what we once were, which blinded us to the way in which we fitted in with a society that was changing. Arsenal remained essentially a pre-war football club, in both outlook and ideology, as the 'Swinging 60s' began. We were in a mess, not sure of what direction to take, and players were starting to prove reluctant to sign for us.

The club said they wouldn't be offering George Swindin a new contract and he left at the end of the 1961/62 season. Swindin had a good first season and also was responsible for bringing in players like Tommy Docherty and George Eastham but it always felt that things weren't far from going belly-up. A fair description of the team would be this: great going forward but just can't defend.

At this time, I became great friends with a young lad called Vince, a massive Arsenal fan. Vince lived quite close to me and turned out to be the son of Joy Beverley, of Beverley Sisters fame. Joy had married Billy Wright, which made Vince Billy's stepson and, in 1962, Billy Wright became Arsenal manager.

I first spoke to Vince one afternoon, coming home from school, on the 134 bus from Muswell Hill. England had played an international earlier that day and Vince had a newspaper. So, asking him if he knew the score, we got chatting and discovered we had this strong interest in football. We became firm friends and remain so to this day; I was best man at Vince's wedding. Vince has always been very upright and proper; he never once said a word to me about his stepdad becoming Arsenal boss until it broke officially in the news.

When I did finally meet Billy at the family home in Barnet, he was very nice, very kind. He was a gentleman. I remember him showing me his cabinet with all his England caps in but he was very modest about it. After Stanley Matthews, Billy was English football's most famous player. He'd had a great playing career but when he came to Arsenal, he came as almost a complete beginner. After he retired from playing, the Football Association had asked him to look after the under-23 team and also some of the youth teams but he had never managed personalities in a dressing room before. Billy had captained England and his style was famously undemonstrative: 'I decided early on that captaincy is the art of leadership, not dictatorship. Respect is the hardest thing for a captain to come by and the easiest to lose. I never changed my mind about this.' It was a style he took with him into management and, perhaps, was one that didn't always serve him well. When he was appointed at Highbury, he totally bought into the history and reputation of the club and I think he quickly became very frustrated that some of the players under him really didn't appreciate what it meant to play for Arsenal.

Billy certainly had an impressive profile within the game and, culturally, Billy and Joy Beverley were a bit like the Posh and Becks of their day. I think the board hoped that Billy's appointment might help modernise the image of the club.

He quickly raised everyone's spirits when he signed Joe Baker. Wright had played against a 17-year-old Baker in a friendly between Wolves and Hibs and the memory of it convinced him Joe was worth every penny of the club record fee of £70,000. For almost every one of my generation, Joe was a great hero and almost a brother to us in a really difficult time. He had a charisma and an aura about him that the supporters just loved. He scored 93 goals in only 144 games and in today's transfer market, he would easily be worth £100m. He was relatively small in stature for a centre-forward but opponents knew not to take liberties with him; he famously once laid out Liverpool's much bigger and wider Ron Yeats and became a hero overnight. He was Roy of the Rovers for my generation. Eastham might have been the better player technically but Baker was the talisman of the side. He was always my personal hero and remains for me amongst the greatest players to have played for Arsenal. His time at Highbury was largely wasted though; the team just wasn't good enough. He was part of a brilliant attack alongside players including Eastham, Geoff Strong, Alan Skirton and a young 'Geordie' Armstrong but defensively we were poor; we could score four but concede five. Eastham once reflected that the team, with a better defence, would have been challenging for the title.

Billy never really got going at Arsenal. I think, in the end, he was just too decent and couldn't cope with the criticism; he took it all so personally and maybe his playing career just hadn't prepared him for some of the rough treatment he received, especially from the press, having been so feted as a player.

During this period, 1963 to 1964, I left home and moved in with a friend of mine called Graham Crump. Graham's mum had a large house in Hornsey, where she rented out rooms. I must say that she was very kind to me and charged only £1 per week for sharing with Graham. In order to pay my way, I quickly found employment with Hornsey Borough Council for £7 ten shillings per week, which to me in those days seemed like an absolute fortune. It was hard manual work, mixing cement and then carrying it up to the brickies, but in the chilly winter air it was welcome physical exertion. The brickies also introduced me to the wonders of the English breakfast! A waggon would collect me at the top of the road at 7.30am sharp and then we would go to a café, where everyone would tuck in liberally. The job lasted around six months and, as winter slowly turned to spring, I recognised I wanted to get away and try something different.

That new job turned out to be based in Clacton-on-Sea, Essex, and was just about the best job at a Butlin's holiday camp, namely that of plain-clothed security officer. This was where my grammar school education came in handy – that and my height and build – as the position required the writing of a report following any incidents which occurred on the camp, of which there were many! I would have to say that more of the reports were written about incidents involving my fellow workers than they were about the guests. The job was a great experience and I was kept busy every day. Quite a few of the staff came from cities like Belfast or Glasgow and I knew some of them to be on the run from the police. They were all great company, though; that was until they had had a drink.

In 1963, at the age of only 21, Jack, my brother was diagnosed with multiple sclerosis. None of us knew what MS was at that time. It was absolutely heartbreaking for all of us as we began to learn about this cruel condition. It had begun when Jack first had problems with his vision and it developed from there. He was such a popular guy and had many, many friends (to this day, when I meet people who had known Jack, they all have such positive things to say about him, not least how handsome he was! It is a small comfort to know the memory which outlived him is such a good and positive one).

In 1964, I was 18 and had moved back home to the family in Whetstone. At the time, the economy was booming and jobs were easy to come by – open up the *Evening Standard* and run your finger down the situations vacant section, make a couple phone calls and you were usually fixed up easily enough. Over the next three years, I largely drifted in and out of various office jobs, never really putting down any roots. I had my beloved Arsenal and that was really all that mattered at the time. When jobs are easy to come by, it can, perhaps, give you an air of complacency about security; it's something you can always sort out next year. I always had enough money in my pocket to go to games, home and away. In those days, there was only a small group of just a few hundred hardcore souls following the Gunners away from home and when you are down to those sorts of numbers, somehow it becomes even more intense. It is easy to become obsessed when your team are winning every week but something strange happens when you've no chance of seeing your team become successful, challenge even. What drives you on? Arsenal brought me the most intense mood swings and, consequently, it became the same for those people, family and friends around me, too; those 90 minutes on a Saturday afternoon set the tone and mood for the whole weekend, perhaps longer, until the next game.

In some ways, it was a subsistence existence, but then a piece of sound judgment on my part, or good luck, call it what you want, resulted in a massive financial boost. It was a Saturday morning and I was meeting up with a Tottenham-supporting friend, a close friend called Brian Sylvester, and I was on my way with him to White Hart Lane, as Arsenal had been knocked out the cup and weren't playing that day. There was a betting shop in Whetstone, Hector Macdonald, which we had to walk by. I had £6 in the world until next pay day but, holding back six shillings for the admission to the game and various fares, I decided to invest the remaining £5 14 shillings on a complicated bet known as a 'Heinz' due to it consisting of 57 different accumulated bets of one shilling each way on a selection of six horses. We hung around in the betting shop for the first two races and enjoyed a decent start as both horses came in. Quickly making our way to the ground, we called into a bookie's on Tottenham High Road, where we followed the next two races – and both of them came in, too. Four races in and I already had a decent winning bet but, as it was close to kick-off, we left and went into the ground, making our way to my friend's usual spot on The Shelf. Fortunately, one of the guys around us had a transistor radio and. as the match kicked off, my bet was causing as much interest in the crowd around us as the football and when the result of the 3.15pm came in, it was another winner! I was well and truly in the money now, with just one race left, the 3.30pm. Now, literally everyone was crowded round the radio to hear if I could pull off my bet. It is a truism of life that while we might begrudge others their successes, if it involves getting money out of a bookmaker, it generally gets everyone's support. Then, as we listened to the final race, Tottenham went and bloody scored and the cheering drowned out the radio as the result drifted out of it and away into the sky along with the goal celebrations. It was all too much for me. So, leaving the ground, I headed straight back to the bookie's on the High Road and belting straight in, I took one look at the blackboard where the name of my selection had been chalked up as the winner. I'd done it, pulled of my bet, and for me, then, it was life-changing. The winnings totalled nearly £700. To put that into perspective, the same payout in 2023 would be more than £18,000. In 1964, it would buy you a brand new Mini with a nice little sum left over. I managed to get to Hector Macdonald's before it closed but, not surprisingly, they didn't have enough money on site, so we arranged for me to pick it up on Monday morning. In the meantime, I took my friends out that evening for a slap-up meal at The Golden Egg on Oxford Street.

I duly returned on the Monday morning to pick up my winnings and I was met by the manager. He knew I always used the *Daily Mirror* to study form; so, trying to make the best of a bad job for himself, he asked if he could contact the *Daily Mirror* to see if they would be interested in the story and get a bit of publicity for his bookie's, too. That was fine with me. So, the next morning I was off to the newspaper's offices in Holborn, where I was interviewed and had a photo shoot, both of which resulted in a big feature article in the following day's paper and I received a further £100 for my troubles!

So, with just short of £800 burning a hole in my pocket, I returned to the daily round of office jobs, of which there were quite a few. None of them had any great prospects but they suited me at the time and they provided me with enough money to do what I wanted to do, too. This mainly meant following Arsenal and going out with the various young women I worked alongside! Back in those days, women usually had very little or no interest in football but the one's I used to see, and there were two I had more serious relationships with, both lovely young women, were quickly made aware of Arsenal and the Gunners' importance to me and my life.

One of my jobs provided me with some eye-opening life education. For a while, I was employed at the world famous Liberty store on Regent Street. Although I wasn't aware of it when I started there, a very high proportion of men working at the London store were gay and, so, I felt it prudent to establish right from the start that I was definitely heterosexual. I met some absolutely smashing guys there and the stuff they told me could be both sobering and amusing. I learnt a lot about their community, the need for secrecy and caution and how generally they went about their lives, with secret signs and code words. Homosexuality wasn't decriminalised in the UK until 1967 although in the years leading up to then, perceptions might have been very slowly changing for the better. However, to some people, the bullies and the less enlightened, the gay community was still a target for their ignorance and physical hatred. It couldn't have been easy at all to lead a life when you were always feeling you had to live in dark corners and act clandestinely. But they regaled me of some great stories and some of the antics of leading film stars and actors of the period were especially eye-opening. It was a daily education to be beneath the roof of that store.

In the spring of 1964, during another disappointing season for Arsenal, I was out early one morning to catch a bus when I bumped into Billy Wright at one of the old milk vending machines. By then, Billy knew me very well and he shared with me what felt like absolutely sensational news. He said: 'I'm sorry it's been such a difficult season but I have got some good news. We are going to sign three players: Don Howe, Frank McLintock and Gordon Banks.' I couldn't believe my ears! I was off to play football that morning; the team were a mixture of Arsenal and Tottenham supporters and I couldn't wait to tell them.

In truth, Don Howe, although only around 29 when he signed, was already losing mobility; he could knock a good pass but he had no pace. Frank McLintock suffered when he first arrived, too keen, perhaps, to make his mark; he was a man very much in a hurry. He had played with better players at Leicester City under Matt Gillies – in a better team, too – and looked a bit lost when he first arrived at Arsenal. He was so competitive, though it worked against him at times; you would see him chasing the ball all over the park and, of course, he would end up out of position.

The proposed signing of Gordon Banks actually turned out to be a good illustration of the temperamental difficulties which held Billy back. Banks was keen to leave Leicester, believing he was worth a rise in his weekly pay, and Wright made it clear to the goalkeeper that Arsenal wanted him. What developed was quite similar to how Whittaker had dealt with Danny Blanchflower; the initial assurances started to sound thinner and Banks was left feeling that he needed to telephone Billy every couple of days to check all was well. Billy kept assuring him everything was okay and it just needed some more time but eventually Banks had to be told the transfer wasn't going to happen and here's the thing; Billy didn't have the heart to tell Banks straight, he asked his wife to tell him that there wasn't going to be a transfer. A very nice man, but temperamentally just not suited. Once the chips were down, he had no safety net, no Arsenal pedigree and no club coaching or management credentials. Vince and I never talked about Billy; it must have been very hard to see his stepdad managing a struggling Arsenal.

Billy does, however, deserve much credit for some of the younger players he developed – Sammels, Radford, Armstrong, Storey, Simpson ... the list goes on. So, we have to say that Billy had a great bearing on the successes of 1970 and 1971; those trophies were won with players Wright developed. But that doesn't detract from the many disappointments under him.

Billy left in the summer of 1966 and turned his hand to broadcasting. It was a sad ending, really, for someone who had been an Arsenal fanatic as a child. Turning around Arsenal's fortunes was a big job and Billy, being so sensitive to criticism, probably found the whole experience excruciating at times. It had been a bold choice to appoint him and, ultimately, a gamble too far.

In 1965, my brother, Jack, got married and the wedding function was held at a hotel in Kensington. During the evening, I had popped over to the De Vere Club, where a friend was having a 21st birthday party, and when I got there, out of nowhere, this very attractive girl appeared.

A couple of weeks later, I was in a coffee bar in Wigmore Street with friends, a place we often went to, usually after leaving a club on a Saturday night, when I spotted this same girl again. She was talking to someone I knew, so I had the ideal opportunity to go over and introduce myself. Her name was Judith and she was beautiful. She had been born in Palestine, prior to the establishment of Israel, to Austrian parents who had left their homeland in the 1930s as the situation there had grown more dangerous and unpredictable. Her parents had returned in 1952 to Austria, where Judy had trained to become a hairdresser. Her elder sister, Hanna, had, meanwhile, come to live in London and, with Judy not being especially happy in Vienna, Hanna invited her sister to come and live with her in her flat in Muswell Hill.

After chatting for a while, my friend and I duly arranged to meet up with Judy and her friend as a foursome on the evening of the 1966 World Cup Final.

I had always intended to go to the final and now that England were playing, it seemed all the more reason. Vince, Billy Wright's stepson, contacted me to say the FA had been in touch with his stepdad and there was a ticket for the final for me if I wanted it! Vince confirmed there would be a car, provided by the FA, to collect me at 1pm from my home in Whetstone. The car duly arrived and I was very impressed to see it was a beautiful, large, black limousine. The next surprise came when I got into the vehicle: once inside, there in all their glory were Vince's mum, Joy, and her twin sisters, dressed in identical outfits ... the Beverley Sisters!

I was pleased to think that, in its moment of joy and national celebration, the FA had remembered Billy Wright and his 105 England caps. A few weeks earlier, Arsenal and Wright had parted company, his time as manager of the club a failure. That his reputation as a great English football man, and no less a decent man, lived on in the corridors of power at Lancaster Gate must have bucked him up – a man who, for all his charm and sociability, was sensitive and ultimately, perhaps, unsure of his own worth and abilities.

Later that evening, after England's victory over West Germany, my friend, Brian, and I met up with Judy and her friend and we all went for a meal at London Airport. The four of us then drove to Kensington to the hotel the England team were staying at. The West End was bedlam that night, thousands and thousands of people celebrating England's victory.

The evening was a great success and Judy and I began seeing each other. Her sister, Hanna, was now married and we spent a lot of time at the flat where Hanna and her husband, David, lived, babysitting their children, Jeanette and Tania, most Saturday evenings. I got to know Hanna and David very well and we all really hit it off. David was also a massive Arsenal supporter, so we had much in common. Very quickly, things felt right and I really began to look forward to the future with Judy. If only Arsenal could sort themselves out.

By 1966, the club felt like a mere shell of its once former all-powerful self; it was almost becoming a misery following Arsenal and, yet, I always wanted to be there, always wanted to go. I was there the night we lost 3-0 at home to Leeds United in the penultimate match of Wright's reign, on a night of torrential showers, along with just 4,554 Highbury devotees. The result, the performance and the attendance all added up to a comprehensive indictment of where we were as a club.

The great Arsenal of Chapman, Allison and Whittaker loomed up over us, forever forcing unflattering comparisons for the pale mediocrity we had become. It was now something so blatantly undeniable to me, yet there was still nothing that came anywhere near to being as important to *me* as Arsenal Football Club. I have to admit that sometimes I sincerely doubted the same could be said of the board – they remained *custodians*, but never *supporters*. You expected, or at least wanted, them to feel the same passion for the club as you did, following the team everywhere.

In spite of all the evidence to the contrary, there was still an undeniable social cachet about Arsenal. In 1968, Arthur Hopcraft published a book, which has become recognised as a masterpiece, *The Football Man*. In it, he dissects the relationship between football and society. One focus of analysis in the book is upon the role of the director and he compares Arsenal's chairman, the urbane and Eton-educated Denis Hill-Wood to a young Ken Bates, whom Hopcraft sees as an example of the new class of business tycoon, the 'man in a hurry', beginning to emerge in football boardrooms. Hopcraft references the number of knights and lords of the realm on Arsenal's board and suggests that the club has never lacked for gentry at the top. So, perhaps the board existed too much in their own little bubble, adrift of the changing times and a little too sure of the status the Arsenal boardroom gave them, regardless of what happened out on the pitch on a Saturday afternoon. In short, perhaps they weren't really that bothered.

# Part Two:
# Bertie Mee

## Chapter Four

# 1966/67

WHEN BERTIE Mee came in, initially as the interim manager, he was, despite having an old fashioned profile, actually quite forward thinking. Mee's strengths lay in areas where Billy Wright was weak; for one, he was a brilliant administrator and delegator. When Bertie, the 'bucket and sponge man' was appointed, I was underwhelmed but it quickly began to look like he knew what he was doing and he knew what needed to be done. He cleverly recognised his own limitations, so had the good sense to make brilliant appointments in the coaching department and, within a short space of time, Arsenal showed signs of becoming a team once again.

However, when Mee's appointment had been announced, all the supporters had huge reservations; he wasn't really thought of as a 'football man'. I don't think there were many people throwing their hats in the ring at the time, though. The Arsenal job wasn't the prestigious position it had once been. One of the things the board liked about Bertie was the fact he would be an in-house appointment; he knew the club and the players inside out. Before Wright, you have to go back to Herbert Chapman for an appointment from outside the club.

I think the club needed a bit more discipline and Bertie's rather clipped and military bearing would have fitted in this regard. Being the physio, he must have heard plenty from the players about their frustrations with Wright's methods; they must have opened up to him while being treated, so Mee must have had a tremendous level of insight into each of the players, their characters and what made them tick. Bertie was a very clever man, a good judge of people and a great delegator. Perhaps, though, his greatest asset was that he simply never pretended to be a coach.

Success didn't happen straight away. That first season under Mee, 1966/67, was to prove very uneven in terms of results. This will seem a bizarre thing to say now, given Arsenal's history of achievements since those dark days in the mid-60s, but I genuinely never expected to see Arsenal play at Wembley in a cup final. That was how negative my thoughts were.

However, in that first season under Mee, Arsenal finished a respectable seventh. That alone was encouraging but I think what genuinely stood out was the undeniable progress the team was making in terms of performances. You could sense that something was happening and building. We were starting to look like a quite different proposition to the inconsistent and disorganised team we saw so often under Wright.

By the beginning of Mee's reign, I had begun to socialise with a group of the younger Arsenal players who were around the same age as me. In fact, what must have been a couple of years before Bertie's appointment, I had met John Radford and, through that friendship with John, I was lucky enough to meet a number of the players on a regular basis. I had a friend, Stephanie, who knew that I was an Arsenal fanatic and, being a cousin of John Radford, she set up a meeting with Raddy and the rest is history.

At the time, John was in shared digs with Tommy Baldwin and we all began meeting up at the White Hart pub in Southgate. In those days, Southgate and the surrounding areas was where most of the Arsenal players lived, although not all of them. Guys like Charlie George, Pat Rice and Sammy Nelson all lived in Islington and tended to socialise there and, although we would never have expected to see him in the White Hart, Bertie Mee lived in Southgate, too. Pretty soon, there were quite a few of the players popping in for a pint and a chat; Peter Storey and Jon Sammels, for example. The White Hart, in those days, was Arsenal's unofficial watering hole. It became pretty much a weekly occurrence where we'd meet to discuss the game and life in general. Most of the players at Arsenal were around my age, so an evening in the pub was the obvious choice.

Jon Sammels came across differently to some of his team-mates; his background wasn't your typical footballer's background. He was very polite, had impeccable manners and was softly spoken; probably quite a sensitive man, too. His sensitivity would have contributed to his struggles with the crowd at times. The Highbury crowd would get on his back during his Arsenal days; a fine player, though, a lovely man and he never lost his great passion for Arsenal.

I think most Arsenal supporters at the time would have been surprised if they had met Peter Storey. He wasn't at all like his on-field persona. Peter was actually a very private man, almost a bit of a loner. He was softly spoken, too; people expected him to be a tub-thumper and belligerent but he was the total opposite. Out of all the Arsenal players I socialised with back then, I'd say Peter quickly became my closest friend and still is to this day. We'd speak almost every day and visit each other's houses. Out of the other players, Bob McNab was probably his big mate. Peter was an underrated player; in those days, every team needed the type of player Storey became when he moved from right-back into midfield. When Bob McNab came back on a visit from the States, he told me once that Bobby Moore had said to him that if asked to pick the best XI players he'd played with, he would have named Storey as his defensive midfielder ahead of Nobby Stiles. Peter had started at Arsenal at right-back but, in time, Don Howe thought he could contribute even more in midfield and when Frank McLintock was moved to centre-back, the two of them quickly became the rock that the Double team was built upon. It's probably true in all walks of life that away from the limelight, some big characters are, by nature, quieter, more reserved and undemonstrative; men like Peter left it all on the pitch. He had the most amazing ability to focus; if you gave him a job to do, he would just never let you down.

Storey told me that Bertie had once tried to warn him off me as a friend. I don't really know why but Bertie was apparently wary of our closeness. Bertie didn't really know me but he may have misjudged my motives; perhaps he thought I might be a bit of a hanger-on who could turn Peter's head and get him to lose focus. Whatever it was, Peter valued our friendship and took no notice of Mee's advice about me.

At the time, there were some wonderful characters around, for whom the word 'rogue' was absolutely spot on. One of them was a massive Arsenal man and most certainly a real-life, lovable London rogue: Johnny Hoy, who was the acknowledged leader of Arsenal's 'firm' at the time. Under Hoy, Arsenal became the top football terrace boys in London in the 60s and early 70s, in the days before 'The Herd' and 'The Gooners'. Johnny and his family were Arsenal through and through, lived in Avenell Road and provided digs for numerous Arsenal players: Tommy Baldwin, John Radford, Sammy

Nelson and Trevor Ross. Johnny was a big pal of Charlie George and, by all accounts, a decent footballer himself who just preferred watching Arsenal to playing. His father, Jack, was one of the famous commissionaires at Highbury. Looking back, you can see that football, and Arsenal especially, was in the blood of people like the Hoys; they lived for Arsenal.

George Graham always had a certain style about him. I remember the first time he asked me to join him and his fiancée Marie for a night out, he took me to a pub in the East End, the Blind Beggar on the Whitechapel Road, a pub regularly frequented by professional footballers, such as a young Harry Redknapp, and in those days it had a certain notoriety about it. It was where, six months previously, Ronnie Kray had shot and killed a man called George Cornell from a rival gang. The pub was owned by Jimmy Quill, a well-known and well-connected East End figure who, amongst other things, had been a top notch amateur boxer in his time. Jimmy had gone into business, which included opening some pubs with Bobby Moore at one time. I stayed in touch with Jimmy for a long time but sadly he passed away quite recently. At the time of our night out with George Graham, Jimmy owned two other pubs in the vicinity and after we had visited all three, it ended up being a late and highly enjoyable night.

Mee's first season was a success, and according to the players, that was largely down to Dave Sexton, Arsenal's new coach. The players all talked about him in the most glowing terms; his methods, his vision and the man himself. The players worshipped him. It was probably the first time any of them at Arsenal had really been properly coached. The young players were highly receptive to Sexton and responded to him with enthusiasm. They all told me they were in awe of the training sessions; they'd not experienced anything like it before. His methods were very modern. For instance, he would use films of matches to illustrate how certain situations in games could be exploited or closed down.

The respect the players had for Sexton helped establish Bertie Mee in their eyes, too. All the players took to Dave and when he left, they were very upset. They just wanted to learn and get better. He'd started as a coach at Chelsea and came to Arsenal after a short stint managing Leyton Orient. When Chelsea offered him the manager's position, he felt he couldn't turn it down. I think the Arsenal players thought more effort could have been made to hang on to him but the board's thinking has been to never stand in anyone's way. I recall returning by train from an away game when the speculation about him leaving Arsenal for Chelsea was first breaking and I asked him outright if he was going to take the job at Stamford Bridge. He went bright red but didn't answer me. I knew there and then that he was going and inside a week, he had been installed at Chelsea. He was one of the most painfully shy men I have met; a brilliant coach but he must have found the media-facing aspects of managing very hard work. Anyway, in what felt like no time at all, Sexton had come in, reinvigorated the football side of the club, lifted everyone's hopes and then dashed it all by leaving. We'd had a brief glimmer of the future and then had it snatched away.

To make matters worse, Tottenham won the FA Cup in 1967. However, the final itself was not without its amusement for me because that afternoon I gained a certain notoriety. There is an activity Londoners may be familiar with but which is largely unknown outside of the capital – 'jibbing'. In simple terms, it means getting into events – football matches, big boxing fights, concerts even, without having a ticket. I was a bit of a pioneer of 'jibbing' in the 1960s and eventually I became well known for it. My talent for it got me into many big events and I remember once 'jibbing' my way into a Sinatra concert.

My attendance at the Sinatra show was as a result of a challenge thrown down to me by my oldest friend from school, Nat Bitton, who had been hearing about my growing reputation. The concert was at the Royal Festival Hall and started at 7.30pm. Nat challenged me to get us both in. You need a cool head and perfect timing; that is the essence and in all my jibbing, I don't think I ever failed. If I am honest, on this occasion, I wasn't actually that confident – if you saw the size of Nat, you'd understand. But a cool head prevailed and we both got in.

In 1967, I not only got into Wembley for the cup final without a ticket but I surpassed myself that afternoon. At the end of the game, I managed to get on to the pitch and joined in with Tottenham's lap of honour, hopefully upstaging it. Commentating on the game, Kenneth Wolstenholme mistakenly referred to me as Eddie Clayton, Tottenham's sub that day. The main reason I wanted to do the lap of honour was that I knew that my Spurs-supporting friends would be seeing me and looking on in disbelief. I knew it would detract from our deadliest rivals winning the cup, as all everyone would want to talk about were my exploits rather than their success in what was, after all, a hugely tedious cup final. The irony of my being an Arsenal fan wasn't lost on any of my Arsenal mates. I even told Jimmy Greaves as we trotted round that I was an Arsenal fan, which he found very amusing. When the press picked up on the story, I was soon being referred to as the 'King of the Jibbers'! A couple of years ago, a journalist writing for *The Athletic USA* did a piece on my antics. There have since been some copycats emerge all over the world but I'll always be known as the 'Original King of the Jibbers'.

In 1967, I was offered an opening with a character in the clothing industry by the name of Lenny Shopper. Lenny, who knew my brother, Jack, had recently read in the press about my antics at Wembley, jibbing my way on to the pitch for the lap of honour, and decided that this suggested I had the personality to be a great salesman. He owned Lenbry Fashions, which was situated in London's textile centre in Great Portland Street and was launching a big new range of clothing, which featured one of the hottest stars of the pop music scene, Lulu. Quite quickly, Lulu at Lenbry proved a reasonable success, certainly successful enough for me to start earning some decent money. I worked for Lenny for a while until, in 1968, Judy and I got engaged and, deciding for various reasons that Lenny wasn't absolutely my cup of tea, I left the job. Judy, meantime, was herself earning some very good money as a hairdresser in a salon in Temple Fortune, north-west London, and our thoughts started moving towards settling down and getting married.

It is odd how, when you look back at events, you see how the pattern of your life throws up coincidences. Judy's hairdressing was going great guns; she loved it and would often talk about her clients. There was one lady she was especially fond of, a Mrs Dein, who lived close by the salon. Judy would often pop to Mrs Dein's to do her hair or just to have a cup of tea and a chat. One day, before Judy and I had met, while the two of them sat talking, a lovely E-Type Jaguar had pulled into the drive and a young man got out and came into the house. Mrs Dein introduced her son, David, to Judy. At that time, Judy's English wasn't great and she was still very shy. The son, David, arranged to take Judy out. Later on, she only thought to tell me all about this when David Dein burst into the public domain after buying into Arsenal. That turned out to be their only date but what might have been? Saved from the clutches of one Arsenal obsessive only to fall into the arms of another! I sometimes wonder how Judy thinks it all worked out for her – David Dein or me.

After one brilliant appointment of a coach, Bertie topped it with the appointment of Sexton's replacement – Don Howe. He had begun coaching at Arsenal following the broken leg which brought his own playing days to an end. He had been doing well with the reserves before his step up and once installed as first team coach, he slowly won over the players; their reservations being not Howe himself but their regret that he wasn't Sexton. Howe had two situations to cope with. Firstly, there was the unhelpful air of familiarity with players who had recently been his team-mates and, secondly, the very evident regret at Sexton's departure. Both of these issues were dealt with one day when Howe stamped his authority on the group. During training sessions, Howe noticed that Sexton's name would crop up and references were being made to his methods. One day, it was said once too often and Don cracked. 'Never mention the name of Dave Sexton ever again. I am here now and these are my methods.' He won the respect of the players that day. Like Sexton, Don was one of the young, modern coaches in British football who were bringing innovations into the mainstream of the domestic game. Don proved to be more defensively minded than Sexton but was, perhaps, a better foil for Mee. Howe's organisation and defensive pragmatism worked well with Mee's love of discipline and hard work.

Don and Frank McLintock would always be chatting and discussing tactics and new ideas; theirs was a highly creative relationship. They were also neighbours, literally, and I can picture them chatting over the garden fence planning the Double.

Chapter Five

# 1967/68

IN THE 1967/68 season, we finished down in ninth, which was disappointing after the apparent progress of Mee's first season in charge. There was a significant tactical shift made, which took a bit of time getting used to. Sexton had preferred a man-to-man marking defensive system, which had looked good at first – it was something he brought back with him from his studies in Italy. Howe, in contrast, wanted Arsenal to move to a zonal system. Its strong point as a system is that it allows you to keep your shape defensively much more easily. Within a couple of seasons, Arsenal looked impregnable at times, with some very good defenders playing a system they understood inside out, but initially there was some confusion.

The season will always be remembered for finally seeing Arsenal in a cup final at Wembley after 16 years. It didn't make a lot difference that it wasn't an FA Cup Final but the slightly less glamorous League Cup Final. For my generation of supporters, it was a very significant achievement.

The competition was starting to be taken much more seriously. I think moving the final to a one-off game at Wembley from a two-legged affair helped raise its prestige. Huddersfield provided stiff opposition in the semi-final. We won the first leg at Highbury 3-2. I couldn't get up to Huddersfield for the second leg but I remember catching the game on television thanks to a short-lived experiment, the consequences of which we live with now to a certain extent. A special channel had been created to offer pay-per-view events and one of the first, if not *the* first, game shown on it was our second leg at Huddersfield Town. The channel was only available in south London but we managed to find someone who could receive it and we all chipped in £1 for the privilege of watching the game. There were ten of us in all, so the lady who owned the house would have made a nice profit. We won the game 3-1 and triumphed 6-3 on aggregate and a good night was had by all as we stopped off on the way home to drink to our success.

Leeds United, our Wembley opponents, were clearly ahead of us at that stage; in fact, most people would have agreed they had an outstanding team, but nobody liked them. A lot of people think the vendettas and ill feeling that grew up around the two teams started with this game but it dated back to Leeds' first season back in the top flight after winning promotion. The 1964/65 season was when Leeds became notorious for almost all the things that blight the game now – things like feigning injury, diving, time wasting. None of these things are contemporary developments; Leeds United were doing them all back then. But what really marked them out was the violence. The first time they came to Highbury after winning promotion, they literally kicked us off the pitch. George Eastham was given a thorough going over. George was very much a player built for the 1950s style of play, a physically slight inside-forward, all grace and shimmying swerves. He was booted every time the ball went near him, with one tackle alone from Giles nearly cutting him in two. And it wasn't just Eastham. All over the pitch, Leeds were kicking us. There's no question they were an outstanding football team; too good to have to do all the nasty stuff. Revie was a cute manager and he was backed by a self-made millionaire by the name of Reynolds. They always seemed to be able to attract the promising youngsters, even when they were in the Second Division. No, nobody back in those days liked Leeds United.

Although Leeds presented a tough challenge, I knew from speaking with the players that Arsenal went into the game strongly believing they had enough to beat them. The feeling was that Leeds might think they were favourites but we weren't going to be browbeaten or intimidated. Players like McNab, Storey, McLintock – these guys had some bottle. They were no one's pushovers and probably relished the battle that teams like Leeds offered.

The game itself was very tense and very 'competitive'. Leeds scored fairly early, a goal following a corner that even in those days, when referees were more lenient, should have been disallowed for a blatant foul on our keeper, Jim Furnell, and then they proceeded to 'park the bus' for the remainder of the 90 minutes, winning 1-0. It was a game of very few chances and not much of a spectacle but it fitted the pattern of games between the two teams for the next few years; each side was probably the other's worst nightmare.

Nineteen-sixty-eight saw the emergence of Bob Wilson as Arsenal's undisputed No.1. Furnell had been blamed for a bad mistake which had cost Arsenal in a cup tie with Birmingham; the game ended 1-1 as a result of Furnell's error and we lost the replay. He was dropped and never played for us again. Bob had been knocking on the door for a while and when his chance came, he took it. After making a confident start, he never looked back and developed into one of the best, and certainly the bravest, goalkeepers ever to pull on the Arsenal jersey.

A slightly less successful addition to the team was new signing Bobby Gould, who was bought for a club record fee early in 1968. He was direct and loved a battle, a battering ram centre-forward. Just after Gould signed, I spoke to Peter Storey about him; Peter was less than impressed after observing our expensive new centre-forward in training. Peter's analysis really depressed me at the time. I had hoped Gould was going to provide the goals to propel us forward. However, fairly quickly Gould would move on and Radford would move back into a central striker's role from his recent and temporary role as a winger and the jigsaw would become complete.

## Chapter Six

# 1968/69

IT WAS around this time that a few of the Arsenal lads started getting engaged or married; we were all more or less at the same stage in our lives. Judy and I were mainly socialising with Bob McNab and his wife, Carole, Peter Storey and Susan and Frank and Barbara McLintock and the idea of settling down was in the air. So, we set a date for our own wedding – Sunday, 26 January 1969. It was going to be a small wedding and we invited around 50 or so guests. On my side, there was only Jack and his wife, Rosalyn, and on Judy's side the numbers were small, too. My oldest friend, Nat Bitton, was my best man. There was a significant Arsenal contingent, too; Bob McNab and Peter Storey both acted as witnesses to our wedding at the Edgware Synagogue on the day following our 2-0 FA Cup fourth round victory at Highbury against Charlton Athletic, a game both Bob and Peter had played in. I was also delighted to have with me, to share in our celebrations, two of my oldest friends from the 62 Group, Cyril Paskin, and 'Big' Dave Davies; Judy and I had enjoyed many happy times socialising with them both and their wives, Norma and Audrey.

I hadn't been working for a time before we got married but my brother-in-law had arranged a job for me with a firm of estate agents, Arburn Estates in Kilburn, for £10 a week plus commissions. Around that time, there was a sharp credit squeeze and, as a consequence, almost no one could get a mortgage, which, of course, severely affected house sales ... hence no commission for me. Fortunately, with her tips, Judy was regularly clearing £40 a week, which helped to balance the finances. In fact, to this day, Judy still insists I married her for her money!

We were very lucky to commence our married life in possession of our own three-bedroom house in Stanmore, which was bought for the princely sum of £3,800 with the help of both sets of parents. Shortly afterwards, though, the rather imbalanced household finances did become an issue; Judy found out she was expecting our first child. At that stage, this meant a real problem. For, without Judy's earnings, I really didn't know how we were going to pay the mortgage.

So, after giving it some thought, we decided I would leave my job at the estate agent, which was still only yielding the basic £10 a week, and try something on my own. I had a reasonable grounding in the fashion trade, especially women's clothing, as this had been my parents' business. I made the move to go round all the factories in East London and buy up their surplus stock – the over-makes, known in the business as 'cabbage' – and try to sell them on to some of the many small independent retailers in the London suburbs. At the time, I drove a Mini – in Arsenal red, of course – which limited the stock I could transport around, but my wonderful neighbour, Terry, modified the inside of the car and fixed up a rail which went across the entire width of the car and then I was in business. And what business! Very soon, my meagre £10 a week had ballooned into £100 or more a week. My mum gave me some sound advice and I quickly learnt from my own mistakes, too. Any stock I was stuck with, I sold off at markets over the weekends and recovered my money. I was soon able to buy a customised van and, as a result, I could carry so much more, and varied stock, which, in turn, meant more income. This, in time, enabled us to upgrade our home to a lovely place in Edgware.

Ultimately, the 1968/69 season is remembered for one thing: another League Cup Final defeat, this time to Third Division Swindon Town. Although it was a shock, a terrible experience at the time, I can honestly say I had been more disappointed losing to Leeds the year before and I think that was down to the way the team was playing in 1969, with a real sense of identity and purpose. The defeat to Swindon couldn't entirely eclipse the progress the team had made over the previous 12 months.

It was great to get to Wembley again, two years running, and that pleasure was amplified by beating Tottenham in the semi-final. The first leg of the semi-final was played at Highbury and more than 55,000 packed into the ground for what was a really tight game. At Highbury, Tottenham sat back and just defended and I can't remember any clearcut chances. When it looked as if we would have to settle for going to White Hart Lane all square, we scored with a half chance that came out of nowhere in the dying moments of the game; the ball just sat up nicely for Radford and he made no mistake.

The second leg was more of the same, a tight affair and hard with it. Knowles and Radford set the tone with a punch-up early on and it developed into one of the roughest games I had seen. Bob Wilson took some terrible stick, especially from Mike England. Arsenal lost a bit of balance when Bob McNab had to come off injured; we had looked good down our left side, a good outlet as Tottenham turned up the heat. Then Jimmy Greaves scored. He had been really quiet, just like him, then first touch and it's in the back of the net. That made it all square on aggregate and it remained an edgy, tetchy affair right down to the wire when that man again, John Radford, scored one of the finest headed goals I have ever seen. It was right at the end of the game, in the 88th minute. Arsenal won a corner, the box was absolutely packed, everyone moving around trying to get an advantage, and then Radford took off and literally crashed a bullet header into the corner of the net ... fantastic! A wonderful goal and once it was in, that was it – there was no way they were coming back.

After the game, I met the team bus at the Southgate roundabout. You can imagine the mood amongst the players but I especially remember John Radford jumping off the bus and giving me a bear hug.

Twelve months of knowing we hadn't quite done ourselves justice in the previous year's final and now we had the chance to put it right. Once we had overcome Tottenham, there was no way we were not going to bring that elusive first trophy home. No disrespect to Swindon, and acknowledging that one-off games are notorious for a reason, but I just couldn't see Arsenal not winning at Wembley this time.

Just prior to the final – it might have been on the morning of the game itself – there was a prophetic article in the *Daily Mirror*, by Ken Jones; it didn't just strike a note of caution, it caused a real sense of apprehension about the game. Everyone knows about the awful surface the match was played on but Jones insisted that some Arsenal players were genuinely worried about it. Making a visit on the Friday afternoon, they had stood in the pouring rain, watching with horror as drenched and muddied groundstaff fought a losing battle with the pitch which, after staging the Horse of the Year Show, followed by days of torrential rain, was simply a mudbath. The Wembley pitch was renowned the world over as the best football surface anywhere and here Arsenal were in a cup final and playing on a surface which helped neutralise any advantage we might have had. Bertie Mee was quoted as saying: 'The greatest leveller in football is an unpredictable surface ... mud can play havoc with normal form.' Mud stretched from goalmouth to goalmouth. The Football League had even, on the morning of the game, considered postponing it, so shocking was the pitch.

What is slightly less well known is that Highbury had been hit by a flu bug in the week leading up to the final. It was going to be a real slog on that pitch but to have the additional problem of players recovering from something as debilitating as influenza was definitely a potentially game-changing handicap.

Jones's final, extremely prescient assessment was this: 'But [Arsenal] recognise too that they are two divisions superior in status and a Wembley defeat would be a sickening chapter.' Mee put into context the significance of the game to Arsenal and their development. 'We shall be even better next season. That's why it's important to win this match. It's not a question of having a cup. The thing is to achieve a target. It would open the door to other things and then it would be up to us to take advantage of the opportunity.'

What ensued that afternoon was, indeed, a disaster. Oddly, Arsenal didn't actually play that badly. We had nearly all the game and should have won comfortably. Their keeper, Peter Downsborough, made some outstanding saves, including two especially fine ones from Sammels and McNab. When Swindon took the lead, it was, perhaps, inevitable that poor old Ian Ure would be at the centre of it. A mix-up between him and Wilson let them in to go one up and, thereafter, Swindon quite understandably tried to protect their lead. We blitzed their goal but when it looked as if we simply were not going to break them down, their keeper made his first and only mistake of the game and Bobby Gould capitalised to equalise.

Gould's late equaliser felt like more than just a lifeline. There wasn't a single Arsenal supporter who didn't now expect us to go on and win it. At that stage, I didn't give a moment's thought to the pitch and how tired Arsenal's players might be feeling. You look at it and think 'Both teams must be knackered but surely Arsenal must be the fitter of the two sides'. I just couldn't see us losing after getting out of jail with that last-gasp equaliser.

The last thing any of the players wanted was another 30 minutes; Don Howe even went as far as to ask for the game to be abandoned. I certainly didn't share their reservations and, as I have said, not a single Arsenal supporter shared them either. I just couldn't see us losing after getting away with it.

Thirty minutes of torture saw us lose 3-1. After extra-time, I just left the ground, immediately after the ref blew for time. I don't recall much coming out of the Arsenal camp after the game complaining about the pitch or making any excuses. People like Frank McLintock tended to be quite hard on themselves and wouldn't ever look for excuses.

There was actually no hangover from that defeat. I don't suppose Bertie or Don would have let the players feel sorry for themselves. Unquestionably, we were having, up until that point, a really good season. There had been a very big step forward from the previous season and it was important we didn't lose that momentum. The run-in to the end of the season after the Swindon game suggests they got over it pretty quickly. After the League Cup Final, we had a run of seven games unbeaten, conceding just two goals.

The defence that season was beginning to take shape. Bob Wilson, Peter Storey, Bob McNab, and Peter Simpson all seemed to have made their positions their own and the only issue about the defence was who was going to be Simpson's partner in the centre. It had been either Terry Neill or Ian Ure but neither was proving to be the ideal foil for Simpson's calm and elegant authority. Peter had the most wonderful left foot and you could tell he was a converted midfielder. He had those two telling hallmarks of a top player: time on the ball and the ability to make it look simple. Muddied and bloodied centre-backs tend to get noticed more easily but Peter was elegance itself.

Ian Ure was a wonderful competitor, no doubt about that; he gave it his all and was a really tough man but he always had a mistake in him. Terry Neill, too, as likeable as he was just wasn't quite up to it. Ure or Neill would always be the weak link in that defence.

Gould was a trier and gave it his all but he wasn't the guy to score us the goals to win us things. As the season drew to a close, centre-half and centre-forward remained the two problems for Mee and Howe to solve. We didn't realise it at the time but the answers to both these problem positions were already at the club.

## Chapter Seven

# 1969/70

MONDAY, 29 September 1969, the happiest day in the lives of Judy and myself: our first born son, Danny, was born at Bushey Maternity home. We just couldn't wait to have our first child. I had been standing outside the delivery room for hours, waiting for the birth to be confirmed, and when, eventually, I heard the first cries of our new baby, I was elated and, in the excitement of the moment, I was sure I had heard the nurse calling out to Judith the word 'girl'. Before going in to see mother and baby, I had time to phone both families and tell them we had a baby girl. I was, therefore, totally astonished when the nurse came to me and said: 'Martin, come and see your lovely son and Judy.' It turned out the nurse had said 'Good girl' to Judy as the baby was being delivered. Once my head got around it all, I went in and saw my boy for the first time. Mother and baby were both fine and I was overjoyed. It meant another quick telephone call to set the record straight and to tell proud grandparents they had a grandson and not a granddaughter. Eventually, everything became clear, although I think everyone thought I had gone off my head a bit in the heat of the moment! Once home, Judy's mum came over from Vienna to help out. All parents will understand just how much love we had for Danny; perhaps his being the first amplifies that love just ever so slightly.

It would be no exaggeration to say that Bertie Mee might have been sacked at the end of the 1969/70 season if he had been judged on domestic form alone. We loitered around mid-table and, along the way, seemed to lose some of that hard-won resilience while, at times, we never really looked like scoring, either. In one run of ten matches quite near the start of the season, we only managed two goals. It was a big disappointment after the optimism of the previous season.

In the late 60s, European competitions like the Fairs Cup weren't such drawn-out affairs as now; in fact, we found ourselves in the semi-finals without really needing to break sweat. In truth, Glentoran, Sporting, Rouen and Romania's Dinamo Bacau represented a relatively low bar but Ajax in the semi-final was a challenge of a different order.

In 1970, everyone was already talking about Ajax. The two games Arsenal played against them were an education; I had never seen football like it. By the late 1960s, English football had begun to get bogged down; it was very organised, fitter and tougher. The British game had shed itself of that old up and at 'em approach; solid defending was now the priority and getting the ball forward quickly and directly. We saw it up and down the country every Saturday afternoon. It wasn't the Ajax way at all.

The Ajax philosophy, 'Total Football', sought to undo rigorously organised defences by manipulating space and it was in the fluid spontaneity of Ajax's attacking play that this European 'new wave' won its admirers. In 1970, they presented Arsenal with a formidable obstacle and a challenge the Gunners would never have encountered in the fast and furious world of English football. Arsenal's response was 90 minutes of unremitting intensity when they harried, challenged and chased down their opponents, eventually subduing them and then undoing them, recording a 3-0 first-leg victory.

Despite the three-goal reversal, all the Ajax stars of the future stood out that night – Cruyff, Neeskens, Krol – but the star of the show, the man that even Johan Cruyff singled out that night, was our own Charlie George: 'He'll be as good as Di Stéfano one day.'

We negotiated a difficult second leg over in Amsterdam, which was, incidentally, my first foreign trip following Arsenal – indeed, the first time I had ever flown in my life. We went from Luton Airport which in those days was little more than a field with a shed in it. A good defensive performance held Ajax at bay and although we lost the game 1-0, we advanced to the final, 3-1 on aggregate. There, we would meet Anderlecht in another wonderful clash of styles.

From an attacking point of view, Ajax and Anderlecht were two of the best, most powerful teams around. Ajax were easy on the eye but, of the two sides, Anderlecht were possibly the more powerful. I remember after the first leg in Belgium, which we lost 3-1, the Arsenal players all telling me about Anderlecht's two forwards, Mulder and the skipper, Van Himst, saying they were a whole different class of player to what they were used to.

Despite the strong impression Anderlecht had made, I know our lads felt they had a really good chance back at Highbury. Ray Kennedy's late goal in the first leg had given us a lifeline and after the game, Frank McLintock gave the dressing room the kind of speech which, according to Bob Wilson, resulted in everyone leaving Belgium with the firm conviction that we *would* turn it around at Highbury. Once back in London, that conviction grew in the days between the two legs until all the players were absolutely convinced Arsenal would win. They knew that they simply had to – it was such a big occasion for the club. When the game came around, they were so fired up that I don't think any team could have stood in their way.

A lot of people think 'pressing' is a modern development but Arsenal in 1970 were one of the best-ever pressing teams. I am not sure Anderlecht could believe the intensity with which we went at them from kick-off; they must have known they were in for one hell of an evening and, as the game wore on, Arsenal just seemed to get faster and stronger and the crowd louder and louder. Highbury was very tense at the beginning but once that first goal had gone in, the noise was unbelievable. It felt like four walls of sound surrounded the pitch and for poor Anderlecht it must have seemed that noise and energy was coming at them from every corner of the ground. The 'Highbury roar' was back. It was definitely the noisiest I ever heard the old ground.

The conditions were poor; the pitch was muddy and cut up right from the start. It certainly meant that Anderlecht were going to struggle to play their game but it was going to be energy-sapping for our boys, too. It was such a very British night: a fast and furious cup tie played on a mud heap before a baying crowd. While the roars and cheers rolled around Highbury, Arsenal fought like they have perhaps never had to fight before; just thinking about it sets the heart racing again. It was such a wonderful, wonderful night.

The first goal was a fantastic effort from young Eddie Kelly. After Anderlecht had failed to properly clear Armstrong's corner at the Clock End, Kelly shimmied one way, drew two defenders, turned inside on to his right foot and, leaving their keeper, Trappeniers, totally flat-footed, scored from outside the penalty box with a wonderfully shaped shot high to the keeper's right. Highbury erupted; the noise almost blew a hole in the sky. It was the perfect time to score, with over an hour left. Anderlecht couldn't have fancied it. The Belgians were a very classy side but given the conditions and the mood Arsenal were in, I think we would pretty much have done for any team that evening.

With 15 minutes to go, George Graham worked it to Bob McNab down Arsenal's left; Bob got his foot round the ball and swung it to the far post. 'It was as good a cross as I ever hit,' McNab said to me later. John Radford, hanging in the expectant air, met it and headed the ball firmly past Trappeniers for Arsenal's second. The noise and the outpouring of relief and joy! This moment was the reward for the years of caring so much.

Arsenal were now ahead on away goals and, almost immediately, Charlie George collected the ball and swung a crossfield pass out to the right, which, just eluding the frantic leap of the Anderlecht left-back, Sammels took on his chest, cushioned the speed of the ball and struck it first time. It sailed into the net like the opening shot of a revolution; *this* was Arsenal's time!

That night was without a doubt one of the greatest nights of my life. If you speak with any of the players, they would all say the same. After the post-match reception in the boardroom, which Frank McLintock had given me a pass for, it was off to The White Hart and more celebrations. When we got there, it was so crowded we couldn't get in; people were spilling out on to the pavement. So, instead, I headed to the West End, where an Arsenal friend of mine ran a very prestigious club, and we had a joyous meal and happy evening. The two of us had been through a lot over the years with Arsenal. We reminisced over old games, defeats and setbacks; we could afford to now – this was our moment.

For most supporters, their first trophy is often the one that most totally captures their imagination; a cup, a league title, it doesn't matter – nothing can ever again quite match the unique emotions of winning for the first time.

There was, once again, a wonderful feeling around Highbury and some of that new found optimism was due to the emergence of three young players and an established player who felt like a new signing.

It was 1970 when Frank McLintock dropped back to play alongside Simpson in the heart of our defence. Initially, he was only filling in due to injuries but he soon became absolutely central to Arsenal's system and the source of that unbendable spirit which set us apart. In my eyes, he had every attribute a top class centre-back needed: good feet, strong in the air, he was an athlete, competitive and very intelligent. To a certain extent, he helped Peter Simpson develop, too. Peter was a smashing player but was naturally quiet and shy and might have lacked a bit of confidence but, playing between Frank and Bob McNab, he couldn't have had two better players to guide and support him.

The three emerging talents were Ray Kennedy, Eddie Kelly and the 'King of Highbury' – Charlie George. It is worth remembering, too, how many of the group that would go on to win the Double came through the ranks at Highbury. Winning things with a team of largely homegrown players always gives it added value for supporters.

In addition to the homegrown talents, Mee also did some shopping. In January 1970, Arsenal signed 'the next George Best', the 19-year-old starlet from Hibernian, Peter Marinello, for a club record fee of £100,000. I suspect the club simply had some money to spend and decided to take a punt on one for the future. After a great debut at Old Trafford, when he scored, Marinello found it tougher and tougher. The references to Best obviously didn't help and his head must have been turned. He was a quiet, rather shy lad but soon developed a reputation for having a bit of glamour about him, a bit like a prototype Charlie Nicholas. He was well-liked in the dressing room. He must have been signed to replace Armstrong. Coming to Arsenal at such a young age for a record fee was a lot to live up to; a nice guy, decent player but he was never going to keep 'Geordie' out of the team.

## Chapter Eight

# 1970/71

IN MID-SUMMER, as the players returned from their break, the mood around Highbury was one of optimism. Winning the Fairs Cup had done much to strengthen their belief in themselves. Now, it wasn't just Don and Bertie telling them they were good enough, they had a trophy to prove it. I knew from speaking to the players that Mee and Howe felt that a title challenge was a realistic ambition. The victory over Anderlecht had given an idea of what could be achieved if Arsenal came close to maintaining that standard over an entire season. Crucially, too, the players had enormous belief and confidence in each other; their success had been a victory of the collective.

We had an immediate opportunity to measure ourselves, as we kicked off the season against the reigning champions away at Goodison Park. Our pre-season planning had been disrupted when Simpson picked up an injury. We were lucky, as we had a very able deputy to step in – John Roberts. Frank McLintock described John as physically the strongest man he had ever met. Heralding from Abercynon, a small mining village in South Wales, a smile was never that far away from his face; framed by a shock of blonde hair, he had the look of a genial policeman. The steadiest of 'Steady Eddies', he was tremendous for us and enjoyed a deserved and extended run in the first team. Although a different type of player to Simpson, he just got on with it and we never really noticed Peter's absence.

We picked up another injury during that game at Everton. In spite of his youth, Charlie George was already contributing much to Arsenal's cause. Adored by the North Bank, Charlie added that indefinable 'something' which sets a brilliant team apart from those that are very good. Charlie broke his ankle in a collision with Everton's keeper Gordon West and would be out until just before Christmas.

The previous season, we had started to see a fabulous partnership developing between him and John Radford. Charlie was a great foil for Radford because he would drop off into space and would drag defenders back with him. He had the brains to exploit it, like a modern No.10. A near equivalent from more recent years might be Eric Cantona. He could score goals but there was so much more to his game and, for a flair player, he could look after himself; you soon learnt not to take liberties with George. Charlie was the all-round real deal; a player, remember, who Cruyff talked of in the same breath as Di Stefano!

When Charlie first broke into the team, you could see what a talent he was. He had a shot on him and was a good header of the ball; he scored goals and had an excellent range of passing; great close control and first touch and he was a quick thinker; plus he was hard. He took absolutely no nonsense from anyone and I never saw him pull out of a challenge; he had some good old-fashioned 'attitude' about him. When he started playing, all his mates were on the terraces, characters like Johnny Hoy, and Charlie would strut around the pitch like 'Jack the lad'. I think he loved the reputation. He was well liked in the dressing room but he was very honest to the point of almost making it slightly uncomfortable; he called it exactly as he saw it, which, at times, could lead him to appear outspoken but I think everyone saw he spoke straight from the heart. He was the original rock star footballer.

Over time, Charlie found the 'Jack the lad' image less helpful. He was certainly never a model pro but neither was he ever a problem player; he just wore his heart on his sleeve and I believe that, ultimately, it wasn't his ability but his attitude which held him back. I think Bertie eventually came to the conclusion that he was being asked to bend over just too far in order to accommodate him and, in the end, he couldn't get him out of the club quick enough. It's a story that could be told about a lot of young, brash talents of that era but he was a solid Arsenal boy and a great footballer to watch.

When Charlie was injured, Ray Kennedy stepped up. Ray was more direct than Charlie and played much more alongside Radford. Ray coming into the side might just have made us even more direct; it would certainly have encouraged us to go longer.

An ankle injury kept Jon Sammels out until November and then a fit-again Charlie George put some pressure on his place in the side. Eventually, during the run-in, Mee decided he preferred George Graham and, as a consequence, Jon sat out much of the final quarter of the season. By then, the on-off barracking he could receive from the Highbury crowd was starting to affect him again. He was still there in Bertie's thinking, though, as he would regularly be named as substitute and was in the 12 for the title decider at White Hart Lane. But in the end, perhaps a combination of the crowd's attitude towards him and the fact he might have seen himself slipping down the pecking order, with youngsters like Eddie Kelly emerging, led him to look away from Highbury. It was no surprise that someone like Leicester City manager Jimmy Bloomfield came in for him. Jimmy had been a similar type of player to Jon and he would go on to build one of the most attractive teams in the First Division at Filbert Street. I think Jon was quite attracted to the idea of playing for Bloomfield. Crucially, Jimmy would have had some insight into Jon's experiences at Highbury as he, too, came in for a bit of stick from the crowd during his time as a Gunner. When Jon moved away, it felt strange that none of the really big clubs came in for him. I think Ipswich, his hometown club, tried quite hard to get him but I don't believe he was that interested in Ipswich or anyone else once he knew Bloomfield wanted him; two stylish footballers and decent men. Jon was sensitive, courteous and kind and, in many ways, a man cut from a very different cloth to many of his team-mates. Many years later, at the height of Arsenal's success under Wenger, Jon came over to me at an event and I recall him saying: 'Martin, you have been a fantastic supporter of Arsenal and you deserve to enjoy all the success the club are now having.' I remain very fond of Jon and maintain great warmth towards him – a wonderful Arsenal man.

We made a very steady start to the 1970/71 season, only losing once in the opening nine games, but then came a real bolt out of the blue when we got battered at Stoke City. We lost 5-0 and, in all honesty, the scoreline flattered us. It led to a clear-the-air team meeting. All the players were able to be critical of one another and when that's done in the right way, it can be a positive experience. The players had their own opinions and no one was above criticism; importantly, they trusted and respected each other. On another occasion, I recall Frank McLintock being very critical and Peter Storey reminding him *he* hadn't been playing too cleverly recently, a point Frank accepted.

Within two or three weeks of the Stoke debacle, the team were back on track. We beat Nottingham Forest at Highbury 4-0 and, a fortnight later, beat Everton very impressively by the same scoreline, with young Kennedy contributing five of those eight goals. After the

Everton game, Arsenal would remain in touch with the leaders from thereon in and after mid-November and a typically 'Arsenal' 1-0 win at Ipswich Town, the Gunners would never be out of the top two.

We had made fairly sure-footed progress to the quarter-finals in Europe, too, where we would meet the West German side FC Cologne. We prevailed by 2-1 in a hard-fought first leg at Highbury. The second leg in Germany was a horrible evening and an especially dubious award of a penalty enabled Cologne to progress by virtue of the goal they had scored in north London two weeks earlier. After the game, Bertie was pretty incendiary with some of his comments about the referee and the approach of the Germans and the English press all backed him the following morning; quite skilfully, a setback had been converted into a rallying call.

Our next game was the cup semi-final at Hillsborough against Stoke City. Given the acrimonious defeat in midweek and that Arsenal went in at half-time at Hillsborough 2-0 down, to have then survived that scare is a testament to the spirit in that team. Some teams flounder, others flourish. Arsenal's success was built upon the ethics of a one-for-all mentality – the collective – but I don't think anyone would begrudge the individual acclaim which went to Peter Storey that afternoon. Peter came out after the break like a man possessed and almost single-handedly grabbed the game by the scruff of the neck and took it to Stoke. Although it wasn't his fault, I think he felt he had contributed to Stoke's 2-0 lead when, in trying to clear a Stoke corner, he blasted it against a Stoke player at close range and the ball ricocheted into the roof of Wilson's net. He was everywhere that second half and, even without his two goals, that afternoon we witnessed his greatest performance for Arsenal.

When Peter stepped up to take a spot kick in the dying moments of the game, footballing immortality rested squarely on his shoulders. Peter had nothing to prove to anyone on a football pitch but that moment spoke of courage and an intensity of focus; it was a moment when the whole ethos of that team was captured by one man in a split second. I'd have bet my life on Peter holding his nerve and, indeed, the quietly spoken man from Farnham wrongfooted Banks – a simple kick of a football but it meant the world – and made it 2-2. Arsenal lived to fight again.

In the dressing room after the draw with Stoke, Frank McLintock was adamant the Gunners would prevail that season; looking around him, he saw only a resolution and fortitude that no one else could match. Leeds United and Revie were certainly no bottlers but they had been hunted by Arsenal since the New Year and that takes its toll. The following week, Arsenal beat Chelsea 2-0 at Highbury in a brilliant London derby; just three days after a rousing victory in the replay of the cup semi-final.

We continued to win the games we had in hand over Leeds, while Revie's team dropped points at almost every turn. We got closer and closer to them until they could feel the uncomfortable heat of the red and white pack chasing them down. Then, following victories on the road at Southampton and Nottingham Forest, the Gunners beat Newcastle United 1-0 on 17 April to go top of the table.

An emotion-filled Islington afternoon was nothing, though, compared to the angry, combustible game that same afternoon at Elland Road where the referee, Ray Tinkler, overruled his linesman flagging for offside in the build-up and allowed a West Brom goal that contributed to a 2-1 defeat for Leeds. Tinkler infuriated Revie and his players by insisting Jeff Astle hadn't been interfering with play at the time. Back in the dressing room, they would have learnt of the full implications of their defeat – Arsenal's victory against Newcastle meant that the Gunners had chased them down.

We maintained our narrow advantage, beating Burnley by the now obligatory scoreline of 1-0 before travelling to The Hawthorns and sharing the points in an entertaining 2-2 draw. It was now in Arsenal's hands as we headed into the home straight. But although we had an advantage over Leeds, we still had to go to Elland Road on Monday, 26 April.

The players travelled with a clear belief in themselves which was no bravado. In the spring of 71, Arsenal felt like a juggernaut and everyone else a three-wheeler. It turned out to be a fierce contest, toe-to-toe stuff, two heavyweights slugging it out. Leeds nicked it with a late and hotly disputed goal scored by Jack Charlton; one that Arsenal complained bitterly was offside. Back at the team hotel afterwards, I spoke to Bob McNab. 'I think I played him onside,' Bob admitted. The narrative of the unjust defeat, though, was good PR for Mee to feed the press and let's not forget it was still in our hands. But Bob had surprised me with what he said because he was such an intelligent and calm player, an absolute master of the offside, usually the officer controlling the whole manoeuvre.

We soon put that defeat at Leeds behind us. I sometimes think it was a blessing as, if we hadn't lost at Leeds, we wouldn't have had the opportunity of being able to clinch the title at White Hart Lane.

Our final home game of the season was against Stoke City, a team who we knew bore us a bit of a grudge and the Potters put in the kind of performance which suggested they wanted anyone but Arsenal to win the league. Their combative showing was only defeated by a late goal from Eddie Kelly, who had come on as a substitute for the injured Storey. Leeds won their last game at home, 2-0 against Forest, to lead Arsenal by a point. With the Gunners having a fractionally better goal average, the challenge was clearcut – a clean sheet the following Monday at Tottenham and Arsenal would be champions for the first time since 1953.

During the victory over Stoke City, Peter Storey had limped off. I spoke with Peter in the players' lounge immediately after the game and asked him what his prospects were for Monday night. Peter had a tremendous threshold for pain, a quick recovery time and he rarely missed a game for us. There was no way I could ever imagine Peter sitting out a game like Spurs away with the title at stake. He seemed genuinely doubtful that he would be passed fit to play but this battle was one that any side would want Peter in the ranks for.

On the Sunday, my telephone almost never stopped ringing. The news was getting out about Storey; friends just wanted reassurance and everyone needed to hear it was going to be all right on Monday evening. Despite feeling that Peter was going to come up short in his fitness test, I was extremely confident about the week ahead. I'd seen this team close up for a long time and I think I knew what made them tick, as a group and individually. I had only to cast my mind back 12 months to find evidence that this was a team that could handle pressure: the sheer will to win which had driven them on against Anderlecht had grown over the intervening year. I knew Frank would get them right mentally, too. Frank could be as rousing as Churchill. This was our moment.

On the Monday, I set off early for White Hart Lane and arrived at 4pm for a 7.30pm kick-off. I simply couldn't believe my eyes. The place was just a heaving mass of Arsenal supporters, an ocean of red and white as far as you could see. I read after the game that the police estimated upwards of 150,000 Arsenal supporters were locked out. Some friends told me they had been in Stoke Newington, three miles away, and never got close to the ground; others told me how, despite queuing at the ground from 3pm, they never saw the game.

I headed to Tottenham's main entrance and waited for the arrival of the Arsenal team bus. There was chaos on all sides of me. I watched as absolutely desperate Arsenal supporters tried to buy season ticket books off Spurs fans; the last remaining vouchers were changing hands for upwards of £20 when the season ticket, even if it was a good season ticket, had probably only cost £15.

The Arsenal team bus was massively delayed and didn't arrive until gone 6.30pm. In fact, the players had to leave the bus and walk the last few yards when it finally became stuck fast in the crowded streets. Although it was eating into their preparation time, it must have given the players such a massive boost to see *so* many Arsenal faces; it was just Arsenal everywhere.

Back in those days, the players seemed to have a much bigger connection with the supporters; we identified with the players and they identified with us. As the team bus had crawled its way through the crowds on its way to White Hart Lane and the players looked out at the thousands of beseeching faces, they would have seen people like themselves; they would have absolutely understood who they were playing for that night – not just the club but all these people whose lives and histories overlapped with Arsenal's. They would have understood what this moment meant to the lives all these people would go back to after the game.

Peter Storey, whose injury kept him out of the team, had managed to leave my ticket at the ticket office and, after struggling through yet more queues, I made my way into the ground. This was it, the moment my Arsenal life had been heading towards since I was that little kid playing football in the street; since I had defied my father and gone to the game all those years ago. It was just a football match but so, so much more than *just* a football match.

What I witnessed was quite probably the most psychologically and emotionally intense game I had ever seen or experienced; at the end, I was physically and mentally drained.

When Kennedy scored with barely two minutes left, it didn't really change things; one Tottenham goal would have still handed the title to Leeds United on goal average. Frank always said that once Arsenal got a goal up, we didn't even draw a game, never mind lose it, and it felt like that. The Arsenal boys were magnificent. Each and every one of them. The wonderful Bob Wilson withstood an absolute barrage of physical attacks, standing his ground as Mullery, Gilzean and, especially, Mike England all tried to give him a going over. Bob was outstanding that night.

It was the final game before retirement for referee Kevin Howley and so that I could keep tabs on how long was left, I had set my watch by his whistle. I was checking it regularly and he definitely blew up early. When his whistle was blown, it is impossible to put into words how I felt or what it meant to me. Thousands and thousands of happy Arsenal supporters ran on to the pitch and hoisted skipper McLintock on to their shoulders. It was a kind of joyous chaos I'd never seen or felt before. Arsenal were champions; it was there in the record books forever.

As the players finally made their way through the crowds of back slappers, back to the sanctuary of the dressing room, Bertie Mee came to the front of the directors' box and basked in the noisy acclaim of the euphoric Gunners massed before him. Bertie, looking almost regal in his own moment of success and vindication, waved and acknowledged the crowds.

As all this was going on, I sensed my own opportunity: while all attention was drawn towards Bertie, I hopped over a low wall into the rear of the directors' box and slipped out the back and made my way down towards the dressing rooms. It didn't take long to find; with the noise and the sounds of celebration I was soon inside, joining in. There was laughter and smiles; the muddied and sweaty Arsenal shirts, treasured artefacts, hanging here and laying there, worn with such pride only minutes earlier. 'Play for the shirt' is the eternal and abiding wish of football supporters everywhere; have 11 men ever done more credit to that shirt than these heroes?

I had shared disappointments with them and talked through their ambitions with them; I knew all of them, some of them I knew as close friends, but this was a thoroughly unique moment for all of us. The joy and the unmitigated happiness that radiated from every face forms a memory that comes back to me in all the same clarity as when I lived those moments all those years ago. This was the fulfilment of all my Arsenal hopes since the early years of boyhood.

Sat slightly apart, unnoticed by the majority was Jon Sammels – boyhood Arsenal supporter, gifted Arsenal footballer and a man totally in the love with the club. He had given so much to Arsenal and made as big a contribution to the Fairs Cup success as anyone when he was one of many Arsenal warriors against Anderlecht. Tears ran down his cheeks; for, at the very moment he had worked so hard for these past few years, the moment Arsenal were crowned league champions, he knew he would never play again for Arsenal, the club he loved. It was absolutely heartbreaking to witness. I talked with him for a time and tried to convince him of what I truly believed: that he had contributed as much as anyone to Arsenal's success and completely deserved his champion's medal. I think it helped him a bit but it must have felt like very cold comfort. While his team-mates scaled the heights, poor Jon could only look on.

After leaving the dressing room, I made my way to the Tottenham boardroom, where I heard their chairman, Sidney Wale, make a commendably generous speech congratulating Arsenal while acknowledging just how difficult the evening had been for him and his club. It was, he admitted, a painful experience. Senior players like Mullery and England had faces like thunder but I noticed a very young Steve Perryman, he must have been only about 18 at the time, smiling and looking very relaxed; I remember thinking at the time 'Steve, you don't fully realise the significance of this defeat'.

When I finally dragged myself away, I made my way towards The White Hart. It was absolute bedlam there and I didn't even get close to getting in and, so, moved on to my old pal Derrick Dagger's club, the Pair of Shoes in the West End and enjoyed a fabulous meal and a night of celebration befitting this great night in Arsenal's history.

Being crowned champions certainly relaxed the players in the days leading up to Wembley. John Radford later commented that after winning the league, the players hit the pub and stayed there for two days, dragging themselves back to the training ground on Thursday afternoon.

In those days, the players almost had an 'official' outlet for tickets in Stan Flashman. However, Peter Storey told me he wasn't going to sell his to Flashman and wanted to know if I would like to sell them to my Arsenal friends. Even at a club the size of Arsenal, selling tickets was still a massive perk for the players; the club knew it but turned a blind eye. So, I phoned around my friends and in no time at all, 30 tickets at £5 a go were snapped up, with the cash duly passed on to Peter.

It wasn't the only bit of good news for Peter, either; on the Friday morning, he phoned me to say he had been passed fit for the final.

Some years later, he gave me the full story behind the fitness test. It had been supervised by Bertie Mee himself and was by far the hardest, most demanding fitness test Peter had ever known. Storey's belief (still to this day) was that Bertie actually wanted him to break down and just kept the test going in the hope Peter that would pull up. The thinking behind this was that Bertie wanted to play young Eddie Kelly at Wembley. Looking at it dispassionately, there may be some truth in this assessment. Back then, in 1971, Liverpool were an efficient team whose strength lay very much in their defence. The chances were that they would sit back and, in what was predictably going to be a tight game, Mee perhaps thought that Kelly might have more to offer than Peter. Anyway, not even Bertie would risk dropping a fit Peter Storey for a cup final and, so, after missing out on Monday evening, Peter got to play at Wembley, very much what he deserved after everything he had given to the cause that season.

There was a real carnival atmosphere in the streets around the ground and across Islington and this grew and grew as we got closer to Saturday's game. Everywhere was a sea of yellow and blue, shop windows all proclaiming support and wishing the boys good luck.

Come Saturday, which dawned under clear blue skies, Wembley was soon basking in roasting heat. Arsenal were the better team and really should have won it inside 90 minutes. George Graham shone as bright as the blazing sun that afternoon; it was the perfect setting for his abilities and he turned in a real virtuoso performance, being named man of the match for his efforts. I thought John Radford deserved the honour just that little bit more, though. John was simply magnificent for the entire 120 minutes it took to win the cup. You had the full range of his abilities on display and he showcased just why he was so valuable to Arsenal. Despite the heat, John put on a show of pace, strength, workrate and skill; he was as strong as an ox and knocked the ball into Charlie's path for the boy from the North Bank to bang in the winner.

The moment the final whistle came will stay with me forever: what an achievement, what a week, what a moment! I think everyone was exhausted – the supporters as much as the players.

I wanted to get to the team to be part of the celebrations. I knew Wembley like the back of my hand; I used to 'jib' into every major game played there and, so, over time I got to know the layout behind the scenes, including the location of the dressing rooms. So, as the team were completing their lap of honour, I managed to make it to the tunnel just as they were leaving the playing area and proceeded with them back to the dressing room. When we got there, I vividly remember drinking from that magnificent trophy in time-honoured fashion. The atmosphere in the dressing room was actually slightly more muted than you might expect, given what had been achieved, but I think the players were simply exhausted; mentally, emotionally and physically drained from their efforts of the past few days, not to mention 90 minutes and then extra time in the wide expanse of Wembley in temperatures which had sizzled all day at around 100 degrees Fahrenheit.

Whatever happened now, these men had become the new benchmark; after struggling to bear the weight of the club's history, they had surpassed all that had gone before. The team from 1971 would become *the* Arsenal team we would judge all others against for a very long time.

A clipped and imperious voice suddenly broke across the dressing room: a sergeant major's bellow brought me up short. Predictably enough, Bertie, a man with a long memory, wasn't having me in there and security was duly directed to ask me to 'move along'. It didn't bother me one bit. I'd seen the players, drunk from the cup and, for the second time in six days, I'd celebrated with my beloved Gunners as trophies were secured. *The Times* journalist and great doyen of football writers, Brian Glanville, was in the dressing room at the time and was quite amused by the incident and it got a reference in his report of the game in the Sunday edition. A big Arsenal supporter was Brian Glanville; after publishing his first book at the age of 19, a ghost-written autobiography of Arsenal's Cliff Bastin, he never looked back. He was badly bullied at school because of his Jewish background and often said his love of the Gunners kept him going as a schoolboy.

Anyway, the day wasn't quite yet over. There was a private party, arranged by Stan Flashman, Archie Davis and John Green at the Portman Hotel. It was a fitting conclusion to a few dreamlike days that I doubted I would ever see again.

By the time I got home, I was absolutely exhausted. While all this had been going on, Judy had been the most patient and accommodating of wives and she had chosen this week to visit her parents in Vienna with our baby, Danny. Perhaps anticipating that I would be a bag of nerves and somewhat preoccupied, she'd given me a bit of space to get on with it.

The celebrations would rumble on into Sunday, when the team paraded the two trophies through the streets on an open-topped bus and headed to Islington Town Hall. Beneath yet more sunshine, along with around half a million people, I gave this incredible Arsenal team the tribute they so richly deserved.

## Chapter Nine

# 1971/72

THE BIGGEST story of the season ran before ever a ball was kicked. Don Howe, frustrated and hurt at the lack of recognition from the club, left Highbury for a shot at managing West Bromwich Albion and with him went valued backroom staff like youth team coach Brian Whitehouse and physio George Wright. Howe's departure caused us to lose sight of what our strengths were and helped to sow the seeds of a disharmony which would lead to the premature break-up of our wonderful Double team.

The clarity of thought which had become Arsenal's hallmark was about to be sacrificed for a dalliance with style. McLintock said we lost our 'intensity', while Bertie, perhaps, began to become distracted with a private quest to rebut Arsenal's critics, who carped about our style of play.

It could have all been so easily avoided. When Denis Hill-Wood rose to speak at the club reception, on the evening of the cup final, he lauded Bertie Mee's role in what Arsenal had achieved but there was no reference at all to Don Howe's contribution. I think to Hill-Wood, Howe was merely a good appointment for which Bertie deserved all the credit. Whatever, the chairman's silence became the tipping point for Howe. Some kind of tangible acknowledgment – making Don assistant manager, for example – may well have been sufficient to placate him.

As the official banquet drew to a close, most of the guests made their way to the Portland Hotel, in the West End, for a more informal reception laid on by Stan Flashman, Jimmy Quill and others. I had a long conversation with Don that evening and he outlined just how disappointed he was with the board's attitude towards him. I think he felt taken for granted. Whereas Bertie was 'stiff upper lip Arsenal',

Don bridged the gap between upstairs and downstairs. From the players' perspective, Don was the 'football man' out of him and Bertie; he was the tracksuit man out on the training ground. In a way, a lot of Bertie's authority rested on Don's excellence. I'd have to admit that my talk with Don left me with a very negative feeling, despite the highs of the previous week.

When Don left and became the manager at The Hawthorns, there remained a fair bit of ill-will towards him from the board. I think Don and the players were viewed as very much being 'them', while Bertie, dapper and military Bertie, had been seamlessly assimilated into 'us', with the board.

Don's resignation cast a shadow over the whole pre-season. It became a very messy divorce and it filled the back pages of the papers. The argument was being conducted in public, which felt un-Arsenal-like.

Denis Hill-Wood maintained that Howe had failed to keep him informed of his plans and had shown a lack of 'business courtesy' by taking other members of staff with him. Arsenal's chairman reminded the public that the club had never stood in anybody's way and that Howe could have left with his blessing. When Hill-Wood, by his own admission angered by the whole thing, began to couch his anger in terms such as 'disgraceful', I think Don felt he had to publicly speak out.

In a series of interviews with Ken Jones of the *Daily Mirror*, Howe got his view across. 'I would still be at Arsenal if the club had made it clear they wanted me,' was Howe's line. He insisted that Hill-Wood had blackened his character and been unfair. Both West Brom and Leicester City had requested permission to speak to Howe and Howe had gone as far as to request a meeting with Hill-Wood to discuss Leicester City's offer but Hill-Wood was simply never available for any meeting. Don claimed that the final straw was when he was told by Bob Wall, the club secretary, that the chairman would be unavailable for a week as he was 'racing at Ascot'. Howe's response to this rather dismissive shot across his bows was to hand in his resignation.

Mee and Wall attempted to smooth things over and maintained they understood Howe's ambitions and wished him well but no such expression ever came from Hill-Wood. Frank McLintock tried to persuade Don to change his mind and Bob Wilson commented before Don finally resigned: 'It would be a terrible blow for the club if Don left.'

Howe's replacement was to be reserve-team coach Steve Burtenshaw, who had come to Highbury in 1967 as a replacement for Don when Howe had taken on first-team duties. During his time with the reserves, Burtenshaw had been a notable success, twice winning the Football Combination, as well as the Football Combination Cup and the London FA Challenge Cup. Steve had also played a big part in the development of youngsters like Kelly, George and Kennedy. He was the standout candidate.

Before he, too, left for pastures new, Jon Sammels commented that when he had been dropped and began training with the reserves, Burtenshaw had been extremely encouraging. 'Arsenal has been lucky,' said Sammels, 'in having had two of the best coaches in the country in Dave Sexton and Don and I am sure they will make it a hat-trick with Steve.'

Bertie felt pretty pleased with himself in the summer of 1971. I think his ego went through the roof after the Double and he started to believe he could do it all again without Don. I think that in Burtenshaw, Mee felt that not only did he have a great fit for the role of coach but that Burtenshaw would also be an ally in the stylistic transition he hoped to enact at Highbury.

The players, for their part, all believed that Mee could have done more to keep Howe at the club. They believed Bertie could have made more effort to talk the chairman round had he really wanted Howe to stay. Steve Burtenshaw was well liked amongst the players and had achieved some success. The younger players, especially, were positive – George, Kelly and Kennedy had all been helped by Burtenshaw.

Initially, we got off to a very poor start and, by autumn, we were down in mid-table and never really rallied. The early rounds of the European Cup provided some easy pickings: a 7-1 aggregate success over Norwegian team Stromgodset was followed up with 5-0 aggregate victory over Grasshoppers Zurich. European football could now be put to one side until the spring.

Bertie wanted a more attractive passing game to become Arsenal's trademark style. To this end, he acquired what he believed would be a significant piece of the jigsaw at Christmas when he persuaded the board to break the British transfer record and spend £220,000 on World Cup winner Alan Ball. Ball was 26 and at his peak, a proven world-class midfielder who was as feisty as he was technically talented. He would demand the ball and dictate how Arsenal's play developed.

When Ball made his debut, at Forest on Boxing Day in a 1-1 draw, a game which saw thousands of excited Arsenal fans make the trip to Nottingham, it was, perhaps, significant that the man left out to accommodate Ball was my best mate, Peter Storey; if ever a manager wanted to signal a sea change in approach, Ball for Storey was like shouting it from the rooftops.

The transfer of Ball, while very exciting, seemed an odd one. Clubs in those days rarely sold key players to teams they saw as competitors. The question that kept on going round my mind was: why would Everton *want* to sell him? Ball was part of that revered Everton midfield, 'The Holy Trinity', and a player Howard Kendall, the greatest Everton player of all-time, described as the greatest Everton player ever. Everton manager Harry Catterick would later explain it as merely 'a great bit of business'; it was, after all, a British record fee. Evertonians described the sale as 'seismic' and Ball, himself a Lancashire lad, maintained he never wanted to leave. But for all his undoubted talent and charismatic presence, Ball was a divisive figure; he could be very outspoken and challenging. I think Catterick had probably had his fill of him.

When he came to Highbury, Ball entered a settled, harmonious dressing room; that didn't last long. Bertie Mee had introduced a pay structure at the club which was largely based upon a loyalty bonus. It worked quite simply. For every season you had been at the club as a professional, you received a 10 per cent bonus on top of your weekly salary. So, if a player was paid £100 a week, he would get an additional £10 for each season he had been at Highbury. It effectively meant that the highest earners were, indeed, the most senior players. When Ball signed, that all ended; it effectively moved the goalposts. Ball immediately earned more than any of them and he wasn't shy about letting his colleagues know. So, as soon as he arrived, a little bit of harmony and togetherness was lost. He earned more than club captain McLintock. Some of the younger players were especially put out; these were lads who were established first-team players but Ball was earning far more than any of them.

I can't say I knew Ball that well but I knew him well enough to form an opinion of him. I went out with him once; he, Peter Storey and myself went to Tramp, the nightclub in Mayfair, and it was clear from the start that Ball expected me to pay for him. My position with the players was perhaps an unusual one. I was, after all, 'only' a supporter but I had immediately been accepted as an equal by them all; never, ever had it been implied that I might have to pay for the privilege of their friendship. I've never bought an Arsenal friendship in my life. Indeed, it was, if anything, the other way round; when I had been a bit hard-up, players had, for example, paid for my meals.

Let's be clear, Alan Ball was a great footballer but I don't think Arsenal ever saw the best of him and that is what I focus on, regardless of whether I liked the man. The other players rated him but I think you would be hard pushed to find a voice amongst the players that didn't balance Ball's contribution as a player with the negative effect he had on the dressing room. The issue of his pay undermined the settled harmony amongst the players and, although he came to Highbury quite rightly recognised as a class act, there would have been more than a few players questioning why we had to disrupt a proven winning style of football in order to accommodate him. The team Ball joined was still some time away from hitting its peak. With Ball, we began going down a different footballing avenue entirely.

The season ended disappointingly. Our defence of the league title fell flat and two cup defeats are largely what stand out. The season might have been rescued had we prevailed in the 1972 FA Cup Final. The FA had hoped for a pageant of football to mark the centenary of the first cup final in 1872; perhaps Leeds United v Arsenal wasn't what sprang to mind and the game picked up where the 1968 League Cup Final left off. Ninety minutes of attritional toe-to-toe effort saw Leeds take the cup 1-0 with a headed goal from Allan Clarke.

Geoff Barnett played that day because Bob Wilson had badly damaged his cartilage in the semi-final against Stoke City at Villa Park. Bob went off in the semi-final with some time remaining and the score at 1-1. Big John Radford went in goal and we safely saw out time. Bob was always a bit put out about that injury. As tensions mounted and with Bob writhing on the ground, Peter Storey encouraged him to grit his teeth: 'There's nothing fucking wrong with you, now get on with it.' We won the replay the following Wednesday evening at Goodison Park after a nightmare journey up to the game – the country was in the midst of strikes which had hit the railways.

In 1972, when Danny was nearly three, tragedy struck our family. Great Ormond Street Hospital confirmed the diagnosis that Danny had leukaemia – acute lymphoblastic leukaemia, known as ALL. It is the most common form of leukaemia in children and also the one they have most success in curing. However, their prognosis for Danny made grim listening; they gave him just three years. At the time, Judy was seven months into her pregnancy with our second child. It is impossible to try to conceive how this kind of news is articulated. You just want to love your child even more, if that is at all possible. We went back and forth between home and the hospital as Danny underwent treatment. He was part of a clinical trial based on different combinations of powerful drugs, which enabled the physicians over time to put together the most effective combination to achieve their goal. These trials have resulted in a wonderful improvement in the treatment of sick children these days but it is an improvement which just came too late for Danny. Now they are able to cure the majority of cases where children have the same diagnosis Danny had but, sadly, that wasn't the case for Danny. I spent many nights there with Danny and then went straight off to work in the morning. The side effects and the implications of the treatment Danny underwent could be very cruel at times, even life-threatening. Of course, you feel completely helpless. I don't think there is anything worse than seeing a child, your own child, suffering and you feeling impotent in the face of that suffering. I can't speak highly enough of the hospital and the staff and to them we remain eternally grateful. Judy's parents moved, too, from Vienna to London, to help after the birth of our second child, David, born just two months after Danny's diagnosis. My in-laws were such a wonderful help. They were living just up the road and it meant that they could focus on David while we gave our full attention to Danny. The family celebrations were understandably rather muted – but how Danny loved his baby brother.

It was two years since we had outfought and outplayed the new kings of European football, Ajax, in that Fairs Cup semi-final and I think the memory of just how ferociously Arsenal had taken the battle to them played on their minds. The tie was keenly anticipated and well over 50,000 attended the first leg staged at the Olympic Stadium.

We returned from Amsterdam with a creditable result and very much in the tie. Against a backdrop of horns and firecrackers, we had taken the lead when Ray Kennedy latched on to a weak header back to the keeper. A period of fairly frenetic pressure ensued when Wilson tipped a curling effort over the bar and then Simpson cleared a goal-bound attempt off the line. Pressure from Ajax ultimately bore fruit and the teams went in at half-time all square. An appalling award of a penalty, which nearly turned McLintock apoplectic, enabled Ajax to end the game with a narrow 2-1 advantage.

At the start of the season, I think most of the players felt we had a decent chance of winning the European Cup. There was still the lingering belief circulating in British football that European teams, while technically proficient, didn't like a battle. In many ways, Arsenal's stirring victories in 1970 against both Ajax and Anderlecht were living proof of just how irresistible the brand of fast, physical, committed football played in England could be against even the very best teams from Europe.

I think we all felt that, back at Highbury, the reigning European champions could be taken. Ball was ineligible to play and Radford was out, too, so we started with really only Kennedy up front and Charlie George playing just behind him. The surprise selection was Marinello on the right wing; the young Scot had only started one other game that season.

We started as if we meant it; it was 100 mph stuff and Ajax looked shellshocked only a few minutes in. Arsenal's intensity soon led to a mistake; an Ajax defender dawdled on the ball and Marinello nipped in and was through on goal. Peter scuffed his shot and the keeper, Stuy, saved easily. If that goes in, it's a totally different game. The miss has come to almost define Marinello's career at Arsenal.

After a quarter of an hour, disaster struck. An aimless punt down Arsenal's middle was guided back to Wilson by Graham. As the ball looped harmlessly goalwards, it was suddenly clear that Wilson was out of position and the whole ground watched in horror as the softest of efforts gently bobbled into an unguarded net.

And that was that. Storey was very disappointed; in the dressing room after the game, he felt no one could say they had all left *everything* out on the pitch. In those days, these sort of chances of winning Europe's premier competition rarely came around; back in 1972, there was no sneaking into the competition courtesy of finishing fourth.

The euphoria of 12 months earlier had faded. Mee appeared reluctant to commit to the style of football which had paid dividends for us. It is always difficult to know when to begin the process of rebuilding a football team. The acquisition of Ball was evidence of looking to the future but it came at a cost. I don't think many supporters, if any, gave a thought about style while we were winning the Double.

Chapter Ten

# 1972–1975

### *1972/73*

The 1972/73 season represented the last hurrah for that group of players. In the early spring, we were looking a good bet for an unlikely repeat of the Double. A magnificent victory at Anfield had seen the Gunners go top, victory a week later at home to Leicester City augmented that position and, with progress in the FA Cup, it looked for a while as if we had got ourselves back in to the kind of groove that had proved so durable in '71.

By the time we won 2-0 at Anfield, we had come through something of an identity crisis. Courtesy of Mee's enduring wish to transform us, he had experimented with our own version of 'Total Football'. In some ways, it wasn't quite the outlandish idea it at first appears. What 'Total Football' called for was intelligence. Bob McNab and Frank McLintock were as smart as any footballers I ever met; Peter Storey could read games and situations; Peter Simpson was as comfortable playing in midfield as in defence; Alan Ball could be the 'general' through whom the game developed, with Eddie Kelly as his lieutenant; and, in Charlie George, we had a player who had not long ago been picked out by Cruyff as one of the biggest talents in European football. To his credit, Mee, who in many ways was the embodiment of Arsenal-past, never lost sight of the future. He had once embraced the future of physiotherapy and now he recognised the intellectual *avant garde* of Rinus Michels's football philosophy as the way forward and as the route he wanted to take Arsenal.

It was certainly an ambitious plan; from pragmatism to purity – Highbury didn't know what had hit it. One of Mee's first acts was to restore the young Scottish misfit Peter Marinello to the team at the expense, once again, of George Armstrong. Marinello would start the next 17 competitive matches, which must have been his longest run of appearances for the club by some distance. The experiment didn't last long and was abandoned in late November after a 5-0 drubbing at the Baseball Ground. The performance at Derby had been so abject and the defeat so comprehensive that it came as an irrefutable confirmation that the change of system had led to us losing any sense of potency in our attacking play while looking nothing short of ragged when Derby attacked us. Derby played well that day; Alan Hinton kept putting the ball on people's foreheads and poor old Bob Wilson must have been left to rue the fact that this game was his first back after a long lay-off following his knee injury.

I believe Frank had spoken out against the new system in some heated meetings and the Derby defeat was probably the last straw. I think he most likely traced the problems back to the signing of Ball. Frank and I quite recently talked about Alan Ball and Frank was of the view that the changes Mee implemented in order to accommodate Ball were made far too quickly and a slower evolution would have helped bed in the changes more successfully. Ball's signing, as far as Frank was concerned, completely changed the way we played; now, *everything* had to go through Ball. McLintock has always been keen to point out that we had done pretty well with the old style of play. Frank rated Ball as a footballer but perhaps could never see him as a 'great signing', given the detrimental effect he ultimately had upon how Arsenal went about winning football matches. And then we signed Jeff Blockley.

Coventry City boss Joe Mercer thought that the £200,000 he received for his muscular centre-half Blockley was, by any standards, a 'shrewd sale'. When we signed a player, Peter Storey was my go-to. Peter was honest in his opinions and a very, very good judge of a player – and he was not impressed by Blockley. Frank McLintock never changed his view that Blockley's signing was a disaster for the club. Mee made it explicitly clear that Blockley had been purchased to replace Frank, sooner rather than later. When he signed, he was initially paired with Frank in the centre of defence but quite quickly Frank was to be dropped and Bertie put Blockley and Simpson together. When we played against Birmingham City just before Christmas, Frank, by his own admission, reacted badly to being told he was dropped and unfortunately was heard passing unfavourable comments about his boss within Mee's hearing; and that was Frank done for. Mee was convinced that Arsenal had seen Frank's best days and he needed replacing. Mee rarely changed his mind.

Poor Marinello didn't survive the Derby debacle and was dropped once more, rarely emerging thereafter. McLintock did reappear towards the end of the season when Blockley picked up an injury, getting a run of nine games, but no matter how well Frank played, Bertie stuck to his line that, once fit, Blockley would return. That moment came when we played Sunderland in an FA Cup semi-final. Frank was dropped and Blockley came in and made one of those mistakes in a high profile match that can define a player; an under-hit backpass resulted in Sunderland's opener. We had a couple of good chances – Armstrong hit a post and Ball nearly picked up a rebound – but their keeper, Jim Montgomery, had a blinder. Most Arsenal fans who were there remember Blockley's poor performance above all else.

We only won one more game after that and were left floundering in second spot, wrapping up the season with 6-1 defeat at Leeds United. I believe the story has circulated that Blockley started against Sunderland while still carrying his injury; regardless, to drop Frank for a semi-final to accommodate *anyone* was a brave move.

By now, the loyalty bonus scheme had been scrapped; once Ball had signed, its demise was inevitable. It seems inconceivable that Mee hadn't thought through the implications of Ball's salary.

Blockley was Mee's final big-money purchase and when he eventually moved him on to Leicester City, Mee admitted that the big centre-half represented his worst deal during his time as Arsenal manager. Frank submitted a formal transfer request in March 1973 and eventually moved on to Queens Park Rangers in June for £25,000. It felt a rather ignominious 'backdoor' exit for such an illustrious servant of the club. By submitting a transfer request, Frank did himself out of a testimonial, too, falling just short of the requisite ten years' service. At QPR, he would continue to prove his worth and, in 1975/76, he came close to a sensationally unexpected title triumph with the unfashionable club from west London, two years after Arsenal had judged him to be past his best.

Frank would later testify to Arsenal having lost their focus once Don Howe had left and in the close season of 1973, the man who had replaced Howe, Steve Burtenshaw, resigned, too. It was the shelving of the 'pressing' aspect of our tactical set-up during Steve's period as coach that had disillusioned Frank. Steve moved on to Sheffield Wednesday and his position as first-team coach at Highbury went to Bobby Campbell.

Campbell was extremely likeable but never likely to be the right choice of coach for a team that was becoming slightly bloated and divided. Peter Storey liked Bobby – most of the players did – but I don't think he was ever convinced of his credentials to coach a club like Arsenal. It was always going to be difficult because any coach was still in the shadow of Howe; I think people could see the size of the job developing at Arsenal, too.

## *1973/74*

The atmosphere around Highbury as 1973/74 kicked off matched the negative feeling generally in English football. The national team was at a crossroads and, by late autumn, would fail to qualify for the 1974 World Cup. Sir Alf Ramsey would become yesterday's man overnight. Amongst Arsenal supporters, Mee had started to cut a similarly distant figure to Ramsey.

The season started well; on a sunny day at Highbury, more than 50,000 saw us dispatch Manchester United 3-0. We were a goal up inside a couple of minutes and, on a sweltering day, turned in a really good performance. It was a misleading opening, though; we followed it with defeats at home to Leeds and then Leicester City; sandwiched in between was a 5-0 hammering at Sheffield United. Two weeks after beating United, we were in the bottom three. We would go on to hover around mid-table all season. We were never far from being turned over and we suffered two embarrassing cup exits. Tranmere came to Highbury in the League Cup in October and won 1-0 and then Second Division Aston Villa knocked us out of the FA Cup in a fourth round replay.

As the season drew to a close, Bob Wilson announced his intention to begin a new career in the media. Bob had been a constant presence, barring injury, between the posts for nearly a decade. He was as brave as a lion – bravery well illustrated by his tendency and success in hurling himself at the feet of onrushing forwards. He was probably the best keeper I have ever seen in one-on-one situations.

We didn't have to look far for his successor in Jimmy Rimmer, a somewhat dour and reserved Lancastrian who had signed from Manchester United in February 1974 and proved to be one of Bertie's best buys, as well as possibly the most miserable looking footballer I have ever seen! I think we picked up Rimmer for less than £50,000. Jimmy had made his debut for us towards the end of the 73/74 season in a rare success, a 1-0 win at Anfield. That victory helped the club climb to a position of respectability and finish the season in tenth place.

I can't say I knew Jimmy at all. He didn't appear to be close to any of the players. He was taciturn – friendly but he kept himself to himself. He would be joined soon enough by another signing from Manchester United, Brian Kidd. Both players did well for us; in fact, without them we may have succumbed to relegation in either of the two following seasons. Kidd wasn't that expensive, either. We got both for less than Blockley cost. I am not sure that either player had especially wanted to move to Highbury; they were both boys from the north-west and Kidd, I recall, was particularly homesick. He was known as a bit of a Mancunian moaner, always going on about how much better Manchester was. Neither player settled in London but credit to them both, they did very well for us.

The reason we had moved for Kidd was down to the sale of Ray Kennedy to Liverpool. Ray had had a quiet season, it was true, and had problems with his weight. I think he was probably affected by his off-field problems, too; Ray had separated from his wife and I think this had taken its toll on him. When he left, I know John Radford was upset about it. For Ray's part, he never wanted to go, not even to Liverpool; he would have stayed at Highbury for as long as Arsenal wanted him. Ray is largely remembered for his goal at Tottenham in 1971 when we clinched the title but arguably as important was his late strike against Anderlecht in 1970 in the first leg of the Fairs Cup Final.

There was some real talent emerging in 1974: Liam Brady, Frank Stapleton and David O'Leary, as well as Richie Powling and David Price. I suspect Mee recognised that he had to bridge the gap until these young talents came of age. Signings like Brian Kidd were part of that effort to keep the club afloat for a couple of seasons while these young players matured. When he finally left the club, Mee commented, half wistfully, that the future looked very bright and that the nucleus of a new young team was in place, with only a couple of shrewd signings needed to give the club the chance of winning honours again.

## *1974/75*

Attendance figures show that for 1974/75 the club retained around 16,000 diehard supporters; the rest of the club's support, disgruntled and wavering at the start of the season, quickly haemorrhaged as the autumn turned to winter and the club settled down to a fight for survival. The supporters knew all too well that the club was in decline. Mee appeared to have lost his way and to have no real idea of what route to take other than to hope to survive long enough for the kids to save us and him. Most fans are realistic about the prospects for their club but the complete absence of hope is a real killer.

My connection with the dressing meant I saw and heard things that others didn't. Take Charlie George, for example. Charlie still had wonderful ability but it got evermore buried beneath the effects of injuries and an attitude that came close at times to being almost contemptuous of his boss. Charlie really became obsessed with Bertie and was often letting go far from complimentary observations concerning his manager. When a player believes the manager is the cause of the club's decline, then it feels that the situation is close to being lost.

Charlie is still revered by Arsenal supporters from that era and rightly so. 'Charlie: The King of Highbury!' … a young boy who supported Arsenal, stood on the North Bank and lived his dream. That final season, he rarely seemed to be fit, another point of exasperation for Mee, and, in the summer of 1975, he was moved on.

Charlie was taken to Derby County by Dave Mackay, where he achieved a cult status similar to that he had enjoyed at Highbury. The deal with Derby emerged suddenly, almost out of nowhere, after the press had begun reporting that Charlie, the North Bank hero, had agreed to sign for Tottenham.

It is inconceivable that he could have seriously considered signing for what he would have understood to be the 'enemy' but it suggests the level of frustration and anger he felt. As a young, cocksure player he had, not infrequently, got into trouble for flicking the V's at opposition supporters and you can't help but feel that the threat to move to Spurs was his last defiant gesture aimed at Mee.

Charlie *is* an Arsenal legend and I am delighted the move to Spurs never materialised. Only Charlie knows the truth about it. He was a man who only really saw things in black and white and said things as he saw them with a level of honesty that came close to being reckless. He was a man 'on the edge', a flawed genius who made just one appearance for his country. That single England cap came under Don Revie. After being played out of position, he was substituted on the hour mark and promptly told Revie what he thought of him and his tactics and was never selected again. You've got to love Charlie!

Bobby Campbell had come to Arsenal as coach via QPR and there had worked with a 'diamond geezer' of a player, a real chirpy Londoner who came in like a breath of fresh air for the Highbury dressing room. Looking a bit like a cross between a magician at a children's party and a bouncer, Terry 'Henry' Mancini did a job for us. He was a clever signing, just what we needed. A genuinely warm personality who played with a smile on his face, was proud to wear the Arsenal badge and always played his heart out for the shirt. You could see Terry gave the dressing room a lift and he became a bit of a cult hero. Older supporters will know what I mean with this comment, which is in no way intended to be dismissive, but fans love a 'trier'; I can forgive much but I expect Arsenal footballers to put their heart and soul into a shift when they represent our club. Mancini was a 110 per cent man.

Terry was initially partnered with Peter Simpson, though occasionally a young Richie Powling would sweep up behind him. Powling would go on to have a lot of bad luck with injuries but was, at one time, seen as much a part of the future as David O'Leary. Without the almost continuous run of injuries, Powling could have made it at Arsenal.

We had our moments, even during the very worst of seasons. Not long after Mancini arrived, we went to Anfield and won convincingly 3-1, then followed this up a week later by beating that season's champions, Derby County, by the same score at Highbury. We had a reasonable cup run, too, and by the time we got through to the quarter-finals, we looked a good bet to go all the way. It wasn't to be, though. An absolute mudbath of a pitch at Highbury saw West Ham come and win 2-0. We played well that afternoon. That game saw another low point in Ball's relationship with the club. A week before the cup tie, he and Bob McNab were both sent off in a game at Derby. As a consequence, they would both miss the West Ham game. However, a loophole meant that *if* Arsenal appealed then any ban would be suspended until after the appeal had been heard. Hill-Wood said he wouldn't dream of 'playing the game' and take advantage of an inconsistency in the procedure. Ball was livid and put in his own personal appeal, unsupported by the club. Although Ball was subsequently picked for the tie, he was played in an unfamiliar right-wing role, which it was obvious he wasn't happy about. Peter Storey noted that Ball offered nothing. He didn't show for the ball and if it came to him, he did nothing with it. Ball's attitude was obvious to everyone, Peter told me, but, strangely, not one voice was raised against him after the game.

We limped through to the conclusion of the season, just having enough in the tank to keep our heads above relegation. We had fallen to the very bottom of the table in late autumn but once Mancini had been signed, there was enough of an improvement to survive.

On 14 March 1975, Danny passed away, at home, at the cruelly tender age of just five. He had never been able to go into full remission since the moment he was diagnosed. However, Danny was very brave while he underwent some very harsh treatments and endured the inevitable side effects of such treatments, too. We made sure he had many happy times and that he received a lifetime of love over the three years of his illness. My sister-in-law, Hanna, and her husband, David, together with their children, Jeanette, Tania and Michael, were absolutely the most loving of family around Danny; and he loved them all, too, especially his grandparents, Joe and Berta, and, of course, his younger brother, David.

Danny and Tania had a special relationship; they loved to be with one another. Danny's eyes would light up when he saw Tania. On one occasion, we took them both for a holiday to Bournemouth, which was a great success and brings back happy memories to Judith and myself. We will always be grateful to Tania for the joy and happiness she brought into Danny's life.

It remains impossible to set out in mere words the impact upon you of losing a child: we are reconciled to losing parents but not our children. The loss of Danny remains with me to this day; it will do so to my last day. But in life, we all have to deal with whatever is thrown at us – there is no other option.

We were privileged to have had Danny for those few years at least. He was a beautiful child and, each day, some part of him still managed to shine beyond the reality of his illness and situation. You learn that the wonder of a child can somehow transcend the material reality of their lives. Each day, I look at his photo in our lounge and cannot help but think about what might have been.

## Chapter 11
# 1975/76

AT LEAST Bertie was allowed the dignity of resigning. Anything else would have been a thoroughly unbecoming way to end the reign of a proper Arsenal man, who achieved something no one had ever achieved at Arsenal. When Bertie gave his press conference to announce that he would leave his position as manager after the final game, there was a tear in his eye.

Mee was a very smart man and, crucially, he knew his own limitations. He ran an orderly ship and I think he clearly had the trust of the board. But, by 1975/76, attendances were almost as bad as at the end of Billy Wright's era. Back in the 70s, gate money was about the only source of revenue for football clubs. Although gates were down all over the country, behind the scenes it must have started to become a struggle financially for a club of Arsenal's size. Gates between 16,000 and 18,000 demonstrated just how little interest and faith some supporters had in our immediate future.

The season had opened with a hike up to Burnley; it was a long way to go for what turned out to be the worst game I ever saw. At least we got a point in a 0-0 draw – a match now only remembered for the fact David O'Leary, at the age of just 17, a remarkably young age for a central defender, made his debut; it was the first of his record-breaking 722 appearances for the club.

Bertie bowed out with a 2-1 home defeat to Ipswich Town before a crowd of just 26,000, which, given what he had done for the club, seems a bit sad.

The final word on Bertie: in 1966, I had stood in the pouring rain with just over 4,000 other diehard Arsenal supporters watching us lose 3-0 at home to Leeds United in Billy Wright's penultimate game. Within five years, I had experienced Arsenal winning three trophies. The Double and that famous night at Highbury against Anderlecht will stand for all eternity as Bertie's hugely deserved epitaph and, for what he did for the club, he will always have my respect and admiration.

# Part Three:
# Terry Neill & Don Howe

## Chapter 12

# 1976/77

THE DECISION to appoint Terry Neill as Mee's successor seemed a gamble. Terry had always been a favourite of Denis Hill-Wood's during his time at Highbury as a player but, from a purely football perspective, it didn't really all add up for me. Terry was a very genial and likeable man and, as far as I am concerned, his strong relationship with the chairman worked massively to his advantage during the appointment process.

Terry had built a reputation as a people person. A stint as chairman of the Professional Footballers' Association (PFA) between 1967 and 1970 had given him a platform to display all his charm to great effect. He cut his managerial teeth at Hull City as player-manager after it became obvious he was surplus to requirements at Highbury. He had also served his country, Northern Ireland, as player-manager, too, winning 59 caps and held their all-time appearance record until Pat Jennings beat it. He called time on his playing career at the premature age of only 32 in order to embark upon management full-time. His first full-time managerial job was at Tottenham. Denis Hill-Wood had a very cordial relationship with his Spurs counterpart, Sidney Wale, and Hill-Wood recommended Neill to him. It is remarkable to think that Tottenham sacked their greatest-ever manager, Bill Nicholson, in order to give the job to Terry.

When Mee had announced his departure, the field was fairly open as to who would take his place; no runners had been declared and the betting was all over the place. In the weeks which followed, the name of a young, promising coach, Terry Venables, began to be touted but not before Arsenal had launched, and ultimately failed, an audacious attempt to bring to Highbury one of the tactical heavyweights of European football.

The name which cropped up was so left field. Soon, the back pages of the press were announcing that the club were in advanced talks with the Serbian master tactician Miljan Miljanić. His pedigree was impressive. He coached the imperious Red Star Belgrade and, by the time of Mee's departure, had moved to Real Madrid but was at the end of his two-year contract. Arsenal reportedly offered him a very lucrative deal to come to north London but he opted against it and stayed in Madrid, preferring their one-season extension. The cynical view is that he used Arsenal's interest to convince Madrid to offer him an extension.

I would love to know where the idea to court Miljanić had come from; it was so against the grain of Arsenal's thinking. The idea of Miljanić was revolutionary. I suspect that the man behind the move was either Bob Wall or Ken Friar, general manager and club secretary respectively, but I don't believe the idea would have come from Denis Hill-Wood.

After being offered Miljanić, to be given Terry Neill felt like a letdown. But the likeable Irishman was almost like a son to Denis Hill-Wood and, in the wake of Miljanić staying in Madrid, Terry, at the age of 34, became Arsenal's youngest-ever manager, to go with his record of also being the club's youngest-ever captain.

I bumped into Terry only a couple of days after his appointment – we passed each other in our cars and we both quickly pulled over so we could say hello. Terry was heading to the White House Hotel for a club meeting. I'd known Terry quite well during his playing time at Highbury; he was a nice guy and while it was exciting to think I was on such cordial terms with our new boss, I did retain reservations about Terry being the right choice for the club. I very quickly asked him if he could share with me the names of any players he might be looking at and one name stood out. He told me the club were interested in signing Newcastle United's centre-forward, the charismatic Malcolm Macdonald, but that, from his recent time at Spurs, Terry knew that they were also interested in signing 'Supermac'. Still, it was an ambitious pursuit and certainly benchmarked the calibre of player Neill wanted, regardless of whether we pulled it off.

Macdonald duly signed for, as Hill-Wood stipulated, 'not a penny more than a third of a million' – Arsenal, therefore, paying the unusual fee of £333,333.33. Although he would go on to score a hatful of goals for a couple of seasons, I think even at that stage it was a fairly open secret that Macdonald's knees had gone. The signing was great PR for the club, though; it lifted the spirits of everyone and bought Terry some goodwill amongst his doubters.

With the signing of Macdonald, the writing was probably on the wall for Radford; John had been completely battered in Arsenal's cause for 12 years. After a game, he would be black and blue. By 1976, although he was by no means old, he probably knew himself that he had seen his best days. 'Supermac' was a crowd pleaser and probably put a few thousand on the attendance but I would take Radford in his prime over Macdonald – and I liked Macdonald. 'Supermac' was a popular guy around the dressing room; he was very thick with Ball but, as harsh as it sounds, I thought we could be a better team without him.

I think Terry would have been very well advised to have had a strong figure alongside him in those early days. Terry had a long-standing assistant, someone he described as his best friend in football, Wilf Dixon. Dixon certainly had a strong pedigree; he had been a coach at Goodison Park when Everton won the league in 1970. He had first joined up with Neill at Hull City when Terry realised he needed an older head to guide him. Even though Don Howe returned in 1977, Wilf stayed at Highbury until 1983 as assistant boss.

It became apparent quite quickly that, from a tactical point of view, things were in a mess. If Don had returned 12 months earlier, as Terry took up the reins, then I think that first season could have worked out differently and some of the stories which emerged out of the dressing room of disquiet might never have occurred. I don't think any of the players were even remotely impressed with the level and style of coaching that Terry and Wilf offered. There was the infamous incident when Terry attempted to set out a tactical approach with the aid of toy soldiers. To the older heads, schooled in the coaching of Sexton and Howe, Terry must have seemed rather pedestrian and lightweight.

A decent, and undefeated, four game pre-season, which featured a 3-0 victory against Grasshoppers Zurich with two goals from Macdonald, also saw 'Supermac' paired with young Frank Stapleton up front in all four games. I think Neill probably thought that he knew what he'd get out of Radford, so wanted to take a look at Frank. I already knew, although Frank was highly thought of and admired for his total commitment and dedication, that there remained serious worries at the club about his lack of pace.

Frank was a shy lad, but he gave everything in training and on the pitch. In some ways, he wasn't a natural at all, certainly in terms of athleticism. I know they worked on simple things like his running action to try to get a bit more out of him. But, technically, his game was accomplished and he worked so hard. He was one of the best headers of a football and he worked and worked on his finishing but, while he was mobile and clever with it, he would never beat anyone in a race.

So, when the opening game of the season came around, against newly promoted Bristol City, I wasn't totally surprised to see Radford picked to partner Macdonald up front. It seemed that Neill had made his mind up about Stapleton and had decided to recoup some of the cash spent on Macdonald, agreeing to sell him to Hull City for a fee in the region of £80,000. I think it was pretty much signed and sealed.

We lost that opening game 1-0. I think Radford must have picked up an injury, because it was very quickly all change with Stapleton; the deal was off and poor old Radford didn't start another single competitive match for Arsenal. We played at Norwich in midweek, won 3-1, including a goal from Frank, and that seemed to be it. I imagine Macdonald liked being partnered by Frank, who was so keen and ran all day, doing all the unglamorous work.

There were a few more comings and goings that season as Neill tried to find a middle ground between the young lads coming through and the older hands.

Alex Cropley was sold to Aston Villa for around the fee we paid for him. We all wished him well; a skilful player who had had no luck with injuries since coming south from Hibernian a couple of seasons previous. Two broken legs were testament to his courage; a slight figure who threw himself into 50-50 challenges.

Alan Ball finally became too hot to handle. He was never really a fan of Terry's and I don't think Terry carried sufficient authority to keep Ball in line. He was sold to Second Division Southampton for a modest £60,000 and I think Terry was delighted to see the back of him. Liam Brady has since spoken of his personal regret that Ball was sold, stating how much he had learned from him. Another player to voice his regret at Ball's departure was one of the men only just signed – Alan Hudson. Hudson's belief was that Neill wanted him to play alongside his friend, not replace him. It was a genuine disappointment for Hudson and perhaps one he never quite got over; for, despite the occasional glimmer of his genuine ability, his time at Highbury rarely suggested he was the right man for Arsenal. You never knew quite what you were getting with Hudson and I think it was, ultimately, a bit of an ego signing, by which I mean Terry thought he could get a tune out of Hudson where others had failed. He had a good period in the spring of 1978 but left no real mark befitting of his talent, making just 40 appearances for us. He was always a big risk at £200,000 and when he was sold, still only in his late 20s, we took a £100,000 loss on him.

Peter Storey left, going to Fulham on a free after falling out with Neill when the boss told him to train with the reserves. It was an unbecoming conclusion for an Arsenal great. As an England schoolboy international, he had his pick of clubs but, as an Arsenal supporter, he had chosen Highbury. In March 1977, Bobby Campbell, who was the manager at Fulham, phoned me and asked if I would speak to Peter about a possible move to Craven Cottage. Fulham, despite having George Best and Rodney Marsh playing for them, were dangerously close to the relegation zone. A move was quickly sorted out and, to his dying day, Campbell always maintained that it was Peter Storey who saved Fulham from relegation that year.

The 1976/77 season also saw Arsenal break their record for the longest run of successive defeats – eight in all. In the middle of this sequence, Terry made another signing which, at first glance, looked like a cross between desperation and stopgap but, in time, turned out to be one of the most inspired signings of his reign. Willie Young, who would go on to be a folk hero at Highbury, was picked up from Neill's old club, Tottenham, for £45,000. Willie would become very effective and one half of one of our best centre-back partnerships alongside David O'Leary. He was played out of position at left-back for his debut, which we lost 4-1 at home to Ipswich, and it didn't go well for him. After the match, he gave a good account of himself, though, in an altercation with some of our own supporters, who had been a bit abusive towards him in the car park. In the next game, he was moved to his authentic position, and partnered Pat Howard, but then O'Leary was back and that was it; for the next four seasons, Arsenal's central defensive pair was O'Leary and big Willie Young.

Coincidentally, I chatted with David O'Leary recently about Willie and he spoke as highly as he always has of his old partner. David was a slight figure for a centre-back and, despite being tall, was not especially commanding in the air. He dovetailed brilliantly with

Willie; they each had strengths the other lacked. O'Leary was easier on the eye, a ball-playing defender with great pace who could easily cut it in modern day football but Willie was all action, flailing arms and legs beneath a mop of red hair and was as hard as granite. It's a fact that O'Leary and Young never came close to getting the credit they deserved. A brilliant partnership and Willie comes close to being Terry's best buy.

At one stage, it looked like we might lose every game left that season but we eventually rallied and finished the season in eighth place. After two relegation battles, that was progress of a kind but, by the end of the season, Terry had probably used up what little goodwill he enjoyed. He lost considerable credibility in the eyes of his players when, after being knocked out of the cup 4-1 at Middlesbrough, he let off steam to the press, claiming Arsenal had played like a 'team of dustbins'.

One of the younger players coming through with whom I struck up a very warm friendship, which continues to this day, was O'Leary. David was a very quiet young man, reserved and very courteous. It sounds a bit old fashioned to say, but you could tell he came from a very nice family; he had a good, solid background. David had a real thirst for knowledge; he wanted to learn and get better. He must have been a coach's dream. He was always in the right place and gave away very few free kicks. In my view, he is one of the few players around in the late 70s who could quite easily play today.

It emerged that Terry had been in touch with Dave Sexton about him making a return to the club. Since his time at Arsenal, Sexton's reputation had blossomed. At one stage, I heard that Sexton's return to Highbury was practically signed and sealed. It would have been a great move. However, Manchester United offered him the manager's job at Old Trafford at a much higher salary and Dave went there instead.

Terry was known as a persuasive man and he must have used all his charm in getting Howe's return past Denis Hill-Wood. Distaste still lingered in the boardroom towards Howe and no one had forgotten, let alone forgiven. Don's sortie in football management, when he walked out on Arsenal, had failed when he oversaw West Brom's relegation from the First Division. A successful period as assistant to Jimmy Armfield at Leeds United had led to a return to management in Turkey with Galatasaray, where he led the Lions to a respectable third-place finish.

Although Don appears to have got the job because Sexton decided to go elsewhere, I can see that it's possible that Don was actually Terry's first choice all along. They were great friends; it's just that Terry would have anticipated difficulties with getting the appointment of Don past Hill-Wood. Sexton would have been a great appointment but I was very happy about Howe's return and I know all the players were excited by the prospect, too.

## Chapter 13

# 1977/78

YOU COULD see an almost immediate Don Howe effect. Our defence had seemed porous the previous season but under Don's guidance we conceded just five goals in our first nine league games and kept six clean sheets out of the first 12. It wasn't just our defending which showed promise – we played some good football, beating Forest, who would go on to win the title that season, 3-0, and then beat West Ham by the same score a few weeks later. Things very quickly felt more positive. Don took control of the football side of things to the extent that I believe he would even have had a very big say on transfers.

Jimmy Rimmer had been an excellent goalkeeper for Arsenal; he was the club's player of the year in 1975. So, it took us all by surprise when Terry, out of the blue, signed Tottenham's legendary goalkeeper Pat Jennings, leaving Spurs fans devastated. Perhaps the only people more surprised than Arsenal supporters when the news broke were those of our deadliest rivals.

Jennings had been close to signing for Ipswich Town after falling out with Spurs. Pat later said that he felt hurt by the conduct of the club towards him; he recited an incident, at the end of his last season at White Hart Lane, when he was in the club car park and every member of the board had walked by him without one single acknowledgement. Once Terry had shown an interest, Pat seized it. He would have been a great signing at any price but for us to get him for just £45,000 represented a most monumental blunder by his old club, one they must have rued for years after. In the space of about four months, we had picked up Willie Young and Pat Jennings for less than £90,000.

Rimmer had made no secret of his failure to truly settle in London, like Brian Kidd 12 months earlier, and a move to a club nearer his roots would have looked attractive to him, although he was, by all accounts, surprised, disappointed even, when the move away from Highbury was raised as a possibility. One thing the Jennings transfer underlined was the decent relationship that existed between the two club's boards of directors: the mini-exodus of Neill, Young, Jennings and also a young Steve Walford might not have happened without the cordial relations which existed between Hill-Wood and his counterparts in Tottenham's boardroom, men like Sidney Wale and Arthur Richardson.

Trevor Ross was possibly the first casualty of Howe's arrival; the midfielder was also known to be at loggerheads with Neill in the months before his departure. Ross was sold to Everton for a very good fee, around £170,000. I think Howe preferred the eternally unsung hero that was David Price. To a certain extent, Ross split opinion at Highbury but he went on to have a good career at Everton. In comparison, David Price was a steady, consistent, if undramatic performer. In a midfield which already contained Graham Rix and Liam Brady, there was always going to be room for a 'Steady Eddie' like Price. He gave a better balance to the midfield than Ross.

The acquisition of Alan Sunderland from Wolves smacks most certainly of Howe's direct intervention. Howe was very well informed about footballers playing in the Midlands and, consequently, Sunderland became a high quality addition to the squad. Perhaps Macdonald's knees were already proving a concern and Sunderland offered an insurance policy in the event of Malcolm breaking down?

From day one, Don made a difference; he settled the club down and the players all welcomed his logical, thoughtful approach, as opposed to the helter-skelter which prevailed under Neill. I really liked Don and was delighted to see him back. Throughout Don's coaching career there existed a view that he was too defensive and that his sides tended to play with their handbrake on. Interestingly, David O'Leary said that Don was cautious but not as defensive as George Graham.

Regardless, we played some smashing football that season. We got to the League Cup semi-finals where, despite outplaying Liverpool in both games, went out 2-1 on aggregate, a defeat made worse by Stapleton's inexplicable miss late on. Hudson's second-half cameo against Manchester City in a League Cup quarter-final replay was perhaps his best showing in an Arsenal shirt; he was mustard that night. The man who Brady described to me as a lost soul had, for a while, found a home; on his day, he was one of the most naturally gifted players I have ever seen.

What everyone remembers about that season was the visit to Wembley for the FA Cup Final. Getting to Wembley couldn't have been more straightforward. We didn't need a single replay and Macdonald scored in every round. In the spring, we had a real purple patch, scoring lots of goals; a run of great performances which culminated in a 4-0 victory against a very good West Brom at Highbury. After defeating Orient 3-0 in the cup semi-final – with a couple from Macdonald, both aided by wild deflections on shots that might otherwise have hit the corner flag – we were looking absolute bankers to lift the trophy.

Whatever could go wrong on the day of final against Ipswich Town, did go wrong. All that sharp, incisive football stalled. Jennings had a great game and he needed to; he kept us in it for over an hour before we finally succumbed 1-0. I found out afterwards about all the injuries – not an excuse, no club got to the end of a season in those days without a load of niggling injuries. Almost everyone was carrying a knock and the worst affected was Liam Brady. Had it been any other game but a cup final, Brady wouldn't have been considered. Ten days before the Wembley showpiece, we had played at Liverpool and Liam picked up a bad knock and really shouldn't have played against Ipswich. I believe Hudson came close to blaming Neill for losing us the final because of his team selection but I can't see what else Neill could have done – we didn't have a deep enough squad. Brady, though, could hardly run.

Although it was a disappointing end to the season, there was a lot to be optimistic about and it felt we were a bit ahead of schedule. I still wasn't sure about Macdonald and I don't think Howe was, either. Don wanted his team to press and work hard and that just wasn't Macdonald's way. By his own admission, Malcolm was a selfish footballer, he just wanted to score goals and he was very good at that, but he was never going to give you the all-round contribution that Radford and Kennedy had given the team in 1970 and 1971 and that was the benchmark. I thought Macdonald was lucky to have Stapleton alongside him doing all his running and taking all the stick up front for him.

## Chapter 14
# 1978/79

THE FIRST game of the season saw us draw 2-2 at home to Leeds. Despite dropping a point, the game really confirmed my belief that we were in good shape. Brady began the season playing the sort of football he would continue to play week in, week out; he reached a level of virtuosity against Leeds that, at times, was unplayable, scoring twice in the process, one penalty and a wonderful second goal that in shape and precision was a carbon copy of his much more famous goal at Tottenham a few months later. He just never dropped his level that season.

Then, four games into the new season and at the age of only 28, disaster struck Arsenal's record signing and swashbuckling talisman, Malcolm Macdonald. We were playing in the League Cup, one of those proverbial banana skins at Rotherham United, where Macdonald took yet another blow to his poor old, battered knee, from which, despite surgery, and several patient comeback attempts, he would never fully recover. A full house at Millmoor cheered the locals on to a 3-1 victory while, for us, the defeat was augmented by Macdonald's injury. I think the hope, initially, was that Malcolm would be back. For a couple of games, his iconic No.9 shirt was kept warm by Steve Walford but by the time we opened our European account, Stapleton had been installed as Arsenal's new No.9 and he would score twice as we beat Lokomotiv Leipzig 3-0 at Highbury.

Stapleton's time had come. He was a fantastic target man with a great all-round game. Sunderland was more mobile and the perfect foil. He could play up alongside Frank or drop back into a five-man midfield, something Don liked to do at places like Anfield. Sunderland was always several players in one and I was a big fan of his. He had pace, was a fantastic finisher and a good header of a ball; Stapleton and him made a near formidable pair up front.

When I met up with Terry Neill at the hotel on the Friday before an away game early in the season, we were chatting and the name of Osvaldo Ardiles came up. I think it was the weekend following Tottenham being walloped 7-0 at Liverpool. Terry surprised me when he told me that, in the summer, he had been approached by Harry Haslam, the one-time manager of Luton Town and Sheffield United who was now a part-time football agent, who had given Arsenal first option on Ardiles and Ricky Villa before they eventually signed for Tottenham. If I am honest, I was quite impressed with what I'd seen of Ardiles and was more than curious as to why he had turned them down. 'We didn't need them,' was Terry's opinion. With Brady, there wouldn't have been room for Ardiles, reasoned Terry. I would have taken Brady over Ardiles every time but the little Argentine was a smashing player who could have helped soften the blow when Liam later moved on to Italian football. Foreign players playing in England were very much a rarity back in the late 70s and Terry and Don may have had quite reasonable doubts about the pair's ability to assimilate into the rough and tumble of English domestic football. But, just for a moment, consider that by the end of the season our midfield might have been: Ardiles – Talbot – Brady – Rix. With the Argentine replacing Price, it could have been the final piece of the jigsaw.

Terry totally understood my devotion to Arsenal, a devotion which could bring me into opposition with him. I could give Terry quite a hard time at AGM's and be critical of something that had, or hadn't been done, but to his credit Terry never held it against me. Some strong battles lay ahead of us though.

There was a welcome return to European competition that season – the first time since 1972. We rubbed our hands in anticipation but ended up with three trips behind the Iron Curtain. The club offered the opportunity to fly with the official party for a small premium. I was able to do this for all three games and the trips were chastening experiences. Leipzig, Split and, finally, Belgrade. In the late 70s, if there were more depressing places to visit than these three cities then they were kept well hidden. The prevailing image was of old, damp concrete and bleak-looking people. The streets were mostly full of soldiers and these soldiers, whether on duty or off, spent much of their day openly drinking vodka, so you learned to keep your head down and out of trouble.

Our first round, second leg tie against Lokomotiv Leipzig was a great success. After beating them 3-0 at Highbury in the first leg, we played brilliantly to win 4-1 in the second leg. Loko's coach, Heinz Joerk, spoke warmly of Arsenal's two performances against his own team, describing Arsenal as 'already one of the favourites to win the UEFA Cup'.

As destinations, Split and Belgrade were no greater beauties than Leipzig in those days. In the second round, a 2-1 defeat in Split was turned around at Highbury courtesy of a truly sublime chip from Willie Young in the dying minutes, which underlined that Young, all brawn, elbows and last-ditch tackles, nursed deep within him a proper footballer who rarely got an airing. With Young, you only saw the defender, the traditional stopper; we rarely saw the footballer and, as a consequence, he was underrated. He could pass it as well as he could clear it into Row Z. He was well thought of inside the game, whole-hearted and genuine; I don't recall him really hurting anyone. However, when he battled lads like Joe Jordan or Cyrille Regis, you'd watch through your fingers!

The victory over Hajduk Split wasn't without its downside. The Yugoslavs seemed intent on progressing to the third round, even if it meant kicking Brady all the way back to Split. They had two players sent off but also got Brady to snap and retaliate and he, too, was dismissed. Liam said the experience taught him a lesson; he was a marked man and would need to get used to that kind of treatment. He would now miss the next two games, against Red Star Belgrade.

A narrow 1-0 defeat, following a scrambled goal, in the first leg in Belgrade set up the return game nicely. A point of interest from the game was to be found in the Red Star team, with one Vladimir Petrović playing with all the grace which would be routinely booted out of him during his brief sojourn in an Arsenal shirt a few years later.

Back at Highbury, in a tight second leg, Sunderland levelled the aggregate score at 1-1 with a firm header at the far post, underlining once again what a weapon the aerial route was for English sides in Europe. Once they needed to, the Yugoslavs started to play and, with the clock running down, an exquisite little backheel from Petrović set up Red Star's equaliser and that was that.

As Christmas approached, a decent run in the league, including a fighting 1-0 victory over Liverpool, saw us well placed to push on. On the last Saturday before Christmas 1978, we made the short journey down the Seven Sisters Road for a north London derby; it would turn out to be an exhilarating trip. Arsenal won 5-0 with a performance of powerful football and 'that goal' by Brady. Arsenal were brilliant that day; the result really didn't flatter us. And what is there left to say about Brady's goal? He showed in a couple of seconds his full worth – a crunching ambush of a tackle to win back the ball from Peter Taylor and then this boomerang of a missile curled into the top corner about 20 years before Roberto Carlos's goal was heralded the world over. Carlos's strike was from a dead ball, with a run-up; Brady's was from open play in the middle of the hurly-burly of a north London derby.

Early in the New Year, we started out in the FA Cup in the same city as the previous year, Sheffield. That season we had set out with a 5-0 romp at Bramall Lane and this time we were drawn at United's city rivals, Sheffield Wednesday, of the Third Division. When we braved the long journey north, amidst freezing heavy snow, I wouldn't have predicted that I would spend all my spare time over the next three weeks shuttling backwards and forwards up the motorway until those dogged Yorkshiremen had finally been defeated. What a wonderful advertisement for English cup football it turned out to be. It was a genuine privilege to be in attendance at all *five* matches.

The first game, at Hillsborough, was one of only four third round ties that beat the weather. It was a horrible pitch to play on and a real leveller. There was snow banked up all over the place, quite a bit of which got rolled into snowballs and thrown at Pat Jennings. Despite the disparity in league positions, I think we were glad to get away from Hillsborough with a draw and a chance to play them on a decent surface back at Highbury in the replay.

The predicted romp never materialised and but for an 88th minute Brady strike to equalise Wednesday's goal on the stroke of half-time, we would have fallen at the first hurdle. We created a few chances but never really came to terms with Wednesday's five across midfield. But goals change everything and when Brady seized on a mistake by Chris Turner, probably the only mistake the Wednesday keeper made in the entire series of games, I instantly turned to my friends and confidently stated: 'We'll win the cup this year.' It was a throwaway comment, I know, but I absolutely believed it.

When extra time ended with nothing to separate the teams, Wednesday boss Jack Charlton was reluctant to toss a coin to decide the venue for the second replay and, so, it went to a neutral ground.

With its famous hot air balloon and a location approximately halfway between Sheffield and London, Leicester City's Filbert Street was selected as the ground where the contest would continue.

A misty atmospheric evening under floodlights in the East Midlands was an ideal setting for any cup replay but these contests turned out to be games the like of which we will never see again. What started as a fairly private affair soon gripped the entire nation. A 2-2 draw, which included a wonderful goal from Brady and yet more resistance and another fightback from Wednesday, was followed, two days later, by an even more nerve-jangling affair when six goals were shared equally on a breathless night in Leicester. After four games, the tie was still undecided.

In the middle of the cup saga, we beat reigning league champions Nottingham Forest 2-1 at Highbury, coming from behind to record a real morale-boosting win, which also saw the debut of our new club record signing, Brian Talbot. He had been outstanding against us for Ipswich the previous May at Wembley and had been coveted by Neill and Howe for some time. As soon as we showed interest, I know that Talbot had been very keen to join us. The price was £450,000 and it was money well spent.

Talbot was a real high quality addition to our club. He was the proverbial box-to-box midfielder; he never stopped. The ground he covered freed up Brady and he just never missed a game. Tactically, he forced teams to play to our strengths, too; he made it very difficult for sides to attack the heart of our defence on the ground, his workrate forcing opponents to resort to lumping long balls into our box, which Willie Young would gobble up all day long.

When we found ourselves heading back up to Filbert Street for the third time in seven days, I don't think any of us knew what to expect. I recall one of the headlines at the time said: 'Wednesday drag tortured Arsenal through fresh FA Cup nightmares.' If I am honest, I don't think that was fair to either team. Wednesday played really well and Arsenal respected them totally. They were great games which were a credit to all the players and added to the prestige of the cup. It's a shame that today's fans won't ever get to experience one of those sagas. Penalty shoot-outs are dramatic but comparing that series of games to a penalty contest is a bit like comparing a cricket Twenty-20 game to a Test match. The Wednesday games were full of twists and turns and they were fabulous.

The fourth replay was a bit of an anti-climax; we were two up in no time through goals from Steve Gatting and Frank Stapleton. It was the first time that either team had opened up a two-goal lead. We prevailed and were rewarded with a home tie against Notts County.

At one stage, the fourth-round tie looked as though it was heading for another replay saga but late goals from Willie Young and Talbot, his first as an Arsenal player, saw us through.

The four league games after that County tie are a good illustration of how we couldn't convert our cup form into a real concerted attempt to win the league. O'Leary told me that, at the time, the players were just as perplexed by it as the supporters were. We went to Old Trafford and won 2-0, then were held at home 0-0 by Middlesbrough, then went second in the table after winning 2-1 at QPR, only to fall to a single-goal home defeat to Wolves – two away wins and just one point from two home games. No one could put their finger on why we were so inconsistent.

The fifth round saw us drawn away at Brian Clough's Nottingham Forest, who no one could remember ever losing at home; they had gone 49 games undefeated at the City Ground when we played them. It was a cold and bleak night as the mist rolled in off the Trent over a dreadful pitch. On such a night, you need your gladiators and it was a blow to hear that Willie Young was out injured.

It was one of those games you look back on and you can't really believe you survived it, let alone won it. It wasn't that we played poorly, we didn't – we fought and battled all night – but Forest played some great football and but for Jennings several times, the woodwork, some poor finishing and some old-fashioned last-ditch defending, we could have been buried by midway through the second half. I don't think Forest could quite believe it was still 0-0 when Sunderland carried the ball deep into Forest territory, Anderson gave away a fairly needless foul and Brady's perfectly flighted free kick evaded everyone but Stapleton, whose crisp header left Shilton flatfooted and beaten. By the end, Arsenal's golden shirts were barely visible beneath all the mud. After the game, Don spoke of how all teams that get to Wembley look back at a game when a bit of luck had been required; he said, with a grin and barely concealed delight, that the tie at Forest had been just such a night for us.

The reward for beating Forest was to travel to Southampton for another difficult tie in the quarter-finals. The Dell is another stadium long gone under the march of progress. It was a peculiarity entirely of its own kind; a unique football arena – noisy, cramped and closed in – it was one of the best and most daunting places to visit, especially for a night game, despite its all-time record attendance being only 31,000.

Saints took the lead but a scrambled effort from David Price kept us alive and we went back to Highbury for the replay. Two days later, a couple of outstanding goals from Alan Sunderland were enough for us to win 2-0 and set up a semi-final against Wolves at Villa Park.

Not long before the semi-final, we heard that Brady was struggling to be fit. Arsenal would leave it late to announce their team, perhaps to call Wolves' bluff, knowing what a boost to them it would be to play us without Liam. Twelve months on from the Ipswich debacle, the memory of Brady playing when he was nowhere near match fit caused Arsenal to be cautious about his fitness this time. We desperately wanted him playing but a cup semi-final was no place for passengers.

Arsenal were immense that day. It was a performance full of character and one that made you really proud of the team. Arsenal would not lie down; they fought from the opening minutes, when Pat Rice yelled a battle cry, to the last seconds after two brilliantly taken goals, first from Stapleton and then Sunderland. There were heroes all over the pitch: Willie and David stood firm in defence; Rix knew he had to compensate for the loss of Brady; Talbot covered every blade of grass; and Stapleton and Sunderland worked and worked. Some performances can capture the unique characteristics of a club; that day, a well-earned battle honour was won.

And, so, on to Wembley for English football's showpiece occasion against Manchester United beneath a sky which reminded me of 1971. I went to the cup final with Peter Storey and it was nice for the first time to be able to provide Peter with a ticket after all the hundreds he had given to me. We oozed belief in the opening half; Brady was irresistible. A two-goal advantage at half-time felt like nothing but our just rewards. I think if we had gone out with the same attitude and intent after the break, we could have quickly killed the game with a third and possibly a fourth goal. But we played with a suggestion of fear, knowing what we stood to lose. Those fears led to negativity and we began to sit deeper and deeper. I suppose the longer it went on at 2-0, it seemed the sensible, cautious thing to do but we probably invited United back into the game and, just as they started tying yellow ribbons on to the cup, we gave away two dreadful goals.

The decision to drop and play deep wasn't Don's. David O'Leary said it was instinctive, to protect what we had the longer the second half went on. Liam famously joked that he was so knackered he was just trying to take the ball as far from our goal as possible and get to extra time, so he just ran with the ball with no thought for anything but killing time. But, as he spotted Rix charging up on his outside, he laid off an inch-perfect pass for him to send over a booming cross which Sunderland, gambling at the back post, caught on the half volley, sending the ball goalwards to, unbelievably, nestle gently in the net. A fleeting silence – then bedlam, pandemonium and the pure, unmitigated joy of the football supporter. No one, least of all the players, really knew what to do, so they just raced around – the eternal image is of Sunderland running. It was one of the greatest moments I have ever experienced – never had an Arsenal success come with such extreme emotions.

The cup which was famously won with almost the final meaningful kick of the game was won, too, ten times over in moments against Wednesday, Forest, Southampton and in the semi-final. The memories of 1978 had been banished. After one of the most dramatic journeys to the final, we then won the cup with *the* most dramatic finale Wembley has ever seen.

## Chapter 15

# 1979/80

THERE WAS a photo shoot at Highbury to herald the start of preparations for the new season. The cup, polished to a military brilliance that even Bertie would have approved of, caught the sunlight and shone radiantly. The day was all smiles as everyone took their turn with the trophy and perhaps the biggest smile was on the face of our newest player: John Hollins, who was happy to tell anyone who would listen just how proud he was to have signed for the Gunners and how much grander, how much on a different level, Arsenal were to Chelsea. He was a really inspired signing; despite being 33, he was still really fit and, after costing next to nothing, we got 127 appearances out of him. It was almost impossible not to like John; he was very popular throughout football. After he had finished playing, he worked on Great Portland Street and we would sometimes meet for lunch.

In 1979/80, Arsenal were magnificent. In the end, the disappointments couldn't have been greater but it stands still as one of our proudest seasons and, though there was no trophy to confirm it, one of our greatest achievements. Arsenal in 1980 became 'history men' and proved that there is a glory that transcends winning. If 1979 was all about the FA Cup, then 1980 was a story of blood, sweat and tears, of brutal failure and of the pain of loving and losing.

Liam's departure became the long goodbye. I didn't know Liam as well as I knew David O'Leary but I knew him well enough for him to talk unguardedly about things. So, let's be clear about one thing; Liam Brady didn't *want* to leave Arsenal. There were two key issues for him, as I saw it: firstly, the young lads who had come through the ranks at Highbury all tended to be taken for granted by the board; secondly, he could see how close we were to being a very good team and he was frustrated at the level of investment the board were prepared to make. 'Good enough' had become the mantra, which precluded the signing of those one or two players who might mean we close the gap between us and teams like Liverpool.

I think Liam hoped he would be made to feel more wanted by Arsenal and that the club might have worked harder to keep him. He was our one, truly world class player and, effectively, the board let him walk out the door. We would revisit all this again 12 months later, having learnt nothing, when Frank Stapleton would leave in the same circumstances as Brady.

David O'Leary could completely understand Brady wanting to try his hand in Italian football and neither was he critical of his mate Stapleton but his firm view is that Frank should never have been allowed to sign for United or any other English club.

Neither Liam nor Frank ever actively looked to leave; if they had been offered what their status merited two years before the end of their deals, I believe there is a very good chance both would have signed new contracts. If we had retained Brady and Stapleton, with the outstanding Kenny Sansom soon arriving and with an upgrade on Price, we were ready to match up to Liverpool.

The statistics from 1979/80 are mind-blowing to modern football followers brought up on squad rotation and having two top players for every position. We played a record 70 competitive football matches – nearly two Premier League seasons in one. Brian Talbot started every single match, which, come a chaotic end to the season, were sometimes played Saturday, Monday, Wednesday and Saturday. Between 2 April and 19 May, just 47 days, Arsenal played 17 games, which equates to a game less than every three days.

Although the season ended in heartbreak, there were games we talk about still, performances we shall never forget. I am moved every time I think of that season. My own stats for the campaign aren't too shabby; I missed just four games, saw every cup game, which amounted to 27 extra matches, attended every away European tie, including the final, plus the Charity Shield. However you cut it, it was a monumental season for the club.

We finished fourth in the league, got to the League Cup quarter-finals, played in the FA Cup Final and European Cup Winners' Cup Final, yet ended empty-handed. We didn't even get a place in the following season's UEFA Cup!

After the Christmas period, which included a north London derby win on Boxing Day and a fighting New Year's Day victory away at Southampton courtesy of a Willie Young header, we found ourselves tucked in in third spot as we prepared to defend the FA Cup.

Progression in the FA Cup and the Cup Winners' Cup were smooth and, by mid-March, we found ourselves in the semi-finals of both competitions. The second leg of our European quarter-final was the coldest football match I have ever attended. We had beaten Gothenburg, managed by a young Sven-Göran Eriksson, 5-1 at Highbury in the first leg, which all but rendered the second leg academic. Still, I decided to go with a group of friends, who all left the stadium at half-time and headed back to their hotel complaining of being frozen. I've never left a game early in my life, so I stuck it out and enjoyed what I could of a goalless affair.

That game in Sweden was nearly my last. If the snarling cold (it was minus 22 degrees) didn't get you, then the Swedish plumbing would. Returning to my hotel after the game, I was so bitterly cold that I ran a bath; it was far too hot and I nearly cooked.

Between 9 April and 1 May, Arsenal played either Juventus or Liverpool a total of seven times and we didn't lose one of them; a period which, perhaps more than Wembley 79, marks the real zenith of Terry Neill's reign at Highbury.

Before we met Juve at Highbury on the Wednesday evening, we had a north London derby on the Bank Holiday Monday at White Hart Lane and it is a game that never fails to anger me. Given that we had a European semi-final only 48 hours later, we had asked if Tottenham might agree to a postponement. Tottenham unequivocally refused our request and when we submitted our team sheet, which was admittedly a second string XI, they let it be known that an official complaint would be made to the Football League for us not selecting our strongest team, which was, in those days, a formal requirement.

Arsenal played them off the park. Paul Davis made a commanding debut and Willie Young played on for the whole game with a broken nose sustained in the first half. Right at the end, we suddenly went 2-0 up and held on to record a fantastic 'up yours' 2-1 victory. Could you imagine any other club behaving in that manner? Their behaviour was appalling and I don't think enough was made of it. Tottenham paraded themselves as a very second-rate outfit. I can wholeheartedly say that few victories in over 70 years of following Arsenal have given me, and still give me, as much pleasure.

With Tottenham's best wishes ringing in our ears we welcomed Juventus to Highbury. At the final whistle, it stood all square. It was an encounter which left a sour taste in the mouth and a game which easily fitted the tradition of angry Anglo-Italian contests over the previous few years.

Around 15 minutes in, disaster struck. Steve Walford tried to loft a ball back to Jennings when it was easier and safer to simply put it out of play. The pass resulted in putting Bettega clean through on goal and Talbot had no option but to bring him down. Cabrini took the kick and Jennings, saving brilliantly to his right, could only push it back to Cabrini and, from six yards, he fired it into the roof of the net.

Some moments after his contribution to the first goal, Bettega played an altogether less savoury role in the worst incident of the match – a tackle on O'Leary which shattered our man's shinpad and absolutely incensed the Arsenal bench. Neill would go to town on this incident after the game and a battle of words ensued, which eventually drew in the patrician old Etonian, Denis Hill-Wood. So heated did it get that Juventus let it be known that the safety of Arsenal fans 'couldn't be guaranteed' in the 'backstreets of Turin'. David told me after the game that, but for the shinpad, his leg would have been broken and David is not a lad given to exaggeration.

We plugged away and then, in the 86th minute, a ball to the back post from a Brady free kick was headed back goalwards by Stapleton and, under pressure, facing his own goal, Bettega could only nod it firmly past his own keeper – karma! It was really nothing more than we deserved. In the end, 1-1 seemed fair, though their away goal meant it was now just that little bit more daunting a second leg when we travelled, perhaps more in hope than expectation, to Turin.

I went with a group of friends to Italy, although we ended up sitting apart during the game. The Stadio Comunale wasn't an especially well-appointed or welcoming stadium but it felt like a ground that had seen things; it had a story to tell.

It was a game of cat and mouse. Arsenal tried to force it, while Juventus sat back and, from the first minute, played for the 0-0 daw that would see them through to the final. The crowd got noisier as the game progressed. With ten minutes remaining, Arsenal turned to a young lad from Bermondsey. 'Go and get us a goal, Paul,' was his only instruction.

History presents an opportunity to record your place in it rarely, if at all. Paul Vaessen, in football as in life, would have few chances to secure his legacy but when it came, he grabbed it.

The noise, the drums and the chanting, all stopped at exactly the same moment while an eerie silence descended. Zoff stood abject with his head in his hands; one Juve defender lay prostrate in the net alongside the ball, put there seconds before by Vaessen.

With ten minutes to go, Italian professionalism looked to have outsmarted Arsenal heart and endeavour. Paul's goal was in the 88th minute. Alan Sunderland had made a decoy run to the near post, almost sensing that Rix, after a surging run to the byline, would go long to the back post where Vaessen waited, unmarked. One sideways nod of the head was all it took for Paul's star to ascend and blaze in the Turin sky with an intensity rarely equalled.

Denis Hill-Wood loved it and was intent on making the most of the moment. He waxed with almost Churchillian lyricism about the fortitude of the club's players. 'They never know when they are beaten,' he said between grins, going as far as to compare them favourably with the 1971 Double team. The significance of the moment could be seen captured in the smiles of Vaessen and his team-mates back in the dressing room and later at the hotel as Arsenal celebrated in good old Anglo-Saxon style.

While we were heroically becoming the first English team to ever win in Turin, we also fought Liverpool in an FA Cup semi-final series which almost ran as long as the previous season's tie against Sheffield Wednesday. The games followed no pattern but ebbed and flowed; one game Arsenal were on top, the next Liverpool.

The first game at Hillsborough ended 0-0, with Talbot coming closest to a goal, hitting the bar with a chip late on. The first replay, at Villa Park, saw Liverpool take the lead through David Fairclough but, within minutes, Arsenal hit back as Alan Sunderland, racing through in a one-on-one with Ray Clemence, kept his nerve and lofted a chip over the stranded keeper. The celebrations which followed Sunderland's equaliser were chaotic; supporters danced on the Liverpool dugout while a calmly detached Terry Neill stood on the touchline, his right fist clenched, gesturing to the players while they hugged as a group just in front of him.

The second replay opened with Arsenal taking a first-minute lead and, thereafter, defending and defending until, in the 90th minute, Liverpool equalised. It was a heart-breaking goal that nearly knocked the stuffing out of us. Sensing blood, Liverpool dominated extra time but, with Jennings defiant, we hung on. Trudging out after the game, it felt like a defeat. Three days later, the contest moved to Coventry City's Highfield Road on a night when it felt like Arsenal fans outnumbered Liverpool supporters by at least three to one. The roar when Pat Rice led us out absolutely tore the sky in two; it was a real battle cry. Before the game, legendary former Liverpool manager Bill Shankly had spoken warmly of how well Arsenal had played and acknowledged the clear mutual respect which existed between the players of both clubs and the credit it had done the famous old trophy.

Eleven minutes in, when Liverpool failed to clear a corner, Arsenal suddenly had an overload on the right and, when Arsenal old boy Ray Kennedy lost his footing in the box, Stapleton gently lofted the ball back goalwards for Talbot, pushing Sunderland out of his way, to power home an unstoppable header.

What a long 79 minutes it turned out to be. The noise was deafening, the action intense and almost constantly dramatic. Jennings made one tremendous double save – shades of Jim Montgomery for Sunderland against Leeds in the 1973 FA Cup Final. As the second half drew on, a chant of 'come on you yellows' came from every corner of the ground. The defending, and there was much of it, was resolute: Willie Young headed everything away; O'Leary intercepted and closed down; Talbot ran without stopping; and Brady shuttled from left to right and back again.

The moment you are on the brink of a result like this is the moment it feels furthest away. I couldn't watch but neither could I look away. Then, suddenly, it was over and there was Talbot running arms aloft to Jennings and the two of them embraced. Young saluted to the crowd as supporters ran on, while the press photographers were desperate to catch the morning's back page image. I had watched the game with Frank McLintock and when that whistle went, we spontaneously hugged each other. The celebrations, looking back, had the unmistakable feel of 'job done'. Arsenal had given everything – they had nothing left, nothing at all.

As we walked out into the evening air, now full of laughter, singing and ready to have drinks to toast the magnificent Gunners, the cup final itself felt almost strangely unimportant; it was, perhaps, there at Highfield Road that an exhausted Arsenal had reached their summit under Neill. Nothing could surpass those past few weeks. It was a period of time when Don Howe showed himself to be a truly world class coach – he made sure we met every challenge. One day, the memory of it will fade but not yet, not for me.

Highfield Road is now flattened. The site of our wonderful victory became a housing estate, though the pitch remains a grassy expanse where children might enact their football dreams. I doubt if anyone pretends to be Brian Talbot, though.

We lost both the finals. After a schedule that prompted some bitterness from the players, we were simply not ourselves at Wembley, a game after which Talbot collapsed in the coach and required oxygen. It had been such a hot, energy sapping afternoon, taking nothing away from West Ham, but our season both physically and emotionally caught up with us that afternoon. Given the sweltering heat, I got a few odd looks, too. I'd worn a lucky knee-length fur coat for every FA Cup tie since the third round and, obviously, I couldn't stop now – it wouldn't be sensible. I gamely, for the cause, kept that coat on, sweat dripping off my nose. It's what football makes you do; perhaps routines and superstitions help us control the anxiety of being so invested in something we have no control over?

We lifted ourselves for the Cup Winners' Cup Final, at the Heysel Stadium in Belgium, against Valencia. Indeed, we were the better team and nearly won it with a brilliant effort from Sunderland which was saved spectacularly. But I think we all knew what was coming. The football gods bequeathed a tragedy and Arsenal, so potent just days earlier, were to be the sacrifice.

A dream died that night in Brussels. It went to penalties. Brady missed his kick and then, as it went to sudden death, Rix, a real soldier that season, saw his kick saved, too, when he, like Brady, went to the keeper's left. That was it. These, the barest of bare bones, are sufficient to capture the brutality of that ending. Afterwards, Don Howe sought out O'Leary and Don told him: 'Kempes didn't get a touch – tonight you were the best centre-half in the world.'

We returned to England with yet more games to play. Just 48 hours after the Heysel heartbreak, we played at Wolves, still requiring two victories to secure a place in the following season's UEFA Cup. Somehow, we won 2-1 but the following Monday at Middlesbrough, in a game in which Pat Rice said he lacked the strength to kick the ball ten yards, we lost 5-0. It was Liam Brady's last game for Arsenal.

On the journey back to London, Neill insisted his players enjoy a crate of champagne. There are so many things which touch me still about that month in the spring of 1980: beating Juventus and young Vaessen's goal; the struggle with Liverpool and the ultimate victory; two cup final defeats; and the curtain coming down on Brady's Arsenal career. Victories over Juventus and Liverpool prove what a great team we were – part of the sadness was that we'd never ever see that team again.

## Chapter 16

# 1981–1986

WHEN BRADY left for Italy, he took much more than just his boots with him. Just as the spectre of his move had hung over the club, now the threat of *another* gut-wrenching departure set the tone for the new season.

Frank Stapleton, once the lad who Neill very nearly sold to Hull City for peanuts in 1976, had developed into a centre-forward of extremely high repute. Like Liam, Frank told me he had never *wanted* to leave Arsenal but, also like Liam, that the club had simply not done enough to convince him they really wanted him to stay.

The offers the club eventually made were, in both cases, just too little too late. The situation inflicted great harm on the club and they had brought it upon themselves. By the summer of 1980, Brady and Stapleton, two young men, were already two of the best players in the world in their respective positions; one had left and the other was making it clear that he was off at the end of the season.

The signing of Clive Allen, a teenager for over £1m, seemed exciting. Neill made the point soon after, that effectively Allen was purchased with money that might otherwise have gone to the taxman if we hadn't invested it in a player.

The pre-season quickly showed, though, that Allen was going to be a difficult player to integrate into our established frontline of Stapleton and Sunderland and was clearly not going to get in the side ahead of either of them at that stage. Perhaps he had been signed with a view to being Stapleton's long-term replacement but counter to that, he was more suited to playing *alongside* Stapleton than with Sunderland; in many ways, his game was too similar to Sunderland's and it was Stapleton, not Sunderland, who would need replacing come the end of the season.

We knew left-back Sammy Nelson's time was coming to an end and, apart from Sammy's age, there were increasing tensions between him and Terry Neill. Pat Rice would also leave, after a decade of outstanding service, latterly as club captain, and move to Watford. So, both full-back berths were available. John Devine would take over from Rice but we still needed a left-back and Crystal Palace's Ken Sansom was by far and away the best around. Realising that Allen would most probably represent a lot of money sat on the bench, Neill moved swiftly. Sansom was immediately keen on a move to Arsenal and, with Allen fitting Palace's profile of young players, the swap was set up. In the end, I think the deal suited all parties.

I was volubly questioning the way the club had handled the contract renewals of Brady and Stapleton. By the autumn of 1981, Ken Friar was getting a bit twitchy about the upcoming AGM and, out of the blue, he phoned me. Flying back from a European tie, Ken had asked me for my number. I was curious why he wanted it – perhaps the club were going to invite me on to the board! He'd like to take me out for dinner, he said, with the club picking up the tab. So, we went to Arsenal's favourite hotel, the White House in London's West End, where Ken proceeded to encourage me *not* to make an issue of Brady and Stapleton at the AGM. There would doubtless be press there and we don't want that sort of thing being addressed in public do we, was his theme.

I could understand his point of view and I recognised he had a job to do but the simple truth for me was that the way the club had approached the matter of Liam's and Frank's contracts was not in the best interests of the club and, having the privilege to express my views to such an influential person, I was not going to pass up the opportunity.

Nothing was going to stop me saying what I felt and what I believed to be the best for Arsenal. I liked Terry Neill very much, we had been friends for a long time, but that was beside the point. I felt mistakes had been made and those responsible needed calling out; if it meant going up against a friend, then so be it.

Over the years, Ken had tried this 'soft diplomacy' on me a couple of times; both times were equally fruitless from his perspective. I simply have never let friendships, or my respect for someone and their position, stand in the way of my opinion where Arsenal is concerned.

Around the club, Ken was held in very high regard – he still is – but, when you think about it, it's inconceivable that a club the size of Arsenal could ever have become the fiefdom of one man and that is largely what had happened. In time, I came to appreciate more the job that Ken – and, before him, Bob Wall – had done for Arsenal but what the supporter sees as Arsenal's best interests can often be at odds with the corporate view of the same issue. I tended to be a lone voice at the AGMs but when I did ask something, there was always a chorus of 'hear, hear' – I suspect from people who wanted to ask the same question but just didn't dare!

Ken Friar started in the ticket office as a 12-year-old in 1950, went on to become secretary and, in 1983, became the club's first managing director (eventually, upon his retirement, he was made life president of the club after 70 years' service). When the chairmanship of the club passed to Peter Hill-Wood, I think Ken may have become even more important to how Arsenal went about their business. I think it's fair to say that football may not necessarily have been a big part of Peter Hill-Wood's life had fate not intervened. Arsenal were rather thrust upon him and, to my mind, the responsibility he felt towards the club was a legacy he could have done without. There were times when he rarely attended matches, even at Highbury. The club had a very safe pair of hands in Ken Friar, just as they had previously had with Bob Wall, and the importance of both men can't be overestimated. They were, for many years, the eyes and ears of the club. I may have occasionally disagreed with Ken but I hold him in the highest regard.

I lost my mother, Rachel, in 1982, to breast cancer; she was only 65. Looking back, I can't help but feel that life had not really dealt my poor mum a great hand. Her generation had been assaulted on all sides in so many ways and I don't think she ever really quietened that sense of unfathomable loss. Mum had bravely undergone surgery and all the usual treatments over the course of her illness but all to no avail. My mother, I knew, had doted on me and, despite all the many problems I had given her growing up in my teenage years, we shared a very strong love. My dad had looked after her wonderfully while she was unwell but, with hindsight, I wish I had been able to spend more time with her towards the end. I was just so busy building up my business, which by then had moved to a showroom in the heart of the clothing industry in London, the prestigious Great Portland Street. During the last week or so, when it became obvious mum was losing her battle, I spent more time visiting and helping dad, too; and, for the last couple of nights, I slept on the floor next to her bed but it is perhaps inevitable that we think we could have done more.

Through an Arsenal-supporting friend, I had been hearing that David Dein, who I didn't know at the time, was buying up small shareholdings in the club from supporters – people like myself, who had only bought the shares to feel even more a part of the club and also to have a voice. At that stage, there wasn't really any value in football clubs but I believe that David was picking up on what Irving Scholar had done at Tottenham a little earlier and, as the visionary that he most certainly was, could see potential in his investment going forward. I'd also heard that Dein was a genuinely huge Arsenal fan.

I had spoken to Ken Friar around this time and I was keen to know if he was aware of this development. Ken said that, not only had he not heard a word about this, he had never even heard of David Dein. I'll never know for sure but my guess is that it is likely that Peter Hill-Wood and the rest of the board got to hear first of David's interest through my conversation with Ken.

I think that Dein might, initially, have bought a block of unissued shares directly from the club and then, a year after Peter Hill-Wood, had become chairman, Dein bought the bulk of the chairman's shareholding for £290,250, which left Hill-Wood owning less than one per cent of the club. Hill-Wood's comments upon the sale are now legendary: he thought Dein was 'crazy', for 'to all intents and purposes it's dead money'. Dein eventually sold his holding to Alisher Usmanov for £75m. Dein had seen the future in 1983; by the time he sold his shares, Arsenal had become a money-making machine. In the years following the move to the Emirates, we were the third richest football club in the world.

Peter Hill-Wood's sale of his shares also brought to a close 100 years of his family's involvement in the boardroom. There was nothing left to effectively bequeath to either of his two sons.

It was a Monday morning. Peter Storey had come into our showroom in Great Portland Street to square us off for his weekend takings. Peter told me that, on the Sunday afternoon, he'd taken his wife and boys to Windsor and he couldn't believe how packed it had been with foreign tourists, who were queueing up to ten deep in the clothing shops that were specialising in Scottish-style clothing and, especially, kilts. These are not the genuine kilts worn by men but an adaption made into an attractive ladies' skirt.

Anyway, I went to Windsor the following week to look for myself. Peter was spot on in his description, so the following day I was on to commercial estate agents to see if any shops were available. There were none where I wanted but I did find one in a secondary position, which I took because it was better than nothing. The shop did very well and, over time, I took over another shop in Windsor, this time in a prime location, and enjoyed the best years of the booming tourist trade in the 80s and 90s. It probably would never have happened without Peter's tip-off, so it was a massive 'thank you' to him.

John Hawley and Ray Hankin have come to symbolise the era between the Wembley hat-trick and George Graham's return. After we lost Stapleton, Hawley's name came up in a conversation with Terry Neill and I remember one odd thing Terry said to me not long after Hawley signed. I was saying how uncomfortable Hawley looked, almost as if he recognised himself that he wasn't quite up to it and Terry said: 'Martin, if you pay peanuts you get monkeys'; and I was thinking, but you're the chap who paid peanuts!

My feelings have always been that if you put on an Arsenal shirt and do your best, it's not your fault if that isn't good enough and everyone could see that these two poor guys simply weren't up to it and eventually you have to question the judgment of the manager or coach who signs them and picks them. A year later, the same questions were being asked of another attempt to replace Stapleton – Lee Chapman, who had spent much of his time in an Arsenal shirt looking very uncomfortable.

I'd travelled with a handful of Arsenal supporters to Moscow for a UEFA Cup tie against Spartak in the autumn of 1982. In the hotel after the game, I was sat with a group of players, Lee amongst them. During the conversation, I brought up something which had troubled me, which was when Chapman scored his first goal for Arsenal, a week earlier in a 2-0 win at Coventry City, no one other than John Hollins went up to celebrate with him. Lee seemed pleased I'd mentioned this, while the others looked on rather sheepishly.

Almost from day one, he had struggled at Arsenal; having the club publicly criticise the fee the tribunal had set for him couldn't have helped his confidence and it felt as if everyone had made their minds up pretty quickly about him. While I didn't want to challenge individuals, I still judged it appropriate to put it to the group, believing the incident would have given a very poor impression to anyone outside the club. In truth, I think the players found it quite hard to accept Lee, recognising that he represented a drop in quality from Stapleton – not Chapman's fault and, remember, he was good enough to be part of a title-winning team at Leeds, but a barrier not easily cleared, nonetheless. I remember seeing him make his debut in a pre-season game at Stamford Bridge and commenting to a friend that Chapman didn't seem able to even kick a ball properly – perhaps not an auspicious start to his career at Highbury.

One point from the first four games and for much of the following nine months, we bumped around the lower reaches of the table. We did get to the FA Cup semi-finals, a run which ended at Villa Park. We were one up at half-time but I couldn't see us winning the game, which had very rarely been the case in my years following the Gunners. When I spoke to David O'Leary about it, he was quite sanguine: 'Beaten by the better team.'

The highlight of the season was the quarter-final at Highbury, when we beat Aston Villa 2-0. It is the game wherein Vladimir Petrović fleetingly rose above the swirling, chaotic hurly-burly all about him to score just before half-time. Unlike poor old Chapman, there was no absence of love for the little Serbian maestro amongst his team-mates – they flocked to hug him in his moment of valediction. The goal remains the overwhelming highlight of Petrović's brief Arsenal career. In one game, Terry and Don tried to shout some advice to him but Petrović was just baffled by what he was experiencing and, in broken English, he shouted to the boss: 'I get the ball, they kick me up in the air; I get the ball again and again they kick me up in the air.'

England international Tony Woodcock was an interesting fellow; I thought him a very good footballer, softly spoken and very clued up. He had a very smart and savvy agent, Jon Holmes, who also acted for

Gary Lineker. He did well for us initially but in a better team, I think he would have done it more often; after a while, he didn't really stand out against the sea of mediocrity. Woody lived quite close to me and we would go for a drink together in Radlett from time to time. He once famously scored five goals for us at Aston Villa in 1983 in a 6-2 victory. Within a month, though, we were losing 3-0 at Leicester City with an abject performance and, a few days later, losing at home to Third Division Walsall after which supporters gathered outside the East Stand to chant 'Neill out!' It was the symbolic point of no return for Neill.

By 1983, Paul Davis had established himself in the team with his outstanding technical skills and, despite a slight frame, he became a highly robust midfielder who never shirked a tackle. Another young player who I thought very highly of was Stewart Robson. He would be troubled by a succession of injuries, which was why, when the club received a decent offer from West Ham, they were willing to sell. Without his injuries, I think Robson might one day have captained the club.

The football was frequently of a poor standard, not just at Arsenal, but everywhere. If the game was becoming unlovable, then off the pitch it felt in a much worse state. Football was drifting away from its traditional position at the heart of English culture. Crowds were as low as they have ever been in my time and I think a lot of people were questioning whether they should bother with football. It never crossed my mind not to go. I didn't really worry about football's wider issues. I was so fixated on Arsenal; as long as I had Arsenal, I was happy. There seemed to be a lot more trouble at games, too; reaching a bit of a peak in the early 80s. I can remember seeing Johnny Hoy and his pals in action at other London grounds and I have to admit feeling a certain pride when a group of Arsenal lads prevailed. Because of how it was reported, the trouble probably seemed much worse and more serious to outsiders than it was in reality; to regulars, it was just an occupational hazard and added a bit of an edge to games. I felt I knew my way around a football ground and never felt especially threatened.

In the early 80s, Sammy Nelson and I discussed how the players from the Double team had all drifted apart, so we organised an annual get-together for the 1971 team but, not long after we started, players from other eras heard about it and began to attend, too; Liam Brady, for example, and also Alan Skirton (who, for some reason, was nicknamed 'The Fish'). It was an excellent event for a number of years. Sammy was a bit of a card; a very genial and eloquent man, always with a funny story to hand, he could be singularly charming. Perhaps like anyone who had survived and flourished for over a decade in elite sport, though, Sammy had an edge. He could sometimes lose his judgment after a few drinks and I know he managed to upset John Radford and David Court to the extent that neither ever came again.

We always met at Langan's Brasserie in Mayfair, a place where footballers tended to go. There would be around ten to a dozen of us, usually during the week before Christmas from around midday until kicking-out time, and they were very enjoyable sessions. One star of these get-togethers was Frank McLintock. It was very noticeable that Frank still had magnetism about him, a level of charisma that had in no way diminished since his time as captain at the club. When Frank held court, everyone still listened. Even these days, when Frank and I meet for lunch, people will recognise him and will want to have a word, especially Arsenal people; it's always been like that with Frank. At Langan's, other diners would often come over asking for autographs and generally make a fuss of the lads. When Eddie Kelly and Peter Marinello arrived, it could sometimes get a bit out of hand but it was great to see the old team reunited and able to reminisce for a while.

The Double team were still in demand and these get-togethers created a good opportunity to arrange things. For example, I was able to help organise the appearance of an Arsenal Double XI in a couple of benefit games for the family of Tottenham's Cyril Knowles, who had passed away at a young age.

The mid-80s are remembered for the sacking of Terry Neill and then Don Howe a couple of seasons later. Both of them lovely, Arsenal men but, realistically, it was time for them to go. The football was frequently terrible, some dreadful matches and results, and again the bottom line for the board was that the punters had stopped coming.

We were in the doldrums and even the signing of Charlie Nicholas couldn't help. I think it is remarkable that we signed one of the hottest-ever prospects to emerge in British football and that it can now be almost totally forgotten. Charlie was very skilful and, while he had no great pace, he was a fantastic finisher. All in all, though, he was not the player we were looking for at the time. We were a very grey side back then and Charlie's dashes of colour didn't really add up to much.

It was a great coup to get him, though, especially given Liverpool's interest, but sadly will his career at Highbury ever be more than a footnote in Arsenal's history?

Towards the end of the 1985/86 season, the club were fairly openly looking for a successor to Don Howe and, feeling the club had gone behind his back, he resigned. Arsenal were feeling confident that, at the second time of asking, Terry Venables was on his way to Highbury. I was told that Venables's appointment was 'in the bag' at one stage. There had also been talk of Alex Ferguson. The Aberdeen manager was keen to come to London. The problem was that when Arsenal offered the job to him, they wanted an immediate answer. Ferguson had stepped in at the last moment to oversee Scotland's World Cup campaign at Mexico 86 as a result of the sudden passing of Jock Stein. Ferguson said he couldn't give Arsenal an answer until he got back from the World Cup and, with the offer left hanging in the air, we moved to make an alternative appointment – George Graham. It reflects well on Friar that the three candidates he pursued were Venables, Ferguson, and Graham – perhaps the three leading British coaches of that era.

At the time, Millwall's George Graham was relatively unknown as a manager, despite some good showings under him at The Den, including a promotion to the Second Division; his appointment looked a little speculative when he was compared to the other two candidates who had been considered.

The day George Graham was appointed, my instinct was that Frank McLintock would become his assistant. I telephoned Frank that evening to talk about it. Frank said there was no way George was going to ask him. Frank went on to talk in the most glowing terms about his old team-mate, 'Stroller', who, Frank said, was now a changed man, a totally different proposition to the player he'd been at Arsenal all those years ago. Frank said Arsenal was George's dream job and, he added: 'You mark my words, he'll be very, very successful here.'

Perhaps a close working relationship between George and Frank wouldn't ever have really worked. George is very calm and measured, while Frank can be impulsive and a bit gung-ho. Once George had made his mind up about something, he rarely changed it, while Frank could flip about. George would have been aware of Frank's tendency towards impetuosity. In 1986, the club was in a mess and what it required above all else was singlemindedness. There was also the small matter of George's ego – I don't think he would have wanted another Arsenal hero knocking around.

Theo Foley, who became George's assistant, was the perfect second in command: loyal, diligent, supportive and dependable. The two of them were the typical 'good cop, bad cop' pairing – George would give them a bollocking and Theo would come along and lift them up. All the Arsenal lads held Theo in very high regard.

I phoned George to wish him luck. We went out a few times, just the two of us, to Langan's, and after a drink or two, George would open up a bit. I think he found it useful to get a handle on what supporters were thinking. I did recognise it as a privilege to be able to speak with George on a one-to-one basis like that and to have an open debate which might include opinions on our players; he would sometimes touch on his transfer plans, too.

George started as he meant to go on. A student and devotee of Arsenal's history, George turned around the club he loved. George Graham gave us the wonder years – and the journey is one hell of a ride.

# Part Four:
# George Graham

## Chapter 17

# 1986/87

GEORGE LIVED and breathed Arsenal and, with a group of hungry young footballers, he very quickly brought a sense of pride back to the club. The name Arsenal Football Club meant something again. *He* did that and, for my generation, the next few seasons became the most glorious period of our lives. Very quickly, everyone started to hate us again and, for George, that was a badge of honour – proof we were doing something right. The Wenger years that followed George were amazing but Graham's reign perhaps presented us in our most authentic light. His team was built upon the qualities that ran through all the great Arsenal teams; in terms of style, it was Arsenal through and through and we loved it. If Wenger gave us an era of high aestheticism, then Graham gave us an unremitting blitzkrieg – football, for him, was total war.

George had always been a highly sociable animal and it wasn't unusual to see him out and about at London's top glamour spots. He would have doubtless run into some Arsenal players over the years, lads like Kenny Sansom, and I imagine he would have picked up an idea of the state of the club. George was smart and canny; he would have quietly noted things and let players, well-oiled after a few pints, begin to say things that might otherwise have remained unsaid. When he was appointed, he'd have had a pretty good idea about what awaited him at Highbury.

From the start, the players were impressed by him and his thoroughness. David O'Leary told me that George made it clear that reputations counted for nothing, that for everyone at the club it was day one again. I think it is well documented that his underlying view was that the squad of players he inherited, for the quality and experience they had, were massive underachievers.

George inherited a group of highly talented young footballers and would have liked the hunger, the willingness to listen and learn. From early on, he made it clear that youth would trump experience. George was ambitious, driven by the idea of making Arsenal great again. Apart from anything else, younger players listen more and are more adaptable to new methods.

After ending his playing days with Crystal Palace and a short stint in the North American Soccer League with California Surf, it had looked like he would go out of football. George tried his hand at different things but struggled to find anything suitable; he just wanted to earn a living and was finding it difficult. I recall he had one job with a haulage company where his footballing profile was used to attract new customers but for all ex-players back then it was difficult to bridge the gap between a life in football and one outside of the game; your footballing exploits are very quickly forgotten and soon your name counts for little.

George had retained some links with ex-players. His closest friend in football had been Terry Venables, who was, by then, manager at Crystal Palace and it was Venables who offered him a job coaching the youth team. As good as George turned out to be, there is no doubt that it was his friendship with Venables, rather than any obvious potential, which got him the job. I think George had a bit of imposter syndrome at first but, in spite of that, he clearly had something about him and quickly built a reputation to the extent that when Venables left Selhurst Park and moved to Queens Park Rangers, he made sure he took Graham with him. After a couple of years, George was appointed manager at The Den, with Millwall languishing bottom of the old Third Division. He quickly sorted them out and they achieved safety on the final day of the season with an away win that would become George's trademark: 1-0. He soon guided them to promotion. It was a swift turnaround and he no doubt started to catch the eye of bigger clubs. In May 1986, he succeeded Don Howe at Highbury.

At that stage, I believe there were probably two big factors in George's success as a coach. Firstly, there was that nagging inner voice which compelled him to drive himself onwards and, secondly, the fact he had played under some great coaches and absorbed some useful lessons. His time under Sexton and Howe would have taught him the importance of a firm defensive foundation.

Howe and Sexton were innovative and organised coaches, too. I think George's thoroughness was as a result of experiencing training sessions taken by Don and Dave in his own playing days. I know the players at Arsenal loved Graham's training from the moment he started back at Highbury.

When he began to look at the players, he was guided by an instinct to promote youth but he wasn't obsessive about it; he was quite pragmatic. Tony Woodcock, Paul Mariner and Tommy Caton were all allowed to leave, with youngsters like Niall Quinn, David Rocastle and Tony Adams finding favour.

One sale which did confuse and disappoint me was that of Martin Keown to Aston Villa. Martin, despite being the one standout success story from Howe's final season, was still on his youth team wages and, so, he went to George and asked for another £50 a week on the grounds that he was likely to be a first-team regular. George and Ken Friar baulked at this request and insisted he negotiate but Martin was adamant that he was worth it and stuck to his guns. The club wouldn't budge and he left. As Martin later admitted, he regretted it the moment he realised what he had done.

I had followed Martin's development right through the youth set-up. Over his formative years, it was clear how ambitious he was and he certainly looked as if he had the talent to go with it. Alongside him for much of that journey was another great prospect – Tony Adams – and the battle between the two of them was very intense. Two highly talented young players fighting for the one spot – either could have been Arsenal's centre-back for years to come. Though Martin had just got his nose in front in terms of development and first-team experience, Tony's presence at the club and his very obvious quality must have reassured George that he could do without Keown. Although I didn't know him that well, I had occasionally chatted with Tony's dad, Alex, at youth team games and I knew all about Tony; his pedigree showed through and, even at that young age, he was every inch the type of combative centre-back that would appeal to Graham. George, as will be made clear, was very fond of a centre-back.

It was clear to me that David O'Leary had drifted from the impeccably high standards of his earlier years and looked a bit stale. I think George coming in did him good. I don't think Tommy Caton was ever the right partner for David. David was at his best when he had a combative 'stopper' alongside him, someone who attacked the ball like Mancini or Young, allowing him to sweep up behind them. Either Keown or Adams was the ideal player to play alongside him. For the time being, at least, Adams became that partner and Keown embarked upon the journey that would eventually lead back to George Graham and Arsenal's door some nine years later.

Graham's impact was almost immediate. In his first season, we conceded fewer goals than anyone except the champions and, at one stage between autumn and late winter, went on a 17-match unbeaten league run (22 games in all competitions). Prior to George, we had started to become the embodiment of the 'southern softies' but that image was quickly dispersed as Graham's young guns went about their business with energy, physicality and fight.

That never-say-die attitude was never more obvious than in our League Cup semi-final with Tottenham that season. We had come unstuck in the first leg at Highbury, losing 1-0, and they scored again in the first half of the second leg to lead 2-0 on aggregate. But suddenly, during the half-time break, fortune handed us the greatest motivational leg-up. Never has a public address system ever played such a pivotal part in the outcome of a football match.

With 45 minutes of football *still* to play, Tottenham thought it a good idea to inform their supporters how they could go about obtaining tickets for the final! It galvanised the Arsenal supporters and, likewise, seemed to galvanise the players. It must have been either audible in the dressing room or had been relayed to them because Arsenal came out like an invasion force. Viv Anderson and Niall Quinn scored to tie it up on aggregate and Arsenal continued to lay siege to the Spurs goal.

Arsenal came of age that afternoon as Mickey Thomas, Paul Davis and David Rocastle began to dominate the midfield. The press captured their performance with words like 'courageous', 'energy' and 'fierce' as Arsenal slowly but surely cowed the more experienced Hoddle and Ardiles. One paper commented that, by half-time, 'Davis had made Hoddle look like a tired old man'.

The replay at White Hart Lane saw Hoddle left out – Davis had run him into the ground – and in an atmosphere as frenzied as I have ever experienced, the game kicked off. In was nip and tuck, with Arsenal just edging it. However, on the hour, Allen gave the hosts the lead but the Gunners never faltered and never changed their approach. With eight minutes remaining, Paul Davis seized on the ball inside his own half and lofted a precision pass to Ian Allinson, who had outwitted the offside trap. Allinson beat Spurs defender Gough to the ball and, from a narrow angle, fired it past Clemence. 'Yet another Arsenal comeback,' was how ITV commentator Brian Moore summed it up.

It was all Arsenal now, with the game edging towards injury time. When O'Leary sent a long free kick upfield to the edge of the penalty box, Quinn, as game as ever, challenged but Gough got his head there first; the ball deflected sideways and, fortuitously, into the path of Allinson, who hit it first time. The ball ricocheted to Rocastle, who managed with his less favoured left foot to sweep it home beneath the dive of Clemence and turn one end of White Hart Lane into a rapturous sea of red and white. Arsenal had done it, in the 91st minute of the replay; it was the first time in the three games that the Gunners had got their noses in front. That night, a new, young team stepped out, worthy of the cannon on their chests.

Graham's reign as boss sometimes reads like a *Boys' Own* tale. It is packed with backs-to-the-wall stories of Arsenal fighting their way out of a corner and that evening at White Hart Lane is up there with Anfield and Copenhagen; a rollicking night when a mud-splattered gang of young mates triumphed and announced Arsenal were back.

The final at Wembley, when we overcame Liverpool after going a goal down, saw Kenny Sansom lift the trophy after two goals from Charlie Nicholas – how nice that Charlie's Arsenal career had at least one special moment to hang his memory on.

It is the 1989 Liverpool game that gets remembered but it is those games against Tottenham wherein something magical happened; boys became men. A fierce resistance to accepting defeat would become a defining characteristic of Graham's Arsenal.

Chapter 18

# 1987/88

GEORGE'S PLAYER recruitment for the 1987/88 season was brilliant: he'd snapped up Nigel Winterburn in pre-season and Alan Smith had finally arrived following his end-of-season loan back to Leicester City, while Kevin Richardson, Brian Marwood and Lee Dixon were all added to an ever-improving clutch of youngsters.

Niall Quinn, whom Alan Smith replaced, had performed gallantly as Arsenal's centre-forward in Graham's first season and his 12 goals were a good return. I liked Niall – the sheer enthusiasm of him and the fact he consistently made the most of his abilities. By the end of his career, he had crafted himself into a really efficient centre-forward; he knew his game inside out and perhaps was one of those players who through hard work became a footballer for whom the whole was greater than the sum of their parts.

However, as much as I liked Quinn, at that stage 'Smudger' was undoubtedly a big upgrade. Alan Smith was the sort of clever footballer who could shine in contemporary football. He played for the team, worked hard and used his intelligence. He was a smashing player and a very nice man. Although he put in a shift, he brought a greater technical dimension to our forward play and, for a side which liked to be direct, he was the perfect target man, with a physical strength which belied his slight frame and softly spoken demeanour. To make him absolutely relevant for younger, modern readers, Alan Smith would fit seamlessly into Arteta's Arsenal.

Brian Marwood was signed towards the end of the season and, because of the relative shortness of his stay, he can easily be forgotten. He settled almost immediately and spent most of Arsenal's title-winning 1988/89 season putting the ball on Alan Smith's head from his left wing position. He was an unerring crosser of the ball, from either open play or dead balls, and opportunistic in front of goal, too. Marwood always struck me as so much more of a George Graham footballer than Anders Limpar, who ultimately replaced him. Marwood began his stint with the PFA in 1990, which coincided with his departure from Highbury; I don't know, but I wouldn't have imagined that George would have welcomed his involvement with the PFA.

Kevin Richardson was unfussy and busy; he went about his business like a sniffer dog in the cauldron of midfield, winning his battles and keeping things ticking over. For a player who won the league title with two different clubs, he is strangely underrated. He would come to the fore in the title run-in of 1989, ably standing in for the injured Paul Davis.

Lee Dixon and Nigel Winterburn were the least well-known of the signings. Lee took a season to establish himself in the side. Once in the team, though, he never looked back. Winterburn looked the business almost as soon as he pulled on an Arsenal shirt, despite initially being played out of position. He had been voted Wimbledon's player of the year for four consecutive seasons prior to his move. A man of few words, he would endear himself to the Arsenal faithful with his constant chivvying of opponents, most famously United's Brian McClair. He would come to be known as 'Nutty Nigel' and I loved him – he played with a passion and an unremitting pride at being an Arsenal footballer; all the great Arsenal teams had a bit of Winterburn about them. Fierce and relentless, I never saw him once give an inch in battle. Winterburn always did his duty and he loved defending, too. He was a spoiler in the proper football sense of the word – one of my all-time favourite Arsenal players.

We only picked up one point from our opening three fixtures but a run of six goals in his first eight games for new boy Alan Smith steadied the ship. When we won at Spurs with goals from Thomas and Rocastle, we had climbed to third place and by the end of October, we were top. We looked invincible for a time as we went on a run of ten successive league victories until a double blow tripped us up – successive defeats, at home to Southampton and then away at Watford.

The two best performances, perhaps of the whole season, were saved for the semi-final of the League Cup against a good Everton side. The first leg at Goodison Park was edged courtesy of a brilliantly taken half chance by Perry Groves. Thereafter, we defended resiliently and were helped by Everton missing a penalty. The second leg saw an exhilarating display from Arsenal sweep aside Everton 3-1 at a noisy and rumbustious Highbury. When we hit that sort of groove – and with the crowd so vocal and partisan – we were irresistible.

From Christmas onwards, David O'Leary was troubled by his Achilles; he would sit out games, return and break down again. A rupture to the tendon perhaps required surgery much earlier than when we finally opted to proceed with it and by the time it had flared for a fourth time, it was just too late for him to regain his fitness for the League Cup Final against Luton Town. Missing O'Leary would prove a huge blow and it would provide George Graham with a lesson he would never ever forget.

The final turned out to be a catalogue of 'what ifs'. Our preparations for the game had been overshadowed by the potentially avoidable hit we would take from O'Leary's absence. There were other issues looming, too. Steve Williams had fallen out with Graham and would 'go missing' on the day of the final and effectively seal his exit from the club. Kenny Sansom was looking increasingly disillusioned. Stripped of the captaincy, which passed to Graham's young acolyte Tony Adams, I recall him as being on the edge of things that day at Wembley, scowling and seemingly unfocused. With the signing of Winterburn, and knowing how highly Graham already rated his new left-back, Sansom must have known his days were numbered.

Harford beat three Arsenal defenders to a cross to set up Stein for the only goal of the opening half. After the break, as we attacked the end where the Arsenal supporters stood, we were much livelier. At the midpoint of the second half, the game caught fire. Hayes seized on a loose ball from close range to level things up and, within a few minutes, Alan Smith gave us the lead. When, moments later, Rocastle jinked into the box and was upended by a tired challenge and the ref responded with the award of a penalty, it felt as if we had totally turned the game on its head in the space of ten minutes.

It was, surprisingly, Nigel Winterburn who placed the ball on the spot. In fairness to Winterburn, he placed his kick well but it just lacked a bit of strength and Dibble, guessing correctly, was able to palm it round the post. Come full time, Graham would totally exonerate Winterburn and, instead, credited Dibble with a fine save.

We were so overwhelmingly on top that the penalty miss shouldn't really have mattered. Then, sadly, Gus Caesar had one of those moments: 'Caesar's Folly'. With the ball at his feet, he hesitated, got it stuck beneath him, stumbled and, as the ball ran away from him, he caught his studs in the turf; a second later, Danny Wilson glanced home a free header to level things up. Stein's late winner was the best goal of the afternoon, a clean first-time strike which gave Lukic no chance.

George Graham vowed to never again find himself going into a season-defining game with no real options for an injured senior player. From that moment onwards, Graham pursued a policy, especially where central defenders were concerned, of safety in numbers. Hence the steady purchase of guys like Steve Bould, Andy Linighan, Colin Pates and even bringing Keown back to the club, while we still had Adams and O'Leary. George became a slightly obsessive hoarder of centre-halves.

And what of the game's pantomime villain – Gus Caesar? Well, I tend to take a view tempered with sympathy. Caesar was a footballer good enough to have played for England at Under-21 level. He was known to be nervy and lacking in confidence and it is likely he played at Wembley with his own injury concerns (a hernia and ankle problem) but was desperate to play. He played 44 times for Arsenal and, from what I saw, he never threw in the towel.

George failed to capture his first-choice signing in the summer, Gary Pallister, but picked up Steve Bould from Stoke City. It is amazing to think that George recruited three-quarters of that world-famous backline (Dixon, Winterburn and Bould) in the space of a few months for a combined fee of just over £1m. In his early days at Arsenal, he was a brilliant judge of a footballer and, for two seasons, his recruitment was spot on. That period provides a benchmark against which some of his later signings have to be judged.

When we all came back for the Makita Tournament at Wembley in late summer, everything seemed to have shifted up a gear. Albeit a pre-season affair, a sensational 4-0 annihilation of Tottenham and 3-0 defeat of Bayern Munich 24 hours later were of undeniably high quality.

I'd not had a bet since my younger days but even I was inclined to take advantage of the bookies' generous offer of 16-1 for Arsenal to win the league. So, with £50 duly invested, we embarked upon a season of football that touched extremes of emotion on a number of occasions, for a variety of reasons, and kept us all literally on our toes until Steve McMahon kindly let us all know there was just the one minute left – and even then, it wasn't all done.

Chapter 19

# 1988/89: Part One

IS THERE a more evocative expression in football than 'Anfield 89'? It was football at its finest and most theatrical.

Pre-season had gone like a dream: eight games, seven victories and one draw, scoring 30 goals and conceding just three in the process. Dixon had, at last, convinced George he was ready to be his right-back and Sansom's class had been replaced with Winterburn's punkish aggression and tireless instinct to rattle the opposition. With the full-back berths decided, Graham had only to perm two from the three central defenders – Adams, O'Leary and Bould.

By 1988, Adams's progress had, to a degree, stalled. We all still loved him but there was no getting away from the fact he had suffered a poor European Championships with England that summer. 'Big Tone' was, at times, made to look a tad rustic in the company of players like Marco van Basten.

David O'Leary had always tended to be at his best alongside a centre-half who wanted to attack the ball, so, to me, it looked like a straight choice between Adams and Bould for the final spot in the team. It was at this stage that David went to have a word with George Graham, to suggest that leaving Tony out of the side to face Wimbledon in the opening fixture of the season ran the risk of setting Adams back a bit; George agreed. Although Tony was no shrinking violet, his confidence would have taken a hell of a battering had Arsenal dropped him so soon after a poor showing for England.

However, when the team was announced David was livid – Adams was playing and so, too, was Steve Bould! It was David who was making way for the new the centre-back from Stoke City.

We romped to a 5-1 opening day victory, with a hat-trick from Alan Smith in a very sure-footed performance. O'Leary duly returned for the next few games but, unexpectedly, so did Arsenal's inconsistency. A 3-2 win at Tottenham was sandwiched between a 3-2 defeat at home to Aston Villa and a 2-2 home draw with Southampton. With Arsenal two down to the Saints at half-time, it required a very, very late equaliser from Smith to salvage a point but, as dramatic as that was, it wasn't the biggest talking point to emerge from the match.

At the time, while the game continued, I had no idea that anything had happened off the ball but, later that evening, when the *ITN News* began, the whole world knew that Paul Davis had broken the Southampton player Glenn Cockerill's jaw that afternoon. It was a very strange affair. Paul had no reputation at all for any kind of nastiness – there are some players you can imagine lashing out, players with 'hardman' reputations to maintain – but not Paul; he was steely, certainly, but a nice lad all-round. The first rumours to circulate were that Paul had been racially abused but Paul never sought to suggest it was that; it was just that Cockerill had been all over him from the first minute. Paul later said that Cockerill's treatment went far beyond anything he had previously experienced and that, at the most basic level, Cockerill was just being disrespectful to a fellow pro. Paul said he just couldn't work out what was going on and that, eventually, he made the conscious decision to address it in his own way. Whether Cockerill's actions had been calculated to draw a response, only he would know, but draw a response it did – one Cockerill didn't get up from. It was enough for the FA to fine Davis £3,000 and ban him for nine games – the longest ban in domestic English football at the time.

George used the episode to establish a siege mentality. He became adept at spinning a useful tune out of a bad story. Eventually, the Paul Davis story became another example of Arsenal's ability to court trouble, internalise the fallout and get bigger and stronger. That old, traditional antipathy which the whole of English football had against Arsenal was back. George and his team came to prove time and time again that they enjoyed a challenge and the bigger, the better. There were no reputations that team would retreat from, no citadel we might flinch from storming.

By early November, we were starting to find some consistent form and after beating Coventry 2-0 at Highbury, we had climbed to second spot. Our next two games would prove just what a promising side we were. In an early round of the League Cup, we had been drawn up at

Liverpool and I think a lot of people were looking at the tie to see just how authentic the noise around Arsenal was.

Only a few minutes into the game and Arsenal had pushed Liverpool back. Marwood was having joy on Arsenal's left and, on the right, Merson, Rocastle and Dixon were carving out space and opportunities.

Just before half-time, Bould went into the book for going through the back of Rush and, in a way, it was a fitting final act. Arsenal had bossed the first half, playing some genuinely attractive football, while remaining physically dominant and making sure that Rush and Aldridge didn't get a look-in. Adams and Bould picked their moments well to leave a calling card.

As Liverpool attacked the Kop in the second half, Arsenal again forced them back. But then one bit of magic from John Barnes turned it all on its head. Dancing through our defence as if we were Brazil for that famous England goal of his, he put Liverpool one up.

Parity didn't take long in coming, though. A long ball from Adams was chested backwards by Smith to Thomas, who sprayed it out to Rocastle and, from a narrow angle, he hit the sweetest shot which arrowed into Hooper's top corner. It was nothing more than we deserved.

What had come out of the evening's football was a blueprint for how we *might* go to Anfield and take on Liverpool. I think our performance surprised them; in those days, sides didn't go to Anfield and get them on the back foot.

The following weekend, we travelled to Forest and we went with real confidence, turning in a really strong performance. There was a real thoroughness about our football that afternoon at the City Ground.

After going a goal behind early on, it was soon all Arsenal. A scramble in the box saw Smith guide the ball over the keeper to make it all square at the break. In the second half, Bould scored from a Groves flick-on and then the trusty old Bould flick for Adams allowed the latter to launch himself bravely through a crowd at the back post to make it 3-1 and give Arsenal a firm grip on the game. In the closing moments, Marwood was put through by another excellent Winterburn pass and completed the scoring: 4-1.

We had presented compelling evidence of our promise. We were ruggedly strong at the back; Dixon and Winterburn were tenacious in their defensive duties but also ready to augment attacking situations and were intelligent with it; the midfield had energy, muscle, brains, athleticism and guile; while, in Smith, we had our best all-round centre-forward since Frank Stapleton. The players knew their jobs and they were collectively learning how to win games; they had heart and no matter how many times we went to the well, there was always something there. The players just loved it; you could see how much they wanted to be a part of that team and as for us supporters, this was *proper* Arsenal.

One of many positives was young Paul Merson; he was becoming a one-off maverick whose unpredictability and on-field cockiness was making him look like the player we had once hoped Charlie Nicholas might have turned out to be. Before he ever came close to our first team, I knew what a great prospect he was. He was very highly thought of by the club; I'd seen him playing in youth teams and for the reserves and, crucially, I had spoken to a friend of mine who supported Brentford, where Paul been out on loan. I was told he'd done exceptionally well there, looking a great prospect. In the players' lounge at Highbury, I had had the opportunity to chat with his parents and they were nice, likeable folk, as was Paul. He was appreciated by his team-mates and it was noticeable that there was no malice about him; and, on top of that, he was a terrific footballer. There was no doubt about his quality but, back then, no one really knew about his private life. There was talk of some members of his extended family who might have led him astray; whatever, in 1988 we only saw and only knew Paul Merson the talented young footballer.

David Rocastle had developed season by season and by 1988, he was an outstanding player, probably the star of the team. He was as close to being the complete midfielder as Liam Brady had been. David and Liam were totally different players, with different attributes, but both were equally important to their teams. David supplemented his football brain and his abilities with a seam of granite. He was physically and mentally so tough; you couldn't kick him off the ball, knock him off his game or intimidate him. That smile hid beneath it a core of steel. You wouldn't find anyone in the game that had a word to say against him.

Rocky was more than a legend; he became that much more personal thing – a hero. We are privileged to call David Rocastle one of our own and his story is just one more narrative that makes the 88/89 season such an enduring part of our history.

It proved to be a happy Christmas. A 3-2 Boxing Day victory at Charlton Athletic saw us go top of the league and there were further victories – away at Villa (3-0) and at Highbury against Tottenham (2-0).

The performance at Villa Park was outstanding. Right from the off, we took it to a Villa team enjoying their own good run of form. After only two minutes, a ball into the box from O'Leary was nodded home by Smith and, thereafter, Arsenal took control. What sticks in the mind was the crispness of our passing, our movement and the number of options the man on the ball had. Possession was progressive and the ball was moved fast.

Rocastle capped a display of verve and intelligence with one of the goals he is still remembered for. The ball came to him 30 yards out and, with the Villa keeper off his line, David lobbed it straight back first time to put us two up on 20 minutes. Two minutes from time, Perry Groves capped a scintillating walk-on part with an assured finish to put the game to bed.

In the morning's press, George Graham had been cited as a man on Real Madrid's radar and the quality of our all-round performance that day could only have further enhanced his standing. What was special about our football that year, something we perhaps lost as we morphed over the next few seasons into our '1-0 to the Arsenal' persona, was the fluidity of our movement. When we attacked, defenders got ahead of midfielders, midfielders ahead of forwards and the readiness of Rocastle, Richardson and Thomas to backtrack meant that absent full-backs were never missed. Adams and Bould were wild beasts ready to pounce, which they did with an apparent relish which was almost psychopathic. I think George trusted this bunch of players more than any others he ever had.

A few days later, we went to Goodison Park and played so well that the Everton faithful applauded us off the pitch at the end. It was a convincing 3-1 victory that saw us cement our top spot. It was all the more impressive given it was achieved without either Tony Adams or Steve Bould; O'Leary played and there was an opportunity, too, for Caesar, who delivered an assured display.

There followed a stumble and a stutter but the return of Paul Davis from his ban seemed to settle things down again. Away from Highbury, Liverpool were going on a post-Christmas run. At one stage in February, they languished in eighth spot, an incredible 19 points behind Arsenal, but, crucially, had four games in hand. However, even if Liverpool won all their games in hand, they would still remain seven points behind.

On 2 April, we travelled to Old Trafford for one of what appeared to be the two most difficult of our remaining fixtures. How many times had we done the calculations? *If* we could get something from the game in Manchester …

We had begun to ship a few goals in recent weeks, five alone in our last two home matches. Perhaps the high octane approach Arsenal had maintained throughout the season was just starting to take its toll?

Since early January, O'Leary had replaced Bould at centre-back. It was now that George pulled his tactical switch and, perhaps, even his masterstroke: three centre-backs, with wing-backs. With Bould back in the team, David moved into a position between him and Adams as a deeper, sweeping, third centre-back. There, David could organise and deploy his 'dogs of war'. O'Leary was the perfect man for the role and, with the insurance of two other central defenders, David might even have the chance to roam forward with the ball.

It worked a treat. Arsenal dominated at Old Trafford and, but for a cruel slice of luck, which saw an Adams clearance slice off his boot and balloon up into the air and over Lukic for the most ill-deserved of own goals, we would have come away with the three points we deserved. It had been a dangerous ball in and Adams, guarding the front post, knew he had to deal with it and, at full stretch, could only deflect it. The press seized on it and 'Donkey Adams' was born! The irony was that everyone chose to ignore Adams's goal at the other end, throwing himself into a melee of flying boots to head home yet another Steve Bould flick-on in a crowded six-yard box; the bravest of brave goals. I think that, most seasons, you'd settle for a draw at United.

The incident of the own goal illustrated just what a tenacious player Adams was, for he just took it on the chin and got on with it. Never was there a suggestion that he might hide; he was always there, putting himself forward, dealing with things – he must have had a character chiselled out of stone. There was a fair bit of fallout from it all and he had some stick to deal with over the next couple of seasons but deal with it he did, never flinching, never yielding. His team-mates, his manager and his club's supporters knew his worth; a giant of a man whose pride and passion would never allow him to shirk a challenge. At that stage of his career, if there had been a small seam of doubt or weakness, he would have kept it hidden; later, as he grew as a footballer and a man, he would learn to deal with such setbacks differently but, back then, Adams was our lionheart.

Chapter 20

# 1988/89: Part Two

CLOSE ON 2am, the early hours of Saturday morning, the moon, high over Anfield, looked down, spreading her silvery light upon the empty and silent stadium. It was the quiet hour following an evening of tumultuous events: seismic, era-defining, life-changing football action. It has been written about so many times, talked about a million times more, but it never pales, its fascination never dims, it never feels as if that evening has finally given up to us its very last secret. Was there *ever* such an evening in your football life?

Of our last seven fixtures, we had the distinct advantage that five of them were at home. After beating Everton, we entertained Newcastle United. During the game, although I had a vague idea something was happening away from Highbury, details were sparse and, besides, I was entirely focused on our game and the absolute need for three points. It wasn't until I got back to my car after our match had finished that the awfulness of what had happened at Hillsborough that afternoon really struck me.

On the 15 April, 94 football supporters lost their lives at the FA Cup semi-final between Liverpool and Nottingham Forest. Three more have subsequently died bringing the total number of fatalities to 97; every one of them had simply set out to watch a football match. The Hillsborough tragedy touched us all.

As a fellow football supporter, it did bring it quite close to home; on another day, that could have been my club, our supporters, me and my heart went out to them all. But it didn't for one moment alter anything for me regarding the title; I desperately wanted us to go on and win it. To imply anything different would be dishonest and said for effect. It was that old obsession again: for me, Arsenal were beyond any considerations of right and wrong, so feeling guilty about wanting us to still win the league would make no difference to anything. Reasonably enough, the whole country wanted Liverpool to win the league and, indeed, clinch the Double, as some sort of testament to those who lost their lives. I understood that.

When we all came back to play and watch football again two weeks later, we put five past Norwich. For me, that was important; it demonstrated just how focused we were. A scrappy game at Ayresome Park against Middlesbrough, the scene of so many disappointments over the years, was won with a goal from a forgotten hero – Martin Hayes. That left three games: two at home, both looking like routine victories at any other time of the season, and the final game of the season, the rearranged visit to Anfield. We tried hard not think of the Liverpool game but it still cast its shadow. If we could beat Derby and Wimbledon, then, assuming Liverpool won their games, we could go to Anfield needing only a point to win the title.

The mood around Highbury for the Derby clash was upbeat but very tense. I think we were all trying not to show just how bloody nervous we all were. We had won four on the bounce, though, and not conceded a goal since Adams's unlucky own goal at Old Trafford. A couple of hours later and the mood around Highbury had changed beyond measure. Derby had done a number on us.

Dean Saunders scored a cracking volley in the first half and, after twisting poor old Tony Adams inside out, he induced a false challenge and duly converted the penalty for their second. It was a desperate situation. We had been nowhere near our best of recent weeks. We looked leggy, nervous, weighed down by expectation. Richardson did have two strong headers saved by Shilton, Smith hit the bar with a glorious opportunity and Winterburn hit a couple of his speciality piledrivers which peppered the outside of the woodwork. A late goal from Paul Merson felt like the emptiest of consolations but how grateful we would be for that goal in a couple of weeks.

A few days later, we played our final home game of the season, against Wimbledon, and drew 2-2 in a match which included a thunderbolt from Winterburn with his *right* foot. In the immediate aftermath of the game, it felt like it was over, that we had blown it. And when Liverpool won their penultimate game 5-0 against West Ham, our task was made clear. It was as brutal as it was simple: win at Anfield by two clear goals.

I later realised that what was required was now easier to picture and I think the situation played to our strengths, for we were a side built to take on a challenge. In a way, it was still entirely in our hands; the single point from our final two home games had just shifted the focus from caution to aggression. And while there was *everything* to lose, there was also, simultaneously, *nothing* to lose and as George, with a knowing smile, kept saying: no one outside Highbury fancied us.

I saw David O'Leary at his home in Hadley Wood with my son, Dean, on the Thursday evening before the match. He seemed very calm and relaxed and we chatted about the game in as casual a manner as we could. I told him that I was certain there was going to be a sting in tail. David was quite sanguine about it all; he genuinely thought we could win but the two-goal margin presented an extra step that might just prove a push too far. I knew just how much this meant to him. He had had a fabulous career at Highbury, had been extremely loyal, staying in north London when clubs with better prospects wanted him; from both a football and a financial perspective, there had been times when you wouldn't have blamed him for moving on. But he comes from an Arsenal-supporting family and his dream was to win the league title at this, *his* club. The team was on the up and up under George and likely to stay there but time was moving on for David. Steve Bould was proving to be so much more than a squad player that, perhaps, David thought, quite understandably, it might be now or never for him in terms of his ultimate ambition.

David is an astute reader of situations and people and he recognised that what was required of Arsenal, as a task, suited the mentality of the players. However unlikely it was, if anyone was to go to Anfield and win to capture the league, it was Arsenal under George Graham. We had started the season as a 16-1 chance for the title and I noted that our odds to win by the necessary margin at Anfield were also 16-1. As George said, no one outside of Highbury fancied us.

We drove up to Liverpool early on the Friday, with Dean, whose 13th birthday had fallen the day before, a nephew, Michael Cohen, and friend and Arsenal nut, Phil Sandzer. We were one ticket short, so, upon our arrival in Liverpool, I went to the team hotel and Theo Foley obliged by producing an extra ticket.

I was reassured by the calmness of the players. George was telling anyone who would listen that we'd do it; he thought we would win 3-0. George thought that, because of what was required, everyone would expect us to go out all guns blazing from the off and I think Liverpool expected that, too. George thought 0-0 at half time would be a very decent position.

Time felt heavy on our hands as the day wore on; everyone really just wanted to get on with it. We spent most of the day in the hotel or walking around the dock area. Whatever we did, every time I looked at my watch, the hands had barely moved. In the afternoon, the players all went back to bed for a nap.

If your life depended upon the outcome of a football match, there is no team I would rather have playing for me than the XI who ran out at Anfield in yellow and blue to a wall of noise. In a nice touch from the club, each player ran out with a bouquet of flowers, which were presented to the crowd at all four corners of the ground in a show of respect to the victims of Hillsborough, a gesture appreciated by the home crowd. But that was that; *this* night had to be all about Arsenal.

From the start, we were cautious, taking the measure of Liverpool. We restricted them to a mere handful of long-range efforts – a couple of them had Lukic moving smartly but there was no danger – and, at the other end, we still managed to force the better openings. Dixon and Rocastle were finding space up against Staunton on Liverpool's left side and the best chance of the half, an early header from Steve Bould, ricocheted away to safety. To a great extent, Liverpool had been nullified; with the insurance of O'Leary, we could push Adams and Bould on to Rush and Aldridge, who inevitably dropped deeper, making the midfield even more crowded for the likes of Barnes and Whelan. Richardson, Thomas and 'Rocky', augmented by Dixon and Winterburn, had compressed the midfield so well that Liverpool played largely in their own half.

Though we needed to score, we desperately didn't want to concede, so a tight, goalless first half seemed to be not only what suited us but it was exactly what Graham had predicted. The Arsenal section of the Anfield crowd was boisterous still – the entire half-time break witnessed a non-stop chant of 'Georgie Graham's red and white army', which they could probably hear in the dressing room.

It is the smallest things in football which sometimes cause the biggest waves. Thirty seconds before Smith blindsides Liverpool to glance home our first goal, Rocastle is pumping his fist and shouting. It had been a fairly innocuous high boot by Whelan on Rocastle to bring about the free kick but it felt like the moment when somehow we released the safety catch and a different Arsenal emerged. Alan Smith had said they'd tried that free kick move tens of times in matches all season and it had never previously worked! It did now. Winterburn whipped over a left-footed, in-swinging free kick and Smith gave it the merest of touches. Liverpool surrounded the referee and then the linesman, none of us knew what for – perhaps it just wasn't in their script?

The mood changed immediately: the tempo ramped up, the volume of the crowd increased and tackles, mainly Arsenal tackles, started to fly in. This was now the game we had all anticipated.

Liverpool were slow to react. For all their experience and expertise, they started to look as if they didn't know what to do next. Arsenal channelled their passion and drive into hounding Liverpool all over the park; it was an exemplary lesson in pressing and Liverpool couldn't get their foot on it, Arsenal biting into them time and time again. There was no way out for Liverpool and when we got the ball, we moved it, meaningfully, progressively, always looking to get a midfield runner in, as Smith constantly pulled right or left, making space in his totally unselfish manner.

We were magnificent: crisp, calm and quick. There was a great spell midway through the second half which culminated in a chance for Thomas, picked out brilliantly by Richardson. Mickey has since said he snatched at it – anyway, he got it right next time.

At this stage, we were so on top that the main concern was not a Liverpool breakaway goal but whether we could keep up the tempo, which had been frenetic and non-stop since almost half-time – the most comprehensive example of 'power football' I'd ever seen. George sent on Perry Groves with a little over ten minutes remaining. The introduction of Groves meant we took off Steve Bould and reverted to a flat back four, although Dixon and Winterburn remained more like auxiliary midfielders than full-backs. It meant more space and soon Liverpool were feeding little passes between Adams and O'Leary but that was the chance we had to take.

More end-to-end stuff and there wasn't a single moment of the game now which felt redundant; every pass, every run mattered. This had gone beyond being a football match.

Then, with a mere 60 seconds of normal time remaining, Richardson went down with cramp. It provided for a rarity that evening; a small moment to reflect, gather thoughts and emotions before we were off again. This must be like the moment in battle before the order to charge. McMahon did his 'one minute' trick and the game restarted, now deep into injury time.

So, here we are: it's time for Arsenal to go 'streaming forward in surely what will be their last attack'.

It takes so few words to describe what happens next when a million of them couldn't do the moment justice. I still can't believe that Houghton didn't tackle Thomas or that Thomas left it so late to flick it beyond Grobbelaar. When it came up for grabs, we grabbed it and just would not let it go.

I was straight in line with Thomas's shot; it felt as if time stood still and the ball took all eternity before it nestled in the net. This time, he hadn't rushed it, he waited and he waited and, as Grobbelaar started to move, he just flicked it over the keeper: 2-0. Liverpool players were down on their knees, Arsenal players were running around the pitch and our section of the crowd became a deafening non-stop wave of sheer joy – we jumped, we screamed, we hugged strangers and, lost for words, tried to comprehend what had happened. One man was in control: George Graham stood there with his palms to the ground – 'focus', he mouthed.

There were just a few moments to see out, time enough for Thomas to pop up at the other end and calmly trap the ball and knock it back to Lukic as if he was playing down the park with his mates. Then it was all over.

I think George Graham was the calmest man in Anfield as the whistle blew. If you watch the footage, he is trying to discourage any celebrations in front of the Liverpool dugout. The Arsenal faithful began an ironic chant of 'boring, boring Arsenal'. Dean, my son, was in tears as we hugged but he was not alone. On what was also his son John's birthday, David O'Leary was in tears, too. Soon, David spotted me in the crowd and beckoned me on to the pitch to join him but I couldn't leave Dean, so I stayed put and enjoyed this once-in-a-lifetime moment with fellow supporters. Everything had happened so quickly that it took a while for my emotions to catch up with it all. For a while, I couldn't actually process it. Grown men were crying, strangers still hugging, all barriers down.

Then Adams lifted the trophy and faced towards us in the corner at the Kemlyn Road end, a little corner of Highbury; the trophy caught the warm yellow light from the floodlights and the whole ground applauded Arsenal's captain. That made an impression on me – I can't imagine it happening at too many other grounds. Dean collected his first memento of the night, his seat, and we started to make a move out of the ground.

We made our way to the Liverpool directors' lounge and, after making use of my 'jibbing' prowess to get us all in, I spoke with George Graham. He was still immaculately turned out, looking more like he'd spent the last couple of hours snoozing in the House of Lords. When we spoke, I couldn't do justice to the congratulations I felt were his due. I remembered Frank McLintock's prescient prediction that George would be so single-minded that he *would* bring great success to the club.

I was really keen to see David O'Leary, so we headed down towards the dressing room. When we got there, what a scene; spirits and emotions were running very high indeed. This meant so much to David. It was a total vindication of his choices throughout his long, loyal career at Arsenal; such a nice guy, unassuming, unfussy and non-pushy, a smashing footballer and such a credit to his club. Everyone was on a high and not wanting the moment to end. Dean found another souvenir, the Union flag Tony Adams had draped around his shoulders as he celebrated after the game. I just took it all in. Memories were enough for me and I didn't want anything to get in the way of this; no filter or distance. I couldn't tear myself away; I felt I could stay in that moment forever.

Back in London, the streets around Highbury filled up quickly; emotions bottled up for so long and, even earlier that night, suppressed for fear of falling short, were spilling out and filling the roads and avenues. Everywhere was red and white within minutes of the final whistle; everyone was outside, young and old, veterans of 1971 and even further back, together with kids still too young even to remember the cup win in 1979. It was joyous and spontaneous. Nothing was planned – perhaps no one really thought it possible? What had started in August had only been won less than a minute before its curtain call and what twists and turns along the way. It was won, it was lost but it ended up coming home to Highbury – our first title for 18 years, the greatest football story ever told.

Our journey back down the M1 was fantastic; there were thousands of Arsenal supporters celebrating all the way to London, flags out of windows and horns sounding. We even managed to get alongside the team coach for some of the way.

When the final whistle sounded at Anfield, Peter Hill-Wood is reported to have taken a drag on his cigar and commented urbanely: 'Never in doubt.' I hope it's true; an incorrigibly Arsenal ending to a thoroughly Arsenal night!

Chapter 21

# 1989/90

ONE OF the hallmarks of the title success was the ruthless clarity of Graham's thinking. When the wobble came, he shored up things with his wing-backs and three centre-backs; he kept things simple, created a framework within which the fearlessness of youth might dare to grasp a famous victory. Now, Graham turned his thinking to how to turn the blueprint of the 'Anfield Job' into an enduring takeover of domestic and European football.

It wasn't immediately clear quite where Arsenal could be strengthened in the summer of 1989. Adams, Dixon, Winterburn, Thomas, Bould, Rocastle and Merson all had youth on their side and would only get better. George wouldn't have wanted to frustrate their development by signing a guy who would go straight into the team ahead of them. Alan Smith was so central to how Graham set up Arsenal that I'm sure he would have struggled to identify a better player in Smith's role.

The previous summer we had looked at Tony Cottee but that was when Arsenal were set up to play four-four-two; now, with the three centre-back system, a guy like Cottee would have been wasted playing a wider role supporting the one central striker, who was always going to be Smith, and, in any event, Merson could play wide left or as the supporting central striker. Arguably, the failure to sign Cottee resulted in Merson's emergence ahead of schedule in 88/89. Personally, I think Lineker would have jumped at the chance to join Arsenal that summer and link back up with his old Leicester City strike partner Alan Smith but, again, it would have been at the expense of Merson's development. Graham, instead, went down the route of strengthening the squad in terms of depth, buying two players who added experience and versatility.

Colin Pates joined a growing coterie of central defenders already at the club but, crucially, had experience of playing at right-back, too. Although he would only go on to make a handful of appearances over his three seasons at the club and would wait nearly two years to get anything approaching a run in the team, his seemed a sensible signing at £500,000. He was short for a central defender but he provided cover for the third centre-back position between Adams and Bould and could cover Dixon, too. He was a decent footballer and I never saw him let Arsenal down.

The other signing was Siggi Jonsson, signed from Sheffield Wednesday for £475,000. Jonsson's career at Highbury was over in a flash, amounting to eight games before a succession of back injuries forced him out. In a way, he was a typical Graham signing, someone under the radar. Although I only saw him a few times, there was no doubt the lad could play. He had a good touch for a big man and was powerful. He was unlikely to get in ahead of Rocastle, Thomas, Richardson or Davis but there was something a bit different about him.

The season got off to a woeful start. Full of optimism and a belief that anything was possible, we headed to Old Trafford. In the searing heat of mid-August, United, who had Neil Webb making his debut, ran out 4-1 victors, with Lukic saving a penalty and Webb scoring the goal of the game.

The United game saw us revert to a traditional four-four-two. Bould was the man left out and, given the success of the three centre-back system, the switch was surprising. United away was the sort of game when the three centre-backs would have been in their element, taking the sting out of things. But, deep down, Graham was a four-four-two man. He stuck with it until the end of the year, when he suddenly readopted the three centre-back set-up again.

By mid-February, it was back to four-four-two but this time with O'Leary making way for Bould; only for David to return for a handful of games when three centre-backs were used again towards the end of the season. For a man so renowned for his steady thinking, the season's tactical and formational flip flops are a striking feature and one which goes some way towards explaining the lack of clarity which contributed to a disappointing season.

There were two minor trophies, both unofficial, but neither without their share of satisfaction. In the summer, we travelled to the USA to play Argentinian champions Independiente in an unofficial 'world championship final'. In a massive stadium, 5,000 curious Americans watched 90 minutes of action in which the ball was largely irrelevant; the match was never really able to escape the mutual antagonisms of the English-Argentinian context. Arsenal won an unsavoury game 2-1.

The second trophy was the British Champions Cup, another unofficial contest between the champions of Scotland and England. We travelled to Ibrox Park to play and beat Rangers 2-1 on a filthy night in an atmosphere of real intensity; no friendly, this one. The contest was a great success and one that I thought might catch on.

David O'Leary had his big moment in early November, when the visit of Norwich City marked him breaking George Armstrong's all-time club appearances record. Before the game, Graham and David Dein presented him with a piece of cut glass and, thereafter, the game had pretty much everything, including a fight that was nothing more than your January sales argy-bargy but which the media built up into a 'mass brawl', thus ensuring the FA would be required to take action.

Arsenal won the game 4-3 with a last-minute penalty. Dixon's initial effort was saved but the rebound came back to him and this time, scuffing his shot, he still managed to get enough on it to score the winner. It was Alan Smith who prompted the unruly scenes. Norwich pushed him and when Smudger didn't respond they pushed him again. Smith just walked off, leaving behind him three-quarters of the players walking around each other, posturing. Norwich got fined £50,000 and we got a £20,000 hit. It was something of nothing. The real implications of it were felt 12 months later after the incident at Old Trafford, with the impression that we were becoming serial offenders.

Perhaps, though, that season we just weren't quite angry or focused enough. We maybe lost sight of what we were good at and just didn't get enough of the basics right. 'It's easier to win it than defend it,' as they say. Thomas didn't look as if he had progressed, to be honest and I think Rocastle was already beginning to feel his knees. There were rumours, too, of players not seeing eye-to-eye with George – Richardson, Davis and Marwood.

We got done by the 'plastic' pitch at Oldham in the League Cup and QPR knocked us out of the FA Cup when a decent cup run might have got us back on track. Ultimately, the season fell flat with a fourth-place finish.

For away games, O'Leary always roomed with Tony Adams – the seasoned old pro keeping an eye on the youngster. I don't know quite when it started but I know David tried to talk to Tony about his drinking; in response, Tony would joke about David being born too old.

Adams didn't have the greatest season in 89/90. I used to think that Tony was too caught up in his own reputation as that guy who runs through brick walls. He needed a break, which oddly he would get soon enough at Her Majesty's pleasure, when he could stop and think about his game. Arsène Wenger's impact on his and Arsenal's footballing philosophy a few years later undoubtedly helped him. There was a time when Tony might never have developed into the accomplished footballing defender he became; he was always better than the version he sometimes presented in his younger days.

By the Easter of that season, I knew one area of the side that was in George's mind to revamp. He called me on the phone and was keen to talk about John Lukic and to plant the seed that David Seaman would be an upgrade. I rated John very highly; he was a crowd favourite, too. If George had been looking to bring in any new players, then a new goalkeeper would have been my last guess but George wanted Seaman from QPR. From what I had seen of Seaman then, I agreed he looked a decent keeper but I saw no reason to replace Lukic. I can only think that, when he asked me, George wanted to gauge the effect replacing Lukic might have on supporters but he made it clear he wanted to sign Seaman. As he said later, he viewed Lukic as one of the top three keepers in the division but Seaman, he believed, was the best. It was a pretty ruthless thing to do but, after 1989, he rightly believed he had sufficient credit to make unpopular decisions. I think George wanted to sign him before the old transfer deadline day we had still in those days but presumably QPR weren't keen at that stage and George had to wait until the summer to get his man.

Along with Seaman, Graham signed yet another centre-back, Andy Linighan from Norwich. When Arsenal went in for him, I think he was quite reluctant to leave Carrow Road. I'm not sure if that was a temperamental thing; some players don't necessarily crave the big-club atmosphere. He might have looked at Arsenal – who had Adams, Bould, O'Leary and Pates – and wondered quite where his next game would come from. But, with Arsenal willing to pay £1.2m for him, Norwich chairman Robert Chase made it clear he was off to Highbury.

The third signing of the summer was the one that caught the eye. I heard about the imminent signing of Anders Limpar from George himself. It was in the pre-season, quite close to the start of the new campaign, and we were just chatting generally; I asked George if he was likely to make any more signings. I think that, by the time we talked, the Limpar deal was as good as done, because George spoke with some authority about it. The name didn't really mean anything to me but, crucially, George introduced him by saying: 'You'll love him, Martin. We've signed a real crowd pleaser.' As soon as he said that, I thought, half facetiously: 'That's strange, because you usually get rid of crowd pleasers.' As Brian Marwood had moved back to Sheffield, this time to United, we needed a left-winger or someone a bit unpredictable wide left. Of the two, I'd bet on George taking Marwood every time; he was very much more the typical Graham player, the polar opposite of Limpar, who was definitely a strange signing for George to make in my view.

When Arsenal reassembled in August 1990, all the young lads were a season older and wiser and, crucially, we were a team with something to prove again. Arsenal needed to be more like Arsenal again. In 1990/91, they would steal our points and then steal our captain but this is Arsenal and we did what Arsenal do.

## Chapter 22

# 1990/91

THE SECOND of George Graham's league title successes is prone to being overlooked beside the glamour and sparkle of '89 but, in many ways, it was the more satisfying achievement. It didn't have the drama of a one in a million, against the odds victory in the last minute; in contrast, its unruffled progress was the mark of a team which had the title under its control over the final weeks of the season. The achievement was all the more noteworthy when you think of the tribulations, admittedly largely self-inflicted, that the club, the team and individuals had to negotiate along the way. If 1988/89 had given us George Graham the master tactician, then 1990/91 showcased Graham the spin doctor; the great communicator for whom every setback was a chance to ratchet up the siege mentality. As George famously said: 'It's fine that everybody hates us, it's part of our history.'

When people are indifferent about Arsenal, then it's usually because we are not perceived as a threat. Nigel Winterburn appeared to not only welcome the visceral dislike which, in 1990/91, came equally from the rest of football and the media; he seemed to genuinely glory in it.

We may well have overstepped the mark at Old Trafford but that wasn't going to stop Graham. Once the FA tribunal had sat in judgment on the 'Battle of Old Trafford' and the inevitable deduction of points was made public, leaving us eight points off the top, then George went on the attack, choosing an address to the first-team squad at London Colney to galvanise the players and to negotiate the first of two potential crises.

With phrases at once both commonplace yet loaded with meaning, he struck exactly the right note. 'The media are enjoying it,' he said, 'because nothing normally comes out of Highbury' and, as a consequence, they were all 'jumping on the bandwagon', because, right then, it was 'fashionable to get into Arsenal'. Having established the unfairness of it all, he set out how to go about addressing it: 'Just keep winning matches', he said, because 'we're not second bottom, we're second top ... just think of football and be proud of yourselves.' His final point was that the players must 'stay together as a unit within the club'.

The victory at Old Trafford had been evidence enough of that unity, a 1-0 win which, as the game wore on, was always more comfortable than the scoreline suggested. Limpar's cheeky near-post effort, which caught Les Sealey off guard, with the keeper expecting a ball to the back post, set the tone for a game which we seemed destined to win, come what may.

When the inevitable flashpoint came, it perhaps owed more to the incident involving Winterburn and McClair at Highbury in the cup a couple of years previously than it did to the Old Trafford game itself. Apart from McClair getting a couple on Winterburn as our left-back lay prostrate on the floor and a glancing blow from Limpar on McClair, there wasn't really much to it. The sight of Arsenal and United substitutes and coaching staffs on the pitch, though, gave the whole affair a more serious feel than it actually warranted. The footage that evening on the news, taken from a low camera angle, which caught the confused and congested pitchside, was enough to suggest the FA would be getting the knives out. Media outrage knew no limit for a couple of days, as talk of a points deduction dominated the news.

I was behind the goal with the rest of the Arsenal contingent and the whole incident took place some distance away from us; while I wouldn't go full Arsène Wenger and claim not to have seen it, it seemed something of nothing even at the time.

United away was the ultimate fighting victory. The ramifications left us adrift but it cemented once again the bonds which existed amongst the players. George might not have wanted it to happen but once it had, he made great use of it. There must have been rumblings from the board, so Graham would have had a difficult balancing act to maintain while he worked hard to turn it to our advantage: to whip up the players with indignation and simultaneously placate the board with contrition. There's no denying he pulled it off.

In late November, in the League Cup, United would knock us out at Highbury with an infamous 2-6 defeat but we showed our strong mentality by bouncing back immediately with a great victory over our title rivals, Liverpool. Graham reverted back to his three centre-back system and our solidity and organisation were evident in a barnstorming 3-0 win. We were strong and incisive all over the pitch. The third goal – when a backheel from Merson put Smith through to strike a screamer into the bottom corner – was a goal worthy of beating anyone. Liverpool had been second best throughout and, once again, Arsenal looked as if they had the measure of their illustrious opponents.

After the Liverpool game, Tony Adams made just two more appearances before he became 'unavailable' and the next crisis duly hit Highbury. The imprisonment of the Arsenal club captain for drink-driving was music to the ears of the media. This time, the club took the blow on the chin and avoided any possibility that we could be accused of condoning Tony's actions or were trying to claim any mitigation. I think they got the balance right; they stood by Adams but never mounted a defence of him. There was some criticism that we continued to pay him while he served his sentence but the best and strongest relationships are most certainly based upon a mutual acceptance of 'for better or worse'. Had they cut Adams adrift or publicly distanced themselves from him, then who knows what might have become of him? By his own well-documented testimony, he was in a bad way mentally at the time and drinking had taken such a hold of him that he sometimes played while drunk. Perhaps the club could and should have done more? If they did, behind the scenes, then Tony largely ignored it, continuing to drink until he was ready to accept his problem in 1996. When he *was* ready, he responded like a giant of a man. He may not be the first person to recover from alcoholism, nor the first to be prepared to wash his dirty linen so publicly if it helped someone else, but the wholehearted and humble way Tony went about confronting his demons was extremely creditable; his response when, finally, it came, vindicated the club's decision to stand by him; any other course of action by the club may well have compounded the perilous state he was in and his way back may have been cut off forever.

Whether it was valid or not, a feeling of 'them against us' permeated Highbury; the points deduction and Adams's imprisonment simply fed the primeval instincts and tribal bond we all have as human beings with 'our club'. As a supporter, so much impacts on you emotionally over which you have no control. As Adams would now readily testify, obsessions can be dangerous and unhealthy things.

With Adams out, we not only kept the wheels on the cart but clawed back the deficit and in late January went top, which is where we stayed, bar one weekend, for the rest of the season. We conceded just three league goals during Adams's absence, as first Andy Linighan and then David O'Leary made sure the skipper wasn't missed. Two of those goals came during the only league defeat of the season, at Stamford Bridge when a poor Chelsea team beat an out-of-sorts Arsenal 2-1. Winterburn was uncharacteristically at fault for the first goal and then Chelsea got a late second while Arsenal chased the game before an injury-time consolation from Alan Smith. The defeat saw the last unbeaten league record for the season in English football fall. Steve Bould had gone off injured and in all likelihood, bearing in mind the goals Chelsea scored, we wouldn't have lost if he had stayed on and George Graham would have gone on to become the first 'invincible' manager of the 20th century, 13 years before Wenger did it in the 21st.

After receiving his custodial sentence after we played Liverpool at home, Adams returned in time to make the return trip to Anfield in early March. Graham decided on caution; with Adams back in for Linighan, Bould and O'Leary played alongside Adams in a three.

There were cool heads all over the park for us that afternoon but the coolest and most mature of the lot was 21-year-old David Hillier. Making only his third senior start, Hillier was assured and clever as he clipped the wings of the Liverpool schemer-in-chief, Jan Molby, in a helter-skelter first half. Seaman gave a masterclass in goalkeeping; several saves kept us in the game and one at the feet of Barnes was reminiscent of Bob Wilson at his best. Our big keeper looked unbeatable that day – every inch Graham's 'best keeper in the First Division'.

The second half saw us come much more into it. Merson down our left began to find space and Alan Smith started to drop deeper, pulling defenders with him and creating space behind. It was just such a move which created the opportunity for the goal. Merson played an immaculate one-two with Smith, breaking Liverpool's backline, and, with the return from Arsenal's clever centre-forward weighted perfectly, it allowed Merson to run free, draw Grobbelaar and calmly flick the ball home. Once we had scored, I couldn't see us conceding;

Arsenal's defensive comfort was such that the closing minutes never really felt nervy.

The victory at Anfield put us three points clear with 12 games remaining. The pick of those remaining games were the 5-0 victory at home to Aston Villa and, in thorough contrast, a very hard-fought 0-0 draw against Sunderland at the old Roker Park on a filthy afternoon.

When Liverpool lost 2-1 at Forest, Arsenal were crowned champions before we even set foot on the pitch later that evening against Manchester United at Highbury. Some of the younger players spoke of it being a bit of an anti-climax, not needing to go out and win a game to clinch the title, but it remains for me one of our most satisfying successes: thoroughly professional.

Nineteen-ninety-one felt like a proper Arsenal triumph. For all Wenger's wonderful, aesthetic football, there remains something so archetypally Arsenal about 1991; the fight, the imprisonment of Adams and the dour endurance in the face of it all. Even with points docked, we won the title with two games to spare.

After the United match, which we won 3-1, I was cutting through the marble hall on my way to the players' lounge when Frank McLintock stopped me and suggested I came with him up to George's office for a celebratory drink. When we got there, I said to George: 'This is a great achievement considering we've struggled with midfield.' Rocky's knees had gone and you would be hard pressed to make a case for how Thomas had improved over the last couple of seasons; Davis had been steady, Limpar had had a good first season and young Hillier had certainly re-energised the midfield when he came in for the run-in. George had marshalled his rather depleted resources expertly, I thought, and got a fair tune out of a midfield that didn't really look title quality.

They were all good lads and put the graft in but the title was, perhaps, secured through contributions elsewhere. Alan Smith won the Golden Boot again. Alan was two or three players rolled into one back then. Goalscorer, target man and decent footballer outside the box, too. Merson had the sort of ability it is hard to pigeonhole; away from home, he might play more withdrawn and he could create opportunities just as well as he could finish them. Kevin Campbell gave us some fresh impetus after Christmas when he came into the team, scoring eight times in ten games, and, along with Hillier, he helped us get over the line. Dixon and Winterburn were so dynamic that they often played like auxiliary midfielders. I had to hand it to George – Seaman had been an inspired signing and a brave one considering the quality of the guy he replaced and that Lukic had been a real crowd favourite.

All three signings had paid off. Limpar had made the same impact as Marwood had in 89 but brought a bit of edginess and unpredictability (the same unpredictability that would see him fall out of favour in time) and Linighan, after not really wanting to be at Highbury, proved a valuable deputy for Adams. Looking back, Tony's drink-driving offence occurred in early May the previous year and, with Graham perhaps having been advised that a custodial sentence was on the cards, the signing of Linighan was a prudent bit of business.

One final thing for 1991; just as the season was coming to its conclusion, the two contenders for the crown put their differences to one side and met to support a cause for a player who had starred for both clubs. On 27 April, Highbury staged a benefit match for Ray Kennedy. After the game, I was able to have a chat with Ray; it was when he told me he had never wanted to leave Arsenal, that it had been Mee's decision not his. He said he had loved Arsenal and had been stunned when Bertie told him he was selling him; he had absolutely no thoughts of his own of leaving. Ray was as tough as old boots – you crossed him at your peril. When he first broke into the team, he was still quite insecure and I remember how, despite his fine performances, he would always tell me in the players' lounge: 'I'll be back out when Charlie is fit again.' When we spoke after the benefit match, he discussed how his Parkinson's disease must have begun to attack his body much earlier than any of us had appreciated; Ray mentioned to me that even when he was still at Arsenal, he noticed he was experiencing difficulties tying his shoelaces, which was, presumably, an early sign of the onset of his illness.

It was heartbreaking to note that I was speaking to him a mere 20 years after he scored the goal at White Hart Lane to clinch the title for us in '71. When I first met him as a kid coming in to the Arsenal first team, he was a smashing lad – and he never changed.

Nineteen-ninety-one was George Graham's last league crown, the last time we looked like getting involved in the title race, and, over the following seasons, we became what we were, perhaps, really always set up to become: a truly great cup team. Was that always the logical endpoint for Graham's method and philosophy?

## Chapter 23

# 1991/92

THE 1991/92 season was the end of an era; at the close of the season, the old North Bank terrace was to be demolished and replaced with a new, modern two-tier structure. Highbury was my first football kingdom, a world within a world. The new stand, when it was opened, was fantastic but how many old loyal Arsenal families did the bond scheme price out? How many missed out on their football education on the terraced concrete behind the goal – kids now lost to Arsenal and to football?

Like so many Arsenal supporters, a spell watching from the North Bank was part of my football education – I spent around 13 years watching from there. As a kid, I had cycled to Highbury almost daily to follow its restoration following the bombing in the war, the roof not being rebuilt until 1956. The old Laundry End first saw its name change to the North Bank in 1966/67 and I distinctly remember when a public address message during a cup tie against Bolton asked the fans on the 'North Bank to move forward' – the name was taken up immediately and the 'We're the North Bank Highbury' chant began at that game.

The opening weeks of the season saw the signing of Ian Wright, a cracking own goal from Lee Dixon and inconsistency from a team who appeared unsure of themselves. We shipped 12 goals in the opening seven games (we had conceded only 18 in the whole of the previous league campaign).

Wright's signing initially struck me as a curious one. Wright would prove himself to be the best and most natural finisher I have ever seen play for Arsenal but he was famously a latecomer to the professional game and £2.5m for a 28-year-old seemed a lot of money and a bit of a gamble.

My own view was that George seemed to be almost eradicating the midfield. I think the concept was simple: get men behind the ball, defend in numbers and, once possession was won back, get it forward quickly for Wright, whose pace and tenacity would carve out opportunities. Whereas we had previously sought to get the ball wide for crosses to Smith, now we were playing Wright in from the full-back or wing-back areas of the pitch.

Paul Davis was famously a casualty of this new style of play. Paul has said that he was asked by Graham to do more tracking back but had responded by telling the boss it wasn't his game. George was never keen on feedback and, thereafter, pursued something approaching a vendetta against Davis, dropping him and refusing to sell him. He didn't pick him for months and months, which stunted Paul's career, and I don't think it reflects well on George. Apart from anything else, ignoring Paul was detrimental to the team, as he was our only really creative player.

George was beginning to favour a whole different type of midfielder – Hillier and other guys coming through like Ian Selley, Steve Morrow and Ray Parlour. It felt like George had had enough of midfielders who wanted to carry the ball and work it forward. I think that, in George's mind, that just took away the advantage we had with Wright's pace and directness. Thomas, Rocastle and Davis all carried the ball, gained yards in possession and then moved it wide. George wanted guys to win it back and look immediately for a long ball forward.

If Davis was a casualty, then so, too, was Alan Smith. In the 11 games we played prior to signing Wright, Smith scored 11 goals. For the remainder of the season, after Wright signed, Smith scored just five goals in 40 competitive matches. I know Alan was quite upset about how his role in the team changed once Ian signed; don't get me wrong, he thought highly of Ian Wright, but from the perspective of how the team was set up, Alan was really pushed to the periphery. Smith was a real team player but he felt somewhat marginalised by how suddenly things changed.

This might sound as if I think signing Wrighty was something to regret, but no. I think he was a wonderful footballer; edgy, with a constant desire to prove people wrong. He scored some brilliant goals and at a startling rate. His first for us, at Leicester City in the League Cup, was almost nonchalant. Out of nowhere, he whipped in a 25-

yard effort. It felt like there was no danger but, in a flash, the ball was in the net – how many times did he do that? He followed it up with a hat-trick at The Dell in a 4-0 victory in which he started with his mate David Rocastle – Wright's all-time favourite Arsenal game.

To be fair to Wright, he wasn't just a goalscorer, he could play. He was brave, he could score with head, right foot or left, had a spiky attitude and loved winding up opponents. It was a wonder he had taken so long to break into elite football. I'd spoken with Sammy Nelson about Wright, who had seen Ian during a week-long trial at Brighton when Sammy was assistant manager to Chris Caitlin. Sammy said they couldn't believe what they were seeing; he was banging in goals for fun. Yet, they still didn't give him a contract. I can only assume that there was something which preceded Ian that made clubs wary of him. Perhaps he could allow his single-mindedness to sometimes tip over in nastiness? I don't know and I don't think Ian does, either.

The European Cup briefly shimmered before disappearing amidst recriminations of English naivety and Graham's feeling that we had been tactically shown up and caught out by a more intelligent team. After beating Austria Vienna 6-2 on aggregate in the first round, including a barnstorming 6-1 first-leg victory featuring four goals from Alan Smith, we travelled to Portugal to play one of the greatest names of the European game – Benfica. After we fell behind to a move which beat our offside trap, Rocastle played a sublime diagonal ball inside the left-back and Campbell struck powerfully across the keeper to give us a really encouraging 1-1 away draw.

Back at Highbury, we started quickly and our early efforts were rewarded with a goal from Colin Pates, which put us in a very strong position. But Benfica suddenly began to play and, with a certain Stefan Schwarz looking mobile on Benfica's left, they started to move the ball around at pace. Short passing and man movement began to counter Arsenal's closing down and harrying. At times, we couldn't get near them and instead of dropping and forcing Benfica to play in front of us, we engaged them and allowed them to play around and through us. That said, their equaliser was good old fashioned route one. A long ball from the full-back, a knockdown from the centre-forward and a smashing strike from a midfield runner made it all square at half-time. The second half was end to end. Most of the pressure came from us and we had a golden chance but the ball took a bobble and Smith put it high and wide from a great position. As the game went into extra time, it became stretched and Benfica took the lead when one ball took every Arsenal player out the game. From that point on, Benfica just picked us off as we threw caution to the wind. The third goal put us out of our misery.

George Graham was shattered by it. It left a mark on him for a long time. We had been confident that we would get through. In the first leg, we had probably been the better team but we let the emotion of it all get the better of us back at Highbury. We had chased the game in a very English way – we saw it again and again from English teams as we slowly got to grips with European football after the post-Heysel ban ended. George felt he had let himself down and he vowed never to let it happen again.

Following Wright into Highbury in the late autumn were two more curious signings. First, Graham snapped up Jimmy Carter from Liverpool for half a million, then followed this with the signing of Pal Lydersen for a similar fee from Norwegian side IK Start, with the deal being brokered by the agent, Rune Hauge.

Carter had originally burst on to the scene with Millwall and, when he left The Den to move to Anfield, he was seen as a very hot prospect. Graham had been interested in signing him at that stage, too, but the Merseyside club secured a deal for, I believe, around £900,000. His stock had fallen sharply following a very disappointing spell at Anfield and, failing to rediscover his old form at Arsenal, his signing soon looked to be questionable. But George wasn't a stranger to plucking people out of obscurity and polishing them into diamonds: Dixon, Bould, Winterburn, Marwood and even Kevin Richardson are cases in point.

In fairness, Lydersen came with a reputation for versatility – he could play on either side at full-back, had occasionally turned out at sweeper and even in midfield – but he was never, in all seriousness, going to be competition for either Dixon or Winterburn.

Over a four-year career at Highbury, he made 15 starts and I'd be hard pushed to think of a time when he looked comfortable or even approached being good value for £500,000. At the time, Rune Hauge was just another agent but, in time, that link would help make sense of Lydersen's signing.

Michael Thomas moved to Liverpool for £1.5m. Although Thomas was still young, I think George had made his mind up about him. He never really kicked on at Anfield, either. Given that his development had stalled and George's views on the type of midfielder he wanted, then I think he saw Hillier as being more versatile and the money from the sale of Thomas was a good return for a player whose best work was probably already behind him. One thing you could always say about George was that he knew his mind and once he'd decided, he was quick to act. There was a fairly high turnover of players and it was a pace which quickened the longer his reign lasted. I think George saw some footballers as having a fairly short shelf life and, once the hunger had burnt out, it was time to move them on.

In the FA Cup, we headed to north Wales to face Fourth Division Wrexham and the Red Dragons, largely made up of teenage YTS trainees, delivered upon us the biggest cup shock since Colchester United knocked out Leeds in 1971. With Arsenal one up with eight minutes remaining, Wrexham turned the game on its head with goals from veteran Mickey Thomas and, two minutes later, Ian Watkin. There was still time for a hotly disputed offside 'equaliser' for Arsenal, a decision that is still not clear after all this time. Later that week, I spoke to George on the phone and I was a little taken aback by his response to the defeat. 'At least we're still the top team in London,' he said. It was a wholly insignificant observation. The previous season, we'd been crowned champions and now 'at least we are the top team in London'. It suggests that even the strongest of managers can perhaps lose a bit of belief or confidence when things aren't going so well or after a shock defeat such as this.

After the Wrexham debacle, we didn't score for three games. But George settled them down again and we had a decent end-of-season run, going unbeaten in the last 16 games, and managed to finish fourth, ten points off champions Leeds United. After finding goals difficult to come by for most of the season, we suddenly couldn't stop scoring come the spring: seven against Sheffield Wednesday, four against Palace, four against Liverpool and, to end the season, five at home to Southampton, a fitting send-off for the old North Bank. Had the season lasted another four or five weeks, then who knows what we might have achieved, given our form at the time.

Looking back, it was an odd season; no real shape or flow to it. At its core were the defeats to Benfica and Wrexham – they defined the season's narrative, really. Either side of them, there was only the signing of Ian Wright, which felt like a positive step change.

Meanwhile, although we didn't know its significance at the time, Rune Hauge lurked in the background.

The summer was spent watching rank outsiders Denmark win the Euros, beating Germany in the final with a thunderbolt first goal from John Jensen. I recall the commentator saying: 'Jensen finally gets one right!' At the time, it didn't really mean much to me but, before long, we would all become a bit obsessed with John Jensen's attempts to score a goal.

Over the summer, George would pick up his telephone to be told there was a 'Mr Hauge asking for you', the agent hawking around a midfielder he thought Graham might be interested in.

## Chapter 24

# 1992/93

ARSENAL'S PROGRESS and development under George had always tended towards efficiency, economy and substance over style; and the speed of that journey had quickened in recent seasons. Those early years under George might almost be characterised as 'cavalier'; now, the characterisation was most emphatically 'roundhead', an austere kind of puritan football that largely did away with romance and magic. But, for all that, the team still massively resonated with supporters.

The North Bank had gone and, for a season, it was replaced with the famous mural. On the face of it, it was a good effort at trying to give the impression of normality as the new stand was being built, yet it didn't take long for it to become a source of sharp embarrassment for the club. Given that the Arsenal team had for years now contained probably more black players than any other side in England, and with a growing number of black supporters following the club, it was a bit of an own goal for the painted crowd in the mural to contain originally not one single black face. This was quickly corrected and, though clearly no harm was intended, I am sure that in some quarters it was noted and the implication, however unintended, understood.

In the league, we scored the fewest amount of goals (40) in the whole division, despite having the prolific Ian Wright in our ranks; we lost more games than we won; and we only won two more games than Oldham Athletic, who just escaped relegation on goal difference. However, in the cups that season, we were simply unbeatable – double cup winners, with both the League Cup and the FA Cup coming to Highbury. It was an historic achievement but one which can fit uncomfortably alongside the memory of some of the football we played that year.

## 1992/93

It was David O'Leary's final season, too – concluding with a probably never to be beaten 722 appearances to his name. In the end, it turned out to be a fantastic send-off for him and that David was on the pitch when the FA Cup was won is a source of great pride to him. It was, perhaps, the knowledge of David's impending departure that prompted George into the market to bring Martin Keown back to Highbury. I was delighted by his return, although it cost us £2.3m to re-sign him. It was very much an exception, too, in that George very rarely admitted his mistakes.

Martin was a true warrior and, because of that, it is very odd that George ever let him go; he was a real George Graham player. Many players have testified to how hard Martin was to play against; there was always something a bit Italian in his playing style. In any other life, he would have been an assassin! In comparison, Adams and Bould were both more typically English in their robustness; Keown was altogether more sophisticated in the dark arts. Adams was the least able to hide his fouls. Steve Bould was more surreptitious and, as a consequence, got away with more; when you had been hit by Bould, though, you stayed properly hit.

Keown wasn't the only signing. Before the season started, we had added a European champion to our ranks. Denmark's John Jensen, scorer of their first goal in the final victory over Germany, signed for just over £1m. George had been looking longingly at Palace's Geoff Thomas for a while but, with nothing doing on that front, he signed Jensen instead. For reasons beyond the player's control, poor old Jensen's signing has become rather notorious; for, after Limpar and Lydersen, he became the third transfer to have been brokered by Hauge.

Jensen's goal against Germany preceded him and it felt like he spent the rest of his career at Arsenal trying to replicate it. Jensen is still remembered fondly enough but I can't say I thought a lot of him. He had no pace; in fact, he looked like he could barely run. He could tackle, certainly, and his workrate was second to none; he was a trier and he gave absolutely everything – a great team man – and, for that, no one begrudged him his cult hero status but, in all truth, he really wasn't very good. The pace of English football, especially in midfield, was just too hot for him – he would have looked off the pace in a game of walking football.

We had a lot of quite similar midfield players to whom Jensen was added: Hillier, Selley, Parlour and Morrow. John Jensen was an odd signing and all the more so when you think about the man he passed in the revolving door, the footballer who was leaving Highbury as he was arriving.

George could be ruthless but I don't think anything he did at Arsenal compared to the sale of David Rocastle. 'Rocky' was certainly bothered by his knee and the injury stayed with him after he left Highbury but, in 1991/92, he had begun to suggest he was getting back to full fitness and was approaching his best – 48 appearances in his final season with the club seems to support this. Whether his knee had deteriorated further, I don't know but his sale affected the club emotionally. There wasn't a player – or even an employee – at the club who didn't love David. As David Dein had said, 'Rocky' could have been Brazilian – he was that good. As a footballer, he was immense – flashing feet, guile, intelligence and a smile to disarm – and, as a man, he was a giant. The players were very disappointed and upset. 'Rocky' had been one of the reasons Ian Wright had signed; realising the dream of playing with his boyhood friend from the estates was part of his motivation for coming to Highbury. Leeds United, who had just claimed the First Division title (the last before the creation of the Premier League), signed him for £2m and, ironically, David made his league debut for them against us. Leeds won 3-0 and, with a trademark jinky run, 'Rocky' made the second goal. When George told him he was selling him, David broke down uncontrollably. It was a horrible moment for David but also for the rest of the players. Because of the ongoing problem with his knee, it was probably good business but we lost a little of our soul when David left – no player loved Arsenal more than he did. When he came back to London, signing for Chelsea, he and I would occasionally have lunch in Windsor, where I had my business. He was a lovely man and a great footballer.

My brother Jack had lived with his MS for 30 years but, in 1993, aged only 51, Jack passed away. Over those 30 years, Jack had been granted some long periods of remission, during which he had married and had two children and had been able to continue with his career as a ladies' hairdresser, later running a business selling hairdressing products. We had the joy of being able to share in our mutual love for Arsenal and Jack was able to attend many matches at his beloved Highbury. Over the years, inevitably his condition deteriorated, each attack leaving him slightly worse off physically than the last. Jack was always stoical and as brave as an ox in the face of his illness but I know the final couple of years were especially difficult for his family.

It had been a blow to lose my only sibling and my mother within such a relatively short period of time and those two bereavements left our already small family down to just two; my father and me. In all honesty, for whatever reason, I didn't have an especially close relationship with my father, certainly not in the way I did with my mother, but I completely understood why he was the way he was and, as an adult, forgave him. Growing up, indeed even into adult life, Dad was never able to praise me for any achievement, not once, but I completely forgave him for it. I hadn't really dwelt on this as a child, when you tend to accept things as being the way they are, but I reflected on it as an adult. It was very easy to forgive him, though, especially when I learned from my mum something of his childhood growing up in Poland. He had had a harsh upbringing and, at around the age of five, he had lost his mum, who died while giving birth to his sister, and had been brought up primarily by his grandparents, who had been very orthodox and, consequently, very strict with him. As is, perhaps, the case with all of us, his childhood must have shaped and defined the person he became in adult life.

Thankfully, when he was very close to passing away, at Barnet Hospital, I was able to let him know how much I loved him. I remember he opened his eyes and acknowledged what I had said to him. Those few moments and our exchange of emotions meant so much to me and have continued to do so, especially now that my memories of him are all I have. Forgetfulness can soften the sense of loss, memory can enhance and amplify it but nothing can change it. Dad was 83 years of age when he passed away.

After being released from prison, Peter Storey came to see me in Great Portland Street. Peter had no money, no job and, frankly, very few prospects. So, I suggested to him that I would give him my tourist merchandise, kilts and tartan accessories to sell on sale or return and that he should go to Petticoat Lane, the busiest and most famous tourist market in London, to try and see if he could find a pitch there. He managed to do that very quickly and with his father, Eddie, grafting alongside him, Peter also found himself a stall in Church

Street market, Kensington, on a Saturday. It wasn't long before Peter was earning ten times as much as he did at Arsenal – he was that successful.

Unfortunately, a few years later, Peter had some domestic issues with his wife and things became difficult for him once again. Anyway, at the end of it, he didn't work anymore and finished up with a small debt to me, just a few hundred pounds which he couldn't settle. It bothered him no end; Peter had a lot of integrity.

Not long afterwards, he came to the showroom with a carrier bag in his hand à la Kieran Tierney. He handed me the bag, apologised for not being able to settle the debt and said: 'I want you to have these.' I looked inside and I was astonished. The bag contained Peter's medals and plaque from the 1970 Fairs' Cup and his 1971 Double winner's medals. I told Peter to forget the debt but I would take his medals home for safekeeping. I was concerned that he would sell them for relative peanuts.

I kept them at home and, shortly afterwards, I suggested to Peter that I should hand them over to Iain Cooke, the curator of the newly opened Arsenal Museum at Highbury, for display. So, this is exactly what I did and they remained there for a number of years.

Quite a few years later, Peter had some other difficulties and the only assets he possessed were his medals. I told Peter that, although it would be nice to hand the medals over to his three boys when they grew up, it would be a bit pointless, as he would be splitting up the set. I appreciated that he urgently needed cash and, so, with his agreement, I set about getting offers from memorabilia collectors, with the best coming in at around £20,000, a very substantial sum around 40 years ago. A meeting was arranged at Highbury and Ian Cooke brought the medals from the museum to a corporate box in the Clock End, where Peter duly received his windfall from the collector. We went off for a little celebratory lunch at an Italian restaurant and when we got there, we ran into Arsène Wenger and David Dein. David duly introduced Arsène to both of us. Wenger was already aware of me from the AGMs and I suspect he probably heard a lot about Peter and his Arsenal career from David over the dinner table that day.

In 1992/93, we still had, without question, a brilliant defence and, also without question, the best striker in the league, a player who routinely manufactured the most luminous goals out of the dreariest of scraps. On that basis alone, the success we enjoyed in the sudden death environment of cup football is really no surprise.

We beat Palace 5-1 on aggregate in the League Cup semi-final to secure a place at Wembley against Sheffield Wednesday. Before that game, we had an FA Cup semi-final to navigate – another date with the neighbours.

The game against Tottenham was on a knife edge, a genuine 50-50. It was nice having one final in the bag but losing to Spurs at this stage would clearly take all the gloss of it and I was really apprehensive about the match. In fact, I was so stirred up by the game that my wife had to come to Wembley and watch the match with me; I was that nervous, I needed her to keep me calm.

The match itself was every bit as canny as we thought. We had Hillier, Selley and Parlour close together in midfield. That trio were the perfect choice as a war of attrition started to take shape.

The second half saw us come much more into it; indeed, Parlour started to knock it about nicely and to dictate the play. Wright had a good effort tipped over and when Parlour got brought down by Justin Edinburgh, Merson floated the perfect free kick to the back post, where the irrepressible Tony Adams, pushing Linighan out the way, headed hard and low and gave Thorstvedt no chance. The delight on Adams's face was real and intense; there was nothing choreographed or manufactured – a proper goal celebration. Ten minutes to go and we were one up.

The only hiccup was when Dixon got sent off, bringing down Edinburgh for his second yellow, but Spurs couldn't take advantage of their extra man and we held on to win 1-0 and we were back at Wembley for the FA Cup Final, where we would play the same side as in the League Cup Final – Sheffield Wednesday. Sadly, Dixon's sending-off would cause him to miss the League Cup Final but this guaranteed David O'Leary one final start at Wembley.

The League Cup game was, by a long way, the best of the Arsenal-Wednesday Wembley meetings that year. Wednesday, managed by Trevor Francis, would go on to finish above us in the league that season; they were a decent side but Arsenal, on the big occasion, were a team you could trust.

There was an early scare when Warhurst volleyed against the post. Then Wednesday drew first blood: a half cleared free kick fell into the path of John Harkes, who blasted it beyond Seaman from the edge of the box to become the first American to score in a League Cup Final.

It didn't take long for parity to be restored, though, when an Arsenal free kick wasn't cleared and, running on to the loose ball, Merson hit one which bent further and further away from Woods into the corner.

We were now on top and it was our turn to hit the woodwork. Campbell was through and slammed his shot from a wide angle past Woods but against the inside of the post and the ball bounced back into the keeper's arms.

Just past the hour mark, Merson's cross ricocheted out to Morrow, who hit it low and hard to become one of the most unlikely scorers of a cup final-winning goal.

Famously, at the final whistle, Adams hoisted Morrow in celebration but managed to drop him over his shoulder, breaking his arm. Poor Morrow was on his way to hospital when the medals were being handed out. I think, for everyone, it took a bit of the gloss off the victory. Poor old Morrow, primarily a full-back but also a resolute man-marking defensive midfielder, lost out on the opportunity to really build on his success, missing the rest of the season because of the injury and then hardly appearing the following year, although what was, arguably, his greatest moment in an Arsenal shirt still lay ahead of him.

Ian Wright always spoke of his childish excitement on FA Cup Final day and even as an adult, he was reduced to the wide-eyed wonder of the small boy who sat hypnotised in front of the TV. Arsenal were pretty much at full strength for the game; the only doubt might have been over Linighan, had Steve Bould been fully fit and match sharp, but Linighan got the nod, with O'Leary and Alan Smith our two substitutes.

The match was, without doubt, the worst FA Cup Final I've ever seen. Wright scored his 29th goal of the season, a textbook effort. A free kick was flighted to the far post, Linighan headed it back to the near post and Wright headed, firm and downwards, to put us into the lead.

After the break, Wednesday seemed more energised. Although Bright soon had a goal disallowed, the Arsenal lead wouldn't hold for long. David Hirst, a prolific centre-forward who had missed the League Cup Final, picked up a loose ball in the penalty box and forced it home.

Smith, who had come on for Parlour, had an almost exact replica of the chance he was to bury a year later in Copenhagen, the ball sitting up for him at distance, but this time he could only send it down the keeper's throat. With 90 minutes up, the game went into an even more uneventful 30 minutes of extra time. Graham brought on O'Leary to stiffen things up; Wright was the man to be withdrawn (he was playing with a broken toe) as we went to a wing-backs system. We neither looked like scoring nor conceding and, so, the game petered out.

Leaving the stadium, I was fairly deflated; pleased we were still in it but genuinely disappointed that we had given such a poor account of ourselves in front of a worldwide audience. Walking away from the stadium, I bumped into our old player, Vic Groves; we chatted about the match and Vic agreed that it hadn't been an especially engaging spectacle.

Before the replay, we had what had originally been scheduled as the send-off for David O'Leary, a farewell match at Highbury against Manchester United. David had asked me to be part of a small committee which helped to organise the event. I'd had a thought on how to swell David's pot without costing the club a single penny. That season, despite getting to the final of both domestic cups, at the end of the season everyone who had a season ticket had one spare, unused voucher. With this in mind, I went to see Ken Friar and suggested that the club give season ticket holders the option of either asking for the spare voucher to be credited to next year's season ticket or surrender it, with the value of the voucher added to David's testimonial pot. Ken asked me to leave it with him, as he would need to run it by the board.

When I hadn't heard anything, I phoned Friar and he told me the board had turned it down. After a short while, I thought I might take this up again and I gave David Dein a ring. By this time, I knew David pretty well. I explained the situation to him and said I was disappointed that the board hadn't seen fit to take up the idea. David said he wasn't even aware of the request and added he would get on the case immediately. Dein took the idea to the board and it was adopted. Dein quite properly didn't discuss the situation with me but the implication remains that Friar had never spoken to the board about it.

As I have made clear, Ken was a highly thought of servant of Arsenal and, for many years, had been loyal to the club, especially the board, and energetically pursued what he always saw as the club's best interests but it wasn't a sense of service which always extended to the players. I can recall that some members of the Double side – Peter Storey, John Radford and Peter Simpson, for example – all found him 'unhelpful' when they were arranging their testimonials. Back in the 70s, the testimonial for players was a much more significant thing. It was a means of setting them up for their life after football. However, Ken always acted in the full service of Arsenal and this was never in doubt; it couldn't have been an easy job to do.

Anyway, a decent crowd of over 22,000 turned out to pay their respects to O'Leary and saw a 4-4 draw. Three days later, it was back to Wembley for the FA Cup replay.

It was a horrible evening and, as a consequence, the old stadium looked a bit the worse for wear. An accident on the M1 caused a half an hour delay to kick-off, too. While, in the metaphorical sense, it was Arsenal who drew first blood, in the literal sense it was Wednesday. With the game still at 0-0, Wednesday played a high and hopeful ball up to Bright. Linighan was ideally positioned to run on to the ball to complete his headed clearance, which he did, but in doing so, he met the ball and Bright's elbow simultaneously and his nose was broken. Bright was booked for the incident. Linighan, the quiet man from Hartlepool, soldiered on; he would, ultimately, have his moment of revenge on Bright.

Arsenal hit back in the best possible way: an exquisite little through ball from Smith put Wright away, cutting through Wednesday's defence like a rapier thrust. He ran diagonally to broaden his target and, drawing Woods, he chipped it over and beyond the stranded keeper. Saturday was forgotten and the Arsenal end went wild. Yet again, out of nothing, Wright had created his own situation, his speed of thought and action defeating three Wednesday players. With Ian Wright in your team, you always had a chance.

In the second half, as on the Saturday, Wednesday pegged us back and this time it had a stroke of luck about it. The ball broke to Waddle on their left and when he shot, Lee Dixon threw himself at the ball to block and the deflection took it in an arc away from Seaman and once more the match was all square.

From then on, it became a more familiar end-to-end cup tie. Bright scraped the outside of a post when in a position to do much better and Merson, put clean through, hit a low drive which almost went through Woods, the keeper turning quickly to get a hand on the ball as it squirmed towards the line.

As tensions mounted and fatigue kicked in, the match moved into extra time again. By then, O'Leary had replaced Wright. The first chance of extra time fell to Smith, getting round the back of Wednesday's defence, he hit it low, but Woods got an arm to it and pushed it away.

With just seconds left on the clock and the game destined to be the first FA Cup Final to be decided on penalties, the ball broke to John Jensen 30 yards out and, doing what Jensen did, he went for glory but his shot was half blocked and ballooned behind for a corner. Jensen turned and cursed his luck. From the resulting corner, rising like a Harrier Jump Jet was Andy Linighan and he beat, of all people, Mark Bright to the ball. Linighan, his face blood stained, crashed a header through Woods's hands and over the line; what sweet karma! There was time only for one poorly-taken corner for Wednesday and the whistle blew. Arsenal, the cup kings of England, had done it again.

The poor guy was exhausted and, with his broken nose, Andy Linighan was a fitting hero. Arsenal always seemed to drag themselves, no matter how bloodied or bruised, over the line. It was a result that summed up the team. Just when the drama and excitement of a penalty shoot-out threatened to get the neutral interested, we went and nicked it with a set piece in the last minute.

And what a wonderful finale for O'Leary: to have graced Wembley in his final Arsenal season, to be on the pitch when both the League Cup and the FA Cup were won, was the best of all send-offs. The 1979 FA Cup win had meant such a lot to David and since then he had experienced the ultimate joy of Anfield and the more leisurely success of 1991; but it was with a very Arsenal sense of symmetry that he signed off – a last-minute winner in 1979 and a last-minute winner in 1993 book-ending his trophy-winning career.

He phoned me early the following morning to say he had the FA Cup at his home and I was to get over quickly for some photos, because he had to take it back to Highbury later that morning. With one final act of kindness, the club had allowed David to take the cup home with him for the night after their celebration dinner.

And, so, what a strange, uneven season: a poor one football-wise but one which produced two trophies. You really couldn't fault the commitment and determination of the team; you really could *never* question a George Graham team for strength of character. Whatever might be said about him and his management style, his players would run through brick walls for him.

Chapter 25

# 1993/94

EVER SINCE Benfica had knocked us out of the European Cup in 1991, George had been on something of a crusade. Europe had become his Holy Grail, the yardstick above all others that he wanted to be judged on. He had conquered English football twice and then been proved supreme at cup football but success in Europe had eluded him; in fact, its absence haunted him and left a nagging question hanging in the air that his domestic achievements alone couldn't silence.

When I spoke to O'Leary, who by then had moved to Leeds, he told me that I wasn't to expect anything in domestic football that year because George was focused entirely on the European Cup Winners' Cup; the whole season was geared to success in Europe. It is a singular example of George's obsessive thinking.

The opening of the new North Bank stand saw Coventry City come to Highbury and win at a canter, 3-0 with a hat-trick from Micky Quinn, with balls bouncing off every bit of his ample physique. Despite having a season ticket for elsewhere in the ground, I decided to sit in the new North Bank for this one. If Arsenal were being fine-tuned to compete in Europe, then the less-than-mobile Coventry centre-forward highlighted plenty of areas that needed some work for the more direct English version of the game. We were lacklustre. It didn't help that the North Bank wasn't totally finished and that the club had also begun to replace the terraced area at the Clock End with seats. It was scorching hot, too, and the ground was deathly quiet for the most part.

Second up, we travelled the short distance to White Hart Lane. Arsenal's defence held sway and, with three minutes remaining, a thumping Linighan header was redirected by Wright and we took the spoils 1-0 – and how Wright celebrated!

Eddie McGoldrick made his full debut for us against Spurs, after coming on as a sub against Coventry. The Irish winger worked hard and had clearly been brought in to cover the exit of Limpar but he didn't set the pulse racing. I think George had finally had enough of Limpar and it was no surprise when he was sold to Everton. Eddie didn't warrant quite the level of stick he received from the crowd at times but, equally, he was never going to be introduced by George as a crowd pleaser. You knew what you were going to get from McGoldrick and, by and large, that was exactly what you did get. McGoldrick for Limpar, though, is another very eloquent comment on George's elimination of flair for steady functionality.

As summer faded, we managed to find a bit of consistency and by the opening round of the Cup Winners' Cup, we had climbed to second in the league but goals were still hard to come by and in one run of six league games, we scored one solitary goal. We tamely surrendered both cups, too; Aston Villa knocking us out of the League Cup and Bolton Wanderers beating us at Highbury in an FA Cup fourth-round replay. By all accounts, the Bolton manager, Bruce Rioch, made a good impression that night; his team played a bit of football and in the boardroom after the game, his understated style was noticed by the Arsenal directors.

In Europe, we could do little wrong. The first round saw us knock out Odense 3-2 on aggregate and we then beat Standard Liege 10-0 on aggregate, including a 7-0 romp in Belgium, to secure our place in the quarter-finals. The competition would get serious from that moment on, with Arsenal drawn to play Italian Cup winners Torino.

The 1990s were a golden age for Italian club football. In 1994, AC Milan would complete a hat-trick of Serie A titles and also win that season's Champions League. Inter would win the UEFA Cup, despite only avoiding a domestic relegation by one point. While the traditional giants of Juventus and AC Milan were riding high, they were also now being joined by less fashionable clubs like Sampdoria and Parma. Indeed, Parma in the Cup Winners' Cup (they were the holders) looked a good bet to complete an Italian clean sweep of the three European trophies. Torino would be canny, technical and organised.

Defensively, we were back to our best that season; we conceded 28, the least in the division and ten fewer than eventual champions Manchester United. However, goals for were hard to come by and we scored barely more than a goal a game.

When March came round, Ian Wright was carrying an injury, picked up a month before the Torino tie. When we travelled out for the first leg in Turin, he felt confident of playing. Wright trained the night before the match in the Stadio Delle Alpi but, come the game, he was left out by Graham, much to his disappointment, with Alan Smith preferred. Would Wright's mobility be missed or would Smith's ability to hold up play prove to be a bigger asset?

Torino turned out to be a decent side. At left-back, they had a young Croatian international, Robert Jarni, who went on to be one of the most accomplished players in his position in the late 90s. Indeed, it was Jarni's attacking prowess which shone, his effort from distance causing Seaman his only moment of disquiet. In an interview after the game, Graham was correct in his assessment that 'we were very comfortable ... and David Seaman had very little to do'.

The return leg in north London brought with it a reminder of some of the great European nights of my Arsenal past; the atmosphere was electric – lots of noise and an air of expectation. The pitch in Turin had seemed miles from the crowd and it felt as if the more traditional crowd-on-top-of-the-pitch set-up at Highbury might cause Torino to become unsettled. For us, Wright was back, fresh from a hat-trick against Ipswich in a 5-1 win, and Smith and Merson joined him up front. We opened by playing at pace but with caution and good sense. Torino offered very little and looked like a side who thought penalties their best chance of advancing. By the second half, the game had become bogged down in an ultra-attritional conflict. Torino just wanted to stop us scoring, while we were conscious of the value of one away goal to them. When it looked as if the stalemate might hold, a good old fashioned English set piece did the trick. Davis knocked a high floating ball to drop into the space between defence and keeper and stealing in completely unmarked was Adams, who casually glanced it to the keeper's right. Sending on Keown to shore things up, we never really looked in any difficulties.

It was a thoroughly professional job, one that must have delighted Graham. Arsenal had played with a bit of know-how. Game management felt like a thoroughly un-English aspect of football. Benfica had out-thought us and demonstrated an emotional control we lacked but the Torino match felt like a turning point in our education. Our tails were up and there was a robust sense of belief that it would take a good team to beat us: next up, Paris Saint-Germain.

While the other semi-final saw Parma take on our nemesis of 1991, Benfica, we headed to Paris full of confidence. Before the game kicked off, there was still time for a joke at the expense of PSG's manager, Artur Jorge. He was the owner of a luxuriant moustache which covered his entire mouth. As the TV camera scanned along the bench of Arsenal substitutes, McGoldrick and Miller sat deadpan, staring deep into the camera ... both wearing an enormous imitation moustache.

PSG, back then, were a club who rarely punched their weight. With French international keeper Bernard Lama, Paul Le Guen as a defensive midfielder and David Ginola and a young George Weah up front, they represented a more serious challenge than their record might have suggested. Manager Jorge had won a total of four league titles in Portugal and France and, in 1987, had his greatest moment when he guided underdogs Porto to beat Bayern Munich 2-1 in the European Cup Final.

There was a great atmosphere in Paris, although before the game we had been subjected to some brutal attacks from local youths. In the face of all this, the Arsenal fans were terrific – their support and the noise we made during the game all added to a great atmosphere.

Arsenal turned it into the sort of game George wanted. PSG couldn't really get any momentum. We played fairly conservatively and made sure that when they did run at us, usually through Ginola, they disappeared down crowded rabbit holes. Then, on 35 minutes, Paul Davis floated over an inviting free kick and Arsenal players were queueing up to head it home – Ian Wright, unmarked, gave us a valuable lead, with a flatfooted Bernard Lama only able to watch the ball skip off the surface and inside the post.

Half-time saw the stadium PA playing the usual PSG anthem of 'Allez Paris Saint-Germain', sung to the tune of 'Go West'. A clutch of like-minded Arsenal supporters, myself included, borrowed it and the chant of '1-0 to the Arsenal' was born.

As the game developed, it began to illustrate national stereotypes: Arsenal looked like a good English rugby pack, military and up for a battle, while PSG sought to exploit individual artistry. Ginola did get more of the ball and his battle with Dixon was absorbing. On the whole, Dixon came out on top but, barely five minutes into the second half, Ginola scored to restore parity and it must have been the least Ginola-like goal he ever scored – a near post flick from a corner. In truth, it was a soft goal to give away.

Two weeks later, Arsenal made one change from the game in Paris; Campbell was in for Merson, who was suffering from a sore throat. PSG changed their set-up, unexpectedly leaving out Weah and playing Ginola up top on his own, with the Brazilian midfielder Rai coming into the side. One worry was that, of our starting XI, we had eight players only one booking away from missing the final should we get through.

The early stages suggested that PSG were going to be more adventurous than we expected, with Valdo playing up with Ginola. PSG needed a goal and, perhaps anticipating Arsenal would come out more, looked to exploit more space than had been the case in Paris.

Two minutes in and we nearly threw everything away. Seaman bowled it out for Winterburn but his throw was intercepted and gave PSG a clear run in on goal, only for a superb last-ditch, lunging tackle from Adams to avert the danger at the expense of a corner. That was one life used.

A few minutes later, Dixon whipped over a cross which, although probably intended for Smith, was seized upon by Campbell, who got enough on the ball to beat Lama at his near post. It looked route one but that does Campbell a massive disservice; craning his neck backwards, he executed a really skilful bit of work, at high speed, a yard off the ground.

Then came the 'Ian Wright moment'. So desperate in wanting to make up for losing possession, he stretched to win the ball back and caught his opponent. Wright was on his knees with his head in his hands as the referee flourished a yellow card, meaning Wright would now miss the final. What happened next illustrated what Wright brought to the team. For a while, he was lost, tears streaming down his cheeks. He knew there was no need to make the challenge. The period of recrimination soon ended, though, and Wright continued to play with his heart. This was now his cup final and he gave absolutely everything for himself and more for his team. There were no causes he didn't chase down – he ran and played his heart out. His emotional frailty had turned full circle and was now his strength. It was a masterclass in application and control and Wright, after making the initial error, proceeded to let absolutely no one down. He battled for a cause that, ultimately, was not now going to be his and, in so doing, he demonstrated what it is to play for the shirt and the badge and to play, really genuinely play, for your team. Wright could be a prickly young man, I am sure, but he was always the wayward son you could only ever love – and never more so that night.

The second half saw PSG press but still without creating anything, save one chance which fell to Ginola, but he snatched at it and pulled his shot wide. There really wasn't that much of a storm to weather; we held our shape and said 'there you go, let's see what you can do'. When we had the bit between our teeth, there were few teams who could really hurt us; give Arsenal something to defend and you'd bet your house on them.

The differences between that night against PSG and the game versus Benfica were there for all to see. Graham had got his plans spot on. Arsenal were patient, with Davis, Selley and Jensen scuttling sideways to block gaps, fill spaces and cut down angles and Wright, Campbell and Smith pressing and dropping to help out. It was an absolute team effort and one that only succeeded on the strength of each and every contribution. There were no passengers that night and, whatever was to happen in Copenhagen, I think the performances over two legs against PSG had seen Arsenal slay the ghost of the Benfica setback. Graham had proved, most of all to himself, that he was equal to the different challenge of European football. Of Arsenal, you could say that ugliness had become a virtue. George drove us with a hard and unremitting logic. To opponents, we were a Frankenstein's monster; to us, we were beautiful.

Now, a final awaited us and George had to do it again in a new and different way. Wright, the option who allowed him to draw the punches of harder hitting opponents, to be cautious and patient while we defended on the ropes, would be unavailable to him through suspension. Back in those days, if the first half had been disappointing, the North Bank would chant at half-time 'Georgie, Georgie sort them out' and he often did; George knew what to do. He would know once again.

Copenhagen has become one of Arsenal's most cherished battle honours. We went as underdogs, which suited us. Parma, our opponents, were the new kids on the block in Italy, with a mouth-watering array of attacking talent under the guidance of Nevio Scala, who had taken the club from Serie B to title challengers. Under him, they won the Cup Winners' Cup in '93 and would go on to win the UEFA Cup in '95. They would severely test Arsenal's defensive mettle and their heart for a battle.

Copenhagen is an avenue in our history we don't walk down often enough. Now we can see it as the ultimate destination of Graham's journey: the high water mark before the fall and it is that knowledge which gives the success such poignancy. That night in May 1994 we were all innocent of what the future held.

The Parken Stadium was a riot of red and white; we must have outnumbered Parma fans by around five to one. Off the pitch, it was no contest; we made so much noise, the game might as well have been at Highbury. On the pitch, we had started out on very long odds to win and, if anything, the closer we got to the match, our odds grew longer. Wright was out, Jensen was injured, David Hillier had failed a fitness test and David Seaman was playing with a broken rib. Ian Selley and Steve Morrow came into the midfield and, up front, Alan Smith was left to lead the line on his own. I can't imagine that Graham had anticipated much coming from open play. Arsenal's best chance, perhaps only chance, was going be dead ball situations, although Graham speculated before kick-off that *if* we got a goal, then they would find it difficult to score against us.

That Parma team was a cracking collection of talent: Benarrivo and Sensini in defence; Zola and Brolin floating between midfield and attack; and Asprilla up front. Faustino Asprilla was a magician, lightning fast; this was the Brolin before he put on weight and looked a pale shadow of his young self when he later came to play in England; and Zola, we know all about.

The tone of the game was set in the first minute: a ball from Brolin split Adams and Bould, Asprilla raced on to it and, out of nowhere, Bould launched himself and, sliding in, snuffed out the chance. Soon afterwards, a Brolin header just cleared the bar and then a breakaway from Asprilla set up Brolin, whose shot hit the inside of the post and bounced away to safety. For a while, it was as much as we could do just to hang in; at times, it was white knuckle stuff but the team didn't wilt or fold, they just dug in and kept their heads.

You have to believe don't you and, out of nowhere, Dixon tried to find Merson running from left to right, the ball was cut out and cleared but the skewed clearance went to Smith, who chested it down and hit the cleanest of strikes, in off the post. Twenty minutes in, we'd been absolutely murdered but found ourselves one up.

Seaman made a fabulous one-handed save from Zola as we made it through to half-time. The longer the second half went on, I think

Parma just lost belief that they could score. Asprilla had one lovely jinky run but, just as he pulled the trigger, Dixon made probably the tackle of his life and the ball squirmed away. By the time the ref blew, I think every Arsenal player had asked him: 'How long left?'

The kind of football virtues that rarely capture imaginations prevailed that night in Copenhagen and I wouldn't have had it any other way. Some might call it a success for all that is best about English football but I'd be more specific than that; I claim that night for us – for Arsenal alone. It was a performance that sat proudly in a tradition. Every Arsenal player was a hero, a warrior that night but Steve Bould put in the performance of a lifetime.

When the game ended, it felt like the start of a whole new chapter for our club; little did we know it was almost the end of the affair and we would move on, riddled with acrimony and misgivings.

That night, we had no thoughts for the future. I think that evening saw George's finest achievement and what comes next, while it may chip away at the veneer, can't dent the body of his work at Arsenal. Nineteen-ninety-four was a show of unity, when togetherness and the pursuit of a common goal brought the best out of us. The following 12 months would break hearts and end friendships; it was the hardest year of my Arsenal life and it tarnished my once unadulterated esteem for a friend and a magnificent icon of this great club.

*1966 – myself, Judith and Peter Storey*

*Myself in the middle of the front row, working as a plain-clothed security officer at Butlin's*

*My son Dean, mascot for the day – Graham Rix, Dean, Stewart Robson, and Tommy Caton*

*1974 PFA Awards Dinner. Fourth from the left Bertie Mee, Peter Storey, myself and appearing directly in front of me, Bob McNab*

Dean and myself after seeing Arsenal win the title at White Hart Lane for the second time! This time 2004

The legendary Frank McLintock and myself

Wedding Day! In the centre of the back row is Bob McNab, and to his left is Peter Storey. Both acted as witnesses to the marriage

After winning the Fairs Cup in 1970. Peter Storey, myself, mystery woman and Peter Marinello.

Advising George Graham how best to set up his back four in 1990!

*A fund-raising event for Ray Kennedy in 1990. From left to right: Ted Drake, myself, John Radford, Peter Storey (partially hidden), George Graham, Sammy Nelson, and Bob Wilson*

*Dad, mum, brother Jack and myself*

*In the players' lounge on 6 May 1991, we clinch the league title! From the left: David Rocastle, myself, Charlie George, and Peter Storey*

*The morning after winning the FA Cup in 1993. David O'Leary, the cup and myself*

Socialising with some Arsenal players and their partners in the late 1960s, including (from left to right) Bob Wilson, myself, Bob McNab, and Frank McLintock

Danny Wengrow (23 September 1969–14 March 1975) – what might have been?

Judith and myself – the person who made it all possible

*An ebullient Bertie Mee after clinching the title in 1971*

*Tony Adams, Steve Bould, and David O'Leary after winning the title at Anfield in 1989*

*Thierry Henry turns to celebrate his wonder goal against Liverpool in 2004*

*Busts of Herbert Chapman and Arsene Wenger which stand in the directors' entrance at the Emirates. Each man shaped an Arsenal era and in so doing changed the game in England*

With the cup after the greatest climax to an FA Cup final ever – the five minute final in 1979. From the left: David Price, Willie Young, Pat Rice, Liam Brady, Frank Stapleton (partially hidden), Graham Rix and David O'Leary

## Chapter 26

# 1994/95

WHEN THE end came, it was swift and brutal – completely at odds with the dithering that followed Simon Greenberg's revelations about George taking bungs, which had broken seven weeks earlier, exclusively in the *Mail on Sunday*. In the weeks between that initial article and George's eventual dismissal, on 21 February 1995, the board had only shown an unwillingness to act, maybe an unwillingness informed by legal advice but a reluctance, nevertheless, to act in the face of overwhelming evidence of 'actions taken not in the best interests of Arsenal Football Club'.

Early on the morning of 21 February, all that changed. George was summoned to Highbury, whereupon he was handed a typed notice of his immediate dismissal and given sufficient time to make a couple of calls and clear his desk.

Just eight months earlier, George had ridden the crest of a wave, leading us to European success and receiving the plaudits of football coaches all over the continent for his consummate tactical planning. Now, here he was, ordered out of the club; a more hurried and backdoor departure is difficult to imagine. It certainly wasn't the send-off a manager with six trophies to his credit might otherwise expect.

If you ask a lot of Arsenal supporters of my generation for their favourite era, then I believe most, admittedly not all, but most, would pick George over any other – there was perhaps a stronger affinity with George's Arsenal. There was a real connection between the team and the supporters. Time and time again, they would pull a rabbit out of the hat; that team always had a performance in them, no matter how poorly we were doing in the league. When the chips were down, they knew how to win ugly and win against the odds – and we loved that.

By then, some of the players had their own problems but that just endeared them to us even more. They felt like brothers and sons; you really cared about them. That season, Paul Merson had gone public about his addictions and I remember the terrific reception he got when he came on as a sub against AC Milan in the Super Cup at Highbury after a period of rehabilitation; it took the roof off. I think George has to take a fair bit of credit for creating that bond; they've all said he was a hard so and so but he knew how to get a group of individuals to become a team.

He built a club at Highbury in his own image. George really embraced the values of the club and would refer to them to emphasise what a wonderful institution Arsenal were. That's what makes the ending so tragic; it felt that, at the end, something really magical and special had been spoilt – for him, the club and for us all. I think that's why I was so angry about it.

I'd known George since he had been a young man joining the club as one of Bertie Mee's first signings. At Chelsea, his team-mates called him the 'Cary Grant of football'; his model looks had impressed them and also his calm and polished style of play. His nickname, 'Stroller', caught on at Highbury. I remember using it during a conversation with George and Frank McLintock coming back from an away game on the train but I genuinely can't recall if I had heard it before and was merely repeating it. During his two spells at Highbury, first as the classy midfielder in the Double team and then as the dignified traditionalist manager, I had known him very well, placed complete faith him and his judgment, socialised with him on many occasions and shared insights into his vision for the club but when the axe fell, I was relieved.

Perhaps it was because I liked, admired and respected George so much that I felt so hurt and let down by his actions. Greenberg's story had been so thorough, so explicit in its detail, that, for me, there was no room for doubt. As time has passed, my initial response of intense anger and feelings almost of betrayal have changed into ones of sadness but back in '95, my anger was quite visceral. How could he have done this to Arsenal? Nobody knew the values of the club better than George and he was also the highest paid manager in England at the time (he tended to keep the players' wages on the lower side, which must have given him more bargaining power on his own contract).

The club presumably had waited for the report following the FA's investigation into the allegations and when it did reach them, they probably felt they had no room for manoeuvre. The club felt under pressure to do something and he had to go. As I have said, I had come to that conclusion much earlier. In my opinion, he had damaged the club and that was that – there no coming back from it.

Under George, there had, at least, always been clarity and now it was all just such a muddle. While the allegations of bungs hung in the air, the board surprisingly sanctioned the signings of John Hartson, Chris Kiwomya and Glenn Helder; whichever way you look at it, that is not indicative of a board that seems in any great rush to get rid of the boss. It remains a period that fails to reflect well on anyone at the club.

I suppose what underpinned my own anger was that George had been recognised by the club and its supporters, and very much by myself, as someone who really understood Arsenal Football Club. He traded on the importance of doing things the right way, doing it the Arsenal way, the mystical significance of the cannon on the blazer and the shirt; he was every inch the disciplinarian traditionalist like his managerial mentor and the man who later became his friend, Bertie Mee.

We all make mistakes but that is not to say accountability or culpability can always be mitigated. George paid back the money and took his punishment but his lingering bitterness suggests he hasn't ever quite come to terms with how it played out. I remember him saying in an interview after his sacking that he was only dismissed because we were having a poor season; he insisted that if we'd been top, he would still be there. I have often heard talk that suggests there was an agreement between Graham and the board that he could walk away at the end of the season, head high, and that the club would look after him financially. If that's true, then that could be at the bottom of his bitterness because, in the end, the club were forced into a corner where that couldn't happen. However you look at it, it was a sad and undignified ending to an otherwise great era for the club.

It was a long time before I could think of anything else; the whole affair consumed me and I was ready to react to any views that seemed to defend George's actions. One such provocation I couldn't ignore was when Jeff Powell, writing in the *Daily Mail*, wrote a long piece not just defending George but, basically, criticising Arsenal for sacking him. I felt it was too much and it made me really angry, so I phoned

Jeff. I had known him since his early days in journalism, when he was a familiar face around some Arsenal players during the 1971 Double season. He established a long-lasting friendship with George and it was because of that, I believe, that he aired such views in the article. Our conversation was heated, to put it mildly, but I thought that he was defending the indefensible and I told him so in no uncertain terms. Jeff didn't see it like that and he remained firmly in George's corner.

Many years after that, I bumped into Jeff at a football writers' annual dinner. He was sitting with George and, as I passed their table, Jeff greeted me warmly and asked me to join him for a while to have a chat, which I did. It was probably all part and parcel of being a football journalist to him but, to me, the whole thing was a call to arms.

It was common knowledge that bungs had been paid in football for some considerable time and that the practice was fairly widespread. I don't think George was made a scapegoat but he was unfortunate in that he was the first to be really caught out by a clever piece of journalism. It was probably just the tip of the iceberg and I can't imagine the FA wanted the matter to be blown out of the water – who knows what a wider investigation might uncover? The one-year ban George received from the FA seemed relatively lenient to me. I don't know, but was that because the FA recognised it went further than George and that he was just one unfortunate fly caught in a much bigger web?

In recent times, George seems to have enjoyed a more positive relationship with the club again; they are much more reconciled to each other and I think Arsenal supporters from that era are glad about this. He began appearing at games again, usually with his old mate Frank McLintock. I am happy about this, too, although it doesn't alter my views – views which have largely remained the same over the intervening years. George was a brilliant manager of Arsenal Football Club and, for that, he retains my deep admiration.

The lack of clarity off the pitch was largely mirrored by a lack of direction on the pitch that season. Before his sacking, I think George lost focus. In a run of seasons when the football was poor, 1994/95 was definitely when rock bottom was struck – perhaps the cups had blinded us all to just how bad it had become.

I know George knew this, too, because he was already starting to think about what he needed to do with the team. When I'd spoken with him earlier that season, he talked about rebuilding and he mentioned the defence. He wasn't critical of anyone, he loved those players, but perhaps he thought they had run their course. We had shipped a few more goals than usual that season. I don't think he was talking about an immediate root-and-branch rebuild but he had decided it was time to look to the future. He'd built that defence in more or less one summer for a few quid and he thought he could do it again, probably.

There were signs of change elsewhere, too. The previous summer he had brought in Stefan Schwarz, a different type of player to those we already at the club: it suggested that he *might* be thinking of playing a bit more through midfield. The fact he had signed three forward players just before his sacking also suggested, perhaps, a slight change of emphasis in how Arsenal attacked. Wright had always been the focus of our attack but I think George had started to think we needed a Plan B.

Hartson was a popular lad at Highbury. Guts and heart were what you got from him but he wasn't blessed with pace – it seemed unlikely he would slip in alongside Wright without some changes to how we were set up. Helder, when he was signed, seemed to offer the solution – a traditional winger to feed a traditional centre-forward. It was probably the first time since George's arrival that we needed a major overhaul but you have to question the quality of most of these signings. Helder and Kiwomya were really poor; frankly no better than Carter and McGoldrick. By 1995, George kept getting them wrong. He was building a team to finish mid-table, not challenge for the title.

Once George had departed, Stewart Houston looked after the team with Pat Rice. I don't think Houston changed anything. There were glimmers of the old days, too. The 1-0 win at Auxerre in the second leg of the Cup Winners' Cup quarter-final was a case in point – a performance honed in George's training sessions. Resolute defending and hard work, all capped off with a brilliant individual goal out of nothing from Wright – if ever the essence of a manager's reign was captured in a performance, it was that night against Auxerre.

Star-studded Sampdoria awaited in the semi-finals – a whole different proposition. They came to Highbury for the first leg minus Platt, Gullit, Mihajlović and Vierchowod but still with the dangermen Mancini and Lombardo fit and ready to go. Arsenal's power from set pieces and another inspirational finish from Wright should have been enough to put us in a commanding position but two goals from the

Serbian Jugović, the second following an exquisite defence-splitting backheel from Mancini, left the contest balanced on a knife edge at 3-2 in our favour. It had been a very open game for a European semi-final but Sampdoria weren't your usual Italian side – their strength lay in going forward.

The second leg in Genoa was an absorbing game with real ebb and flow, moments of high drama and an ending when we thought we might just be seeing the most unexpected phoenix ever emerge from a season of wreckage and ashes.

It was likely to be a torrid evening at the Stadio Luigi Ferraris and, with this in mind, Keown was starting; selected largely to sit on Mancini and prevent him from playing in the diminutive Lombardo. Early on, Mancini slipped Keown and fired Sampdoria into an early lead. In fairness to Arsenal, there was no panic; although we already needed a goal, we played sensibly. Our break came not long after the interval when Wright dug the ball out of his feet to direct it beyond Zenga. With a narrow aggregate advantage restored, we now had half an hour to endure.

Those 30 minutes ticked down without much apparent threat and with ten minutes to go, you felt once again that we had the measure of a far superior opponent. Then, in the space of three minutes, the sky fell in: two goals from the teenage Claudio Bellucci. After his efforts, timed at 82 and 85 minutes, we were on our knees. No one knew quite where to look for guidance or inspiration – George wasn't there.

A lifeline that none of us really expected came in the shape of a long range free kick from Schwarz with only a minute or so remaining. Schwarz's effort passed through a posse of players and, skipping of the turf, eluded Zenga's dive to nestle in the corner of the net – three goals in eight minutes.

After 30 minutes of extra-time during which neither team wanted to make a mistake, the game went to penalties. Dixon, Hartson and Adams all converted theirs, while Seaman did his magic and kept enough of them out. In the end, Arsenal simply refused to be beaten. They found a way, just as they had been doing for nine years – George would have been proud of them. It was a bit of a rag-tag performance but, once again, they had overcome. Hartson's bravery for a raw 20-year-old was outstanding and Adams, too, showed the sort of strength and willingness that defined an era now missing its figurehead. Given the state the club was in, the victories over Auxerre and Sampdoria stand as a testament to the resolve and the sheer bloody-mindedness that still existed deep within the psyche of the players. There is no question that George's influence was stamped all over them. Those games stood as an illustration of his achievements but also as a reminder of what we had lost.

They say anger is one of the stages of mourning. The curtain was coming down, the audience leaving and the lights dimming. Nine years of the most perfect theatre had finished. Perhaps my anger at George was in part due to my own sense of loss. He had rediscovered an Arsenal we all thought had been consigned to history; he reconnected the club with its traditional values. Nights like Sampdoria away defined the driven mindset he had brought, instilled and left behind him at Highbury. Defend him or attack him, George led us through the wonder years.

Was the final in Paris against Zaragoza an irrelevance? No, but if you ask me for my memories of 1995, 'Nayim from the halfway line' was only ever a sub-plot; George was always the story. To lose a cup final to a fluke goal in the last minute of extra-time seemed to confirm the end of an era, because Arsenal didn't lose like that under George; we won like that more often than not. On a sultry evening in spring 1995, defeat in the final simply fitted the mood and the narrative.

# Part Five:
# Bruce Rioch

## Chapter 27

# 1995/96

IN THE summer of 1995, if Bruce Rioch was being talked about at all as the next Arsenal manager, then his name was certainly being drowned out by that of Bobby Robson. The ex-England manager seemed certain to be heading to Highbury, with an offer of £2m over five years on the table. Robson was keen to come, although Porto were equally keen to retain him. Robson, it seemed, had one year left on his contract and, thus, was at liberty to activate his release clause – or so Arsenal and Robson thought. Things, however, became more complicated when Porto made clear that Robson had, in fact, two years remaining on his present deal. Arsenal, by then, were convinced that Robson was the man they wanted, so Dein flew to Portugal in order to negotiate his release, being prepared to offer the Portuguese club between £500,000 and £1m in compensation. However, it quickly became apparent that Porto were simply not budging.

Dein was also pushing his own nomination: Arsène Wenger. The two had met as far back as 1989 when Wenger was at Monaco and the Frenchman had made a deep impression on Dein. With a model in his head for growing football as a commodity, Dein was simultaneously starting to see the future shape of the game in terms of how it was played. Wenger, recognised Dein, could be influential in both regards.

Bruce Rioch was certainly highly thought of in the game. He had guided Bolton to two promotions and had done it playing some decent football; and, remember, he had made a good impression on the Arsenal board when he brought his Bolton team to Highbury for a cup replay and won.

Rioch's situation with Bolton was unusual, too. He was notorious for not signing contracts and I am not sure if he ever had one at Bolton. After leading Wanderers to promotion to the Premier League, Rioch had personal reasons for wishing to move down south. His father-in-law had serious health issues and, consequently, Rioch's position at Bolton was becoming untenable; Rioch was leaving Bolton whether or not Arsenal wanted him. Once Robson had become unattainable, and with Wenger viewed as too much of a risk, then Rioch began to have the field to himself. I don't recall any other strong candidates at all.

As a footballer, Rioch had had a reputation for being one of the hardest men around. Coming from a military background, he was organised, disciplined and known to have a very strong ethical code. He called it as he saw it and thought it unnecessary to accommodate reputations or egos. There was a lot to do at Highbury and Rioch was, undoubtedly, viewed as a reassuringly safe pair of hands.

His training sessions were intense and rigorous. He would often join in fully intent upon rattling a few cages with thunderous tackles but he was focused, too, on introducing a more fluid, passing style and there is no doubt that he *did* improve the football at the club.

Feedback from players is interesting: Rioch and Ian Wright couldn't stand the sight of each other; Merson acknowledged, and was grateful for, the support he personally received from Rioch for his addiction problems; Keown states Rioch's training improved his passing and ability on the ball; and Adams admits he might have let Rioch down, having been so caught up with his own difficulties back then that he was largely absent, in a psychological sense, from the dressing room when, perhaps, the new manager had needed him most.

Rioch's feud with Wright was long running and it was probably the most damaging of all the bust-ups he had at Highbury. Rioch had a reputation for falling out with people. Ian Wright was the star man, loved by the supporters. From the moment Rioch held up a training session to suggest to Wright he watch some videos of Bolton's John McGinlay and learn from what he saw, there was never going to be much love lost between the pair. Players have testified to the many arguments and flare-ups between the two of them, often in the dressing room, the worst of which followed our FA Cup defeat at Sheffield United in a third round replay.

Rioch even managed to escalate the feud further by suggesting that Arsenal might be a better team without Wright. It must have seemed an outrageous suggestion at the time but perhaps Rioch might have had a point in hinting at a wider problem. Wright was so formidable a presence that he almost demanded we played a certain way. It was effective but also predictable and, perhaps, we had taken it as far as we could as a gameplan. I think Tony Adams said something similar, not in any way disrespectful about Wright but never-the-less voicing concerns that we might never be successful again, especially in a title race, without a greater variety of options up front other than just Ian Wright.

Enter: Dennis Bergkamp.

The acquisition of the Dutch master gave a tremendous and immediate boost to Rioch's standing. It was a clear and obvious way of signposting the future – a statement of intent – and I can't imagine a more effective way of hanging out an 'under new management' sign for everyone to see.

There has been speculation that Rioch didn't have much to do with the job of convincing Bergkamp to sign, that Dein had done all the leg work and that it was, essentially, his signing. Some have even suggested that Wenger recommended Dennis to Dein. Bergkamp's English agent was Jerome Anderson, who also represented recent signing Glenn Helder. Anderson was a big Arsenal fan and someone I knew very well. I'd spoken to George Graham about Jerome not long after George was appointed at Arsenal. George was sceptical about dealing with him but I convinced him that he was a big Arsenal supporter and wouldn't do anything to harm the club.

Bergkamp's big football hero was Glenn Hoddle, who was, by then, the boss at Chelsea. Initially, it was Chelsea who made the running for Dennis's signature; they wanted to pair him up with Ruud Gullit who they had recently signed. I understand that everything was agreed, the transfer fee and Dennis's personal terms, but at the last minute, when Bergkamp was bringing his family to London, Chelsea admitted they didn't have the money. They left the deal in limbo to a certain extent, as they still wanted him but couldn't pay for him. Up until then, Anderson had not explored his Arsenal connections but once an issue cropped up with Chelsea, he was on the phone to Dein. Dein confirmed the club's interest but asked Anderson to speak to Rioch; Bruce fulsomely echoed Dein's enthusiasm. With that, Dein very quickly arranged a board meeting and the club sanctioned the deal at £7.5m. All this had gone on while Dennis was still driving to the UK. Apparently, he was initially disappointed that Chelsea had pulled the plug, mainly because of his respect for Hoddle, but

Anderson suggested that he go and talk to Rioch before returning to Italy. Fortunately, Bergkamp was totally smitten with the club; he looked round the marble halls and had a long talk with Rioch, with whom he got on like a house on fire.

Bergkamp, in later interviews, was clear that both Dein and Rioch were part of the talks, that both made a number of promises to him, primarily about how we were going to play much more openly. Bergkamp said that, even before arriving at Highbury, he liked what he knew about Arsenal. The recent Cup Winners' Cup success had put them on his personal football map, he admired Ian Wright, saw us as a settled team and he loved the wonderful old ground. He thought Arsenal would do nicely.

Bergkamp's stock had certainly fallen during his unhappy two-year sojourn in Italian football with Inter Milan. Doubts did exist around the size of the fee we paid and, more pertinently, whether Highbury was the right place for him to rediscover the form and panache of his early career. He was joined by David Platt. I wasn't particularly impressed by Platt's signing, not least because I thought the price too high. I think Platt eventually let us down a bit by not seeing out the final year of his contract when his experience would have been invaluable with us back in Europe.

Stefan Schwarz, after looking a very classy midfield operator, had decided to call time on his Arsenal career after just 12 months. Schwarz had become disillusioned by our inconsistency and endeared himself to no one when, on his way out of the club, he said he hadn't realised he was joining a mid-table team!

Progress was steady if unspectacular in those early weeks and months. One thing Rioch deserves credit for was that he got a full season out of Merson, an ever-present that year, and Merson played well, which might partly have been down to the manner in which Rioch supported him off the pitch.

Rioch kept it simple in those first games and, in truth, we looked more comfortable away from home. The 2-0 win at Goodison in the second game was a case in point: one exquisite ball from Bergkamp for Wright to run on to for our second goal was a highlight and harbinger of things to come. You could argue that we were still rather like the Arsenal of the recent past plus Dennis Bergkamp: solid, organised and prepared to get a foot in. However, a 3-0 win at Leeds suggested a new and slightly showy Arsenal were starting to emerge. It included a great goal from Wright; chipping Lukic, when there was really nothing on, was brilliant.

Throughout an up and down season, we hung on to fifth spot and confirmed it in the final game when, with goals from the two big money boys, Platt and Bergkamp, with a screamer, we clinched a spot in the UEFA Cup. It was a very creditable return for Rioch's first season. We had unquestionably played better football and, as the season wore on, with Rioch drafting in Hartson alongside Wright, Bergkamp was able to drop deeper into his preferred role. We had climbed from a 12th-place finish in 1994/95 to fifth a year later; we'd conceded 17 fewer league goals than a year earlier, 32 in all (the best in the division); but, unimaginably, we managed to score even fewer goals, three less in 1995/96 than the dire return in 1994/95.

On a lap of honour after the final game, Wright and Rioch embraced and walked for a while, the very picture of harmony. In the dressing room afterwards, Wright said this was his home, where he was staying, and Rioch dished out credit to everyone and looked every inch the man who had the measure of the task before him.

George had been a big act to follow; it had taken someone who was as sure of themselves as Graham had been. It couldn't have been easy for Rioch – there were a lot of ghosts to deal with.

Rioch, hamstrung in transfer negotiations by the board's post-Graham insistence they do all the negotiating, provided an extensive list of players he wanted for the new season. None of them materialised. A list of his suggestions reads like a *Who's Who* of European footballing royalty: Frank de Boer, Robert Jarni, Alan Stubbs, Bixente Lizarazu, Jason McAteer, Paul Ince, Gary McAllister, Lee Sharpe, Zinedine Zidane, Christophe Dugarry, Les Ferdinand, Roberto Mancini, Attilio Lombardo, Jürgen Klinsmann, Graeme Le Saux and George Weah. A move for McAllister was on for a while but then there were doubts about his age. The final straw for Rioch came when – denied De Boer, Jarni, Lizarazu and Le Saux – he identified Newcastle's left-back Robbie Elliott at £1.5m as someone he wanted but there was nothing doing as far as the board were concerned. What Rioch didn't know was that they had decided, only a few days after he had finally signed his contract, that they no longer wanted him. I understand that it was Danny Fiszman who, after calling time on George, now recognised that the relationship between Dein and Rioch was so poor as to be unsalvageable.

To sack a manager a week before the new season kicks off suggests something is badly wrong. A clue to Rioch's difficulties with signing new players that summer, which was at the root of his frustrations, can be found in how Dein reacted to Ian Wright's transfer request, which was finally provoked when Rioch told Wright he was playing on the left wing. When Ian went to see Dein in his office to hand in a request for a move, the vice-chairman, in turning down the request, told Wright to 'bide his time' – presumably because he *knew* that Rioch's days were numbered.

Some supporters said that Rioch wasn't big enough for the club. I think that is a bit unfair. He took over an aging squad and suffered long-term injuries to Bould and Adams but oversaw a change in style which required him to challenge old, ingrained football habits and still managed to get us back into Europe.

The intensity of the footballing beauty that soon followed has left us blind to a number of positives that emerged from Rioch's one Arsenal season. Chief amongst them is Dennis Bergkamp and, because of the Dutchman, the successful shift from pragmatic football to expansive football began under Rioch.

# Part Six:
# Arsène Wenger

## Chapter 28

# 1996/97

AN UNSCIENTIFIC survey of Arsenal supporters before the 1996/97 season kicked off showed the sort of approval ratings for Bruce Rioch that modern prime ministers would kill for. The Arsenal fanzine, *The Gooner*, found that 70 per cent thought Rioch was doing a decent job. At that stage, so did I – but I trusted that Dein and Fiszman knew best.

When the news broke of Rioch's sacking, I was surprised, certainly, but my thinking was this: Arsenal are not a sacking club – they do not panic; if the removal of the manager a week before the season commenced, which at most times would be viewed as catastrophic, was thought in the best interests of the club, then so be it. Football is ruthless and Arsenal had, at times in the past, possibly been too gentlemanly in how they went about their business.

Dein and Fiszman were both respected figures at the club but they were different to the typical Arsenal board member; importantly, they had made their own money and brought an air of cut and thrust to the otherwise reserved atmosphere of the oak-panelled boardroom at Highbury.

Their ambitions for the club appeared to go beyond the elegant management of decline which, at times since the war, appeared a preoccupation with the board.

Rioch's dismissal can be viewed as an illustration of how the tone of the suited side of the club was beginning to change. In many ways, Dein and Fiszman combined the best of both worlds – old school Arsenal class with the ambition and energy of the businessperson in a hurry – and they weren't going to let Arsenal stand still. That said, while I trusted them, it felt that the whole season had been written off before it began.

Pre-season had been pretty ropey. I travelled up for the Scottish leg of the preparations. As a kid, I'd always promised myself I would see Arsenal at all the big grounds around the world. So, a trip to see us play at Parkhead and Ibrox was too good to miss. We lost both games; we were beaten 2-1 by Celtic and got thumped 3-0 against Rangers in Richard Gough's testimonial. Against Rangers, the team looked really out of sorts; they didn't just play badly, they really didn't look happy. I remember seeing Keown taking his frustrations out on an advertising hoarding – it looked to be more than just an off-day.

The ship had sailed as far as Bobby Robson was concerned; he was to be Barcelona's new manager. Dein had created the opportunity and would finish the project with the appointment of 'his man' – Arsène Wenger.

Back in 1996, it was still the case of 'Arsène Who?' That no one in the English game really knew much about Wenger effectively describes the all-consuming air of provinciality that kept our game apart from football developments in Europe. One Englishman who did know Wenger well, though, was Glenn Hoddle. After playing for him at Monaco, he had seen him at close quarters and the result was that Hoddle viewed Wenger as one of the best coaches in the world; a revolutionary football man to his fingertips, someone who could shape the future of football. Hoddle knew Dein very well and, through that friendship, was able to highly recommend Wenger to Arsenal.

In terms of personalities, the distance from Rioch to Wenger is incalculable; in almost every regard, Wenger was so revolutionary to the English game as to be off the scale. On the Thursday before the new season commenced, Arsène was announced as the new manager, his appointment being ushered in with the news that, at his instruction, we had signed two new French players – Remi Garde and Patrick Vieira. Vieira, who would cost £4m from AC Milan, was the standout signing. At 20 years old, he was already being talked about as a potential French great and had a reputation as a commanding midfielder. Garde moved from RC Strasbourg. The 30-year-old was a very decent footballer, too, but his time with us was plagued with injuries. The appointment of Wenger got everyone talking and the expectation was to grow on the grounds that he would be seeing out his contract with Japanese club Grampus Eight and, therefore, was unlikely to arrive before the end of October at the earliest.

Joining him at Highbury would be a coach who, out of choice, would stay in Wenger's shadow and, when he left, would be able to walk by us all in the street and remain unnoticed: Boro Primorac. The two shared an obsession with fast, progressive football and a love of languages (Primorac spoke eight fluently). Initially, Primorac was seen as the more approachable out of him and Wenger; Paul Merson spoke very highly of him. Primorac shunned the spotlight but had a comprehensive knowledge of football, tactics and players; indeed, it is Primorac who is believed to have first brought the young Vieira to Wenger's attention.

Houston was asked to continue in his caretaker role until Wenger arrived in London but he would soon be off to QPR as their new manager, where he would be joined, ironically, by Rioch as his assistant. Arsenal stalwart Pat Rice held the fort from 13 September until Wenger's arrival. Rice's first game as caretaker boss would coincide with Vieira's debut, too. With Sheffield Wednesday one up at half-time at Highbury, Vieira was introduced shortly after the break and put in a brilliant game-changing performance. This rangy kid sidled on to the pitch and completely took over. His tackling, passing, running with the ball and all-round composure were striking. It was like he was playing a game on the beach. He was so good, you wondered why we had held him back for a few games. In no time, he turned the game and we romped home to win it 4-1. Rice will always have the claim on Vieira's Arsenal debut.

Arsenal's sturdy Englishness was, I imagine, well known to the new manager but another example of it warranted a video being sent to Wenger. The 2-2 draw at Villa Park had featured one of those comebacks which speak of character and something embedded deep within the psyche of a club. Two down with minutes remaining, Bergkamp set up Merson to head home and injury time saw Linighan head an equaliser at the back post. It was, too, the second time in a matter of days that we had staged a comeback – the previous Wednesday, we'd given Chelsea a two-goal start at Highbury and fought back to eventually take the lead, only to surrender it to a late equaliser in a classic 3-3 draw.

By the time Wenger arrived in London, we had hit a bit of form and sat in second spot. By then, Tony Adams's drinking had finally caught up with him mentally and physically and he knew it was time for honesty. His announcement to his Arsenal colleagues came as a bigger shock than perhaps it ought to have; Lee Dixon, for one, admitted to feeling confused by it and his initial reaction was along the lines of: 'You're not an alcoholic, you're Tony Adams captain of Arsenal.'

After Euro 96, Adams, to all intents, went missing, lost in a haze of drinking, self-doubt and self-loathing. The club had, rightly, got some credit for how they supported Merson when he came out about his problems and, again, I think the club got it right as Adams slipped from view and started on his journey back, as far from the glare of publicity as could be managed.

In Adams's absence, our established three-man central defensive set-up was manned by Bould, Keown and Linighan; a system though not entirely favoured by Wenger was intelligently retained by the new boss until, with a summer's planning behind him, he could ditch it and revert back to his preferred flat back four.

So, the club Arsène inherited was, frankly, one of extremes: some dilemmas, some positives and a club now tired from having been in the throes of change and transition for too long. Rioch's attempted revolution had run up against a lack of internal buy-in; now, the new manager needed backing from the board.

Something had to give with the players, too. A squad who were, perhaps, set in their ways needed to shed themselves of a defensive response to change. It helped that no one had ever encountered anything like Wenger in English football before; he was so totally different that it wasn't easy to pigeonhole him. His excesses and enthusiasms seemed to baffle even the hardiest and most robust of our little Englanders. He confused the sceptics and gave no encouragement to those who doubted him.

His first press conference had been such an overwhelming success that, even before he sent out a team to play a match, he had won over most of us. I got a call that evening from a journalist friend called Myles Palmer, who enthused about Wenger. Myles was really impressed by him and was convinced he would be a success at Arsenal. The football agent, Dennis Roach, who had represented Hoddle and also Mark Hateley during their stints at Monaco, knew Wenger and always spoke of him in the highest possible terms as a football man, as a businessman and, also, as a human being.

The media interest in him began to gather pace after his appointment. There was a bit of a frenzy to find out who he was. I don't recall ever hearing anything negative about him. Okay, some lurid and false stories emerged about his private life but I don't think anyone of any merit gave them credence; they were mere tittle-tattle, gossip for people who couldn't handle words of more than two syllables. In terms of football, Wenger was sound, so agendas resorted to fiction.

Looking back, you can see what a task it was to change Arsenal in 1996; the club was a true monolith. That had perhaps been one of our enduring strengths but times were changing; the old blueprint was beginning to feel irrelevant. Dein and Fiszman understood we had no option other than to go full-on Wenger.

It was a good first season; although nothing special, we unquestionably built on the previous year's showing. The most important thing was that Wenger now had a better idea of his players, English football and the ebb and flow of a domestic season. If you take Bergkamp out of the equation, then he largely inherited a squad to play a certain style of football which wasn't his own style. Perhaps that's what any new manager might expect but our squad was about as far away as they needed to be for 'Wengerball'.

One of the casualties would be John Hartson. We sold John to West Ham in February '97 for a very respectable £3.2m. Over the years, I've caused a few raised eyebrows with this comment but, bearing in mind we finished third in that first season under Wenger, just seven points behind eventual champions Manchester United, I think that, had we had hung on to John, if only until the summer, then there might have been a different conclusion to the season. Hartson did give us something different. Long term, he was never going to show the characteristic Wenger looked for most in a forward – pace. Following his move to Upton Park, we lost four times at home, all by the odd goal against Manchester United, Wimbledon, Liverpool and Newcastle; a couple of goals from Hartson in those matches, especially in the key games against United and Newcastle, could have made a big difference.

It was a very creditable beginning; a huge improvement in terms of the football. Bergkamp seemed happier and more effective, too, playing just off Ian Wright. It was the role he would excel at over the next few years as Wenger's chief footballing architect.

In February 1997, we signed a young striker from France, a move which generated little attention this side of the channel, as Nicholas Anelka moved from PSG for £500,000. Despite being relatively unknown in England, in France he was recognised as the hottest prospect from Clairefontaine and PSG were distinctly unhappy at losing him, especially for such a nominal fee. Vieira and Anelka had been signed for a combined fee of less than £5m. It was just the beginning of Wenger's shopping spree, which would see him reshape our squad.

With the close of the season, a sequence of three disjointed and, at times, unsettling campaigns came to an end. The future would be more familiar and consistent: trophies, glory and the most wonderful football that Highbury ever saw. Wenger served up a rich and cognisor diet. The pace of change caught us all out, I think, as we raced headlong into a bright and shiny future.

Chapter 29

# 1997/98

OVER THE summer, a succession of transfers augmented the growing sense of anticipation that was taking hold at the club. Despite most of us knowing next to nothing about the players joining us, I think we had already seen enough of Wenger to trust in his judgment. Everyone knew Vieira had been signed on his say-so and we'd never heard of him. What we did know was that they were nearly all foreign; they sounded emphatically exotic and were making Arsenal Football Club, for the first time in my life, the sexy place to be in European football.

The pick of the buys was Dutch winger Marc Overmars. Despite having won three league titles with Ajax, as well as the Champions League, he never-the-less represented a gamble, joining us after nearly a year off following a bad cruciate ligament injury. However, costing just over £7m, I think we were all excited at the thought of him and Bergkamp in the same team. He was lightning fast and by the end of the season, he looked an absolute bargain, with any lingering worries about his cruciate ligament banished. He was, at times, unplayable and unstoppable.

Not far behind him was the exotic-sounding Emmanuel Petit and in no time, I completely fell in love with Manu! At Monaco, under Wenger, Petit had played as a creative midfielder. More recently, he had featured at left-back. Now, Wenger saw a way of utilising his two different skillsets and sat him alongside Vieira to give us a defensive midfield double act.

Alex Manninger was brought in as understudy to Seaman and proved a highly reliable deputy. Gilles Grimandi arrived, like the pony-tailed Petit, from Monaco and I thought he did a good all-round job. Primarily a centre-back, he could also play at right-back, which he did to great effect when covering for Dixon during the run-in, or as a man-marker in midfield. Grimandi's distribution from the back was good, too, and I think what he offered the team can be overlooked at times.

Wenger also speculated on potential with the signings of Matthew Upson, Luis Boa Morte, Alberto Mendez and Christopher Wreh. None of them ever really worked out but Upson would, in time, prove a solid Premier League defender and Wreh would do enough to keep a fit-again Ian Wright out of the XI that started at Wembley in the FA Cup Final.

Wenger recouped over £6m in departures from Highbury. One sale caused some misgivings – Paul Merson. Wenger wanted to keep Merson but would only offer him a two-year contract. Middlesbrough, who had just been relegated, offered him both more money and a longer contract. We received £4.5m for Merson and when he informed Wenger of his intentions, Arsène, perhaps rather ruefully, told Paul that at Boro he would be on more money than Bergkamp was on at Arsenal.

The first couple of months of the season contained some spectacular moments. Although we dropped a few points, drawing games that later in the season we would have won, overall the campaign began in sensational style. There was Bergkamp's outstanding hat-trick at Leicester City, where his third goal was one of his three all-time best goals; Winterburn's curling missile to win the game in the last minute at Stamford Bridge; the first half at Highbury against West Ham, when Bergkamp just kept playing in Overmars to run on to and score; and Ian Wright breaking the club record for goals scored with a hat-trick against Bolton in a 4-1 victory which saw us go top.

I was still regularly in touch with David O'Leary, who, by then, was assistant manager to George Graham at Leeds United (I can recall David phoning me to say: 'You won't believe it but George has just asked me to be his No.2 at Leeds.' David was quite shocked but clearly he had made a positive impression on Graham when they were both at Highbury). David was hugely impressed by the football he was seeing at Highbury. He was genuinely excited by the stuff Arsenal were dishing up.

In early November, we recorded a 3-2 victory over league leaders Manchester United. Anelka scored his first goal for us and Vieira curled home a venomous effort. United squared it up but Platt headed home from distance with a late effort for a deserved three points.

It was unquestionably great box office but there could be a suggestion of helter-skelter about it with, at times, Vieira and Petit, the midfield shield, anywhere but sat in front of the back four. In some games, it mattered less once we got on the front foot but against the better sides, we could be picked off.

Following the United victory, we dipped, losing at Sheffield Wednesday and then at home to Liverpool and again at Highbury against Blackburn. The Blackburn game was one of those low points which are later recognised as a season's turning point. It was the fourth defeat of the season and all of them had come in a six-week period.

Adams convened a meeting of the players to address the drop in form and put it squarely to the French lads that the defence needed more protection; that they were being caught out of position and we were then being punished. I suspect that everyone just got a little carried away with themselves and needed reminding of the basics. The old hand Adams had seen it all before and he knew that, no matter how much attacking power you had, league titles were won and lost by defences and defending.

Petit struggled, initially, to accept the physicality of the English game, something Robert Pires would later struggle with, too. Petit has commented that he loved the strangeness of the Arsenal dressing room, the big characters it contained, and understood, with time, that it was all part of the extraordinary camaraderie required in the English game to withstand the martial aspects of it. Following a game at Southampton, Petit needed five or six stitches in a knee injury following a wild kick from a Saints centre-half. He was bemused by it all. We had won, he said, but it hadn't felt like a game of football; the ball was always flying over your head.

Bergkamp helped to show the way to Petit. Bergkamp is recognised for his grace, his fluidity of movement and quickness of thought but he could be a tough bastard, too. Elbows, stamps, all the dark arts were in there alongside that silky elegance. I suppose you don't survive two years playing on your own up front in Italian football without the means to look after yourself. Bergkamp found a way to overcome and Petit did, too, promising to get his head down and continue to play football against teams that merely wanted to kick us off the pitch. Interestingly, one thing which helped Manu was a suggestion by the English lads at Highbury that he train without shinpads; it'll toughen you up, they said! In no time at all, he became a ferocious tackler and his partnership with Vieira is rightly celebrated.

On 21 February, we won 1-0 at Crystal Palace; that and the next five league games would lay the foundation for an irresistible run. That spell of six matches saw us win 1-0 five times and draw 0-0 at Upton Park – no goals conceded had become a fashionable badge of honour once again. Ian Wright picked up an injury, although he had struggled since his spat with supporters in the match against Blackburn when he had been booed off by some fans and had continued the argument with them through a dressing-room window. Anelka came into the team in his place and, along with Overmars, provided the sort of searing pace which allowed us to play more as a counter-attacking team.

That run of 1-0 wins featured the most impressive and most remembered victory of the season. We visited Old Trafford on 14 March, sitting in second place, and started to slowly run down United's points lead. So substantial was their lead that a local Manchester bookie had paid out early on bets for them to win the league. What happened in the early Saturday kick-off caused the betting to be opened again.

Two of Wenger's summer recruits were central to our 1-0 victory. Manninger, in goal for the injured Seaman, made two outstanding saves with the score at 0-0; at the other end, Overmars twice came close before scoring the only goal with 15 minutes remaining. United still led by six points but, crucially, we had three games in hand. It was the tenth game of an unbeaten run which would eventually stretch to 19 matches and it meant that the destination of the title was now in our hands. That advantage would be augmented with two more single-goal victories, first against Sheffield Wednesday and then over Wimbledon, a match in which Wreh scored a wonderful goal to win a very difficult game.

For most of the season, the title had looked unlikely but by mid-March, the Double was starting to be talked about. The league was looking like a re-run of the famous overhauling of Leeds in 1971 when the 'southern softies' were reeling in the purveyors of northern grit.

In the midweek directly following the victory at Old Trafford, we went to Upton Park for a cup sixth-round replay. It started badly when Bergkamp took the law into his own hands and elbowed Steve Lomas to get himself sent off and land a three-match suspension. In first-half stoppage time, Anelka scored an absolute belter of a goal, swivelling on the edge of the box and hitting it first time. Ten-man Arsenal held out until the final six minutes, when Hartson levelled for the Hammers. Extra time couldn't separate the teams and, so, it went to penalties. After both teams missed two of their five, it went to sudden death. Tony Adams put the pressure back on West Ham with probably the worst penalty kick you'll ever see and when Manninger dived to his right to turn away Abou's effort, Arsenal marched on.

The reward was a semi-final against Wolves at Villa Park. Arsenal were very strong favourites, going into the game with a run of eight clean sheets in the league behind them. There was no Bergkamp – he was serving the final game of his three-match suspension – and, with Wright still injured, it meant Chris Wreh partnered Anelka up front. An early surge from Vieira drew in Wolves defenders and, slipping the ball to his right, Wreh met it first time and passed it beyond Segers to score the only goal of the game. At the final whistle, you could see how much it meant to the foreign lads, all of whom had grown up watching the English cup final on TV.

In the spring sunshine, the Arsenal of the first few weeks of the season re-emerged and all the fluidity of autumn returned. Bergkamp rediscovered his mesmeric touch, his penetration and 380 degree vision; Overmars was non-stop; Vieira and Petit were bossing the midfield; Adams, Keown and Bould were stepping out and playing like Pirlo.

First up on the title run-in were Newcastle, who also awaited us in the cup final. Two goals from Anelka – who, with every appearance, was proving the reputation which preceded him from Paris to London was no hyperbole – and, at last, a first Arsenal goal for Manu Petit, much to Highbury's delight, sealed a convincing 3-1 victory. Blackburn were swept aside at Ewood Park in a devastating opening 15-minute spell of fast, precise football which saw a Bergkamp strike and two from Parlour to put us three up early on. Anelka got another just before half-time as a potential banana skin proved a stroll.

Wimbledon came to Highbury and were dismantled 5-0 and then Barnsley (with another gem from Bergkamp) and Derby at home were all added to the long run of consecutive victories we were putting together. Nine straight wins had put us four points clear of United with a game in hand. Beat Everton at home and the title was secured. The only downside was that, during the Derby game, Bergkamp – who collected both the PFA and Football Writers' Association Footballer of the Year awards – picked up an injury which brought an early end to his season.

An air of expectancy at our final home game of the season was totally justified and Arsenal didn't let us down. Two goals from Overmars and an own goal had more or less buried Everton and guaranteed us the title before we witnessed a moment previously unimaginable in all my years at Highbury. In one glorious illustration of what Wenger had brought with him to England, Arsenal's two centre-backs were momentarily our two most advanced players on the pitch. Bould jinked, dummied and chipped a delightful ball over the top for Adams to run on to and, after steadying himself and waiting for the whole of Highbury to hold its breath, he smashed it into the net like a rocket.

It was *the* truly iconic moment of the whole campaign, perhaps even of Wenger's 22-year reign. It summed up the difference Wenger had made. Our football had been bejewelled all season with outstanding performances. After a lifetime of convincing myself that I liked it that we were dour, dull and hard to beat, here was a brave new world that challenged all my settled ideas about football and Arsenal.

This was a whole new kind of beauty. This wasn't beauty talked up by the media to bulk up viewing figures; this was authentic. This was something to tell the grandchildren about – wonderful, joyous, beautiful football. When even the hard men at the centre of our defence couldn't resist the allure of beauty, then the transformation was complete.

Winning the cup was a formality. No disrespect to Newcastle but this was always going to be Arsenal's Double! A ten-game winning run in the league, cup replays and penalty shoot-outs had seen us pass every test. It had to be Overmars who opened the scoring and, despite a couple of brushes with our woodwork, our second and killer goal from Anelka felt as if it was nothing more than we expected.

On our bench sat Bergkamp, missing through injury – he would have his time in the cup final sun one day, though – and also Ian Wright, stripped and desperate to get on. It would have been his final appearance for the club before a summer move to West Ham. I wonder if sentimentality could have been given a bit of licence with five minutes to go with a cameo appearance for him. I can't help but believe Ian Wright deserved that last little flicker of love.

In 1998, the wind changed direction across the landscape of English football; because of Arsenal, something changed in the psyche of the most insular of football nations. The irresistible energy of Wenger's team would overcome a stubborn conviction that the 'English way' was best and he would do it with the most English of clubs, too. That remains the irony of it all. Wenger showed an entirely different way was possible and it took him just a season to prove it, with the title and the FA Cup. United would fight back – and credit to them for that – but over the long term, Wenger's ideas would win out. He said young English boys could only benefit from training with players like Bergkamp, Overmars, Vieira and Petit and that, in time, our game would produce these types of players and they would play a style of football that, back then, we couldn't imagine.

Arsène Wenger was the architect of the future; many would follow, but he was its trailblazer.

## Chapter 30

# 1998–2001

### *1998/99*

Before the season began, Wenger commented that everyone always wanted to beat Arsenal and, as champions, that would be no different. He encouraged his team not to worry about anyone else and to simply concentrate on our way of playing. When the new campaign kicked off, I thought we were in great shape: pace, penetration, creativity, resolution and the character to get through the difficult times. Just like Wenger, I thought we could – and would – do it all again.

Around the edges, the squad changed a bit. Platt left after a disappointing three years of injuries. A younger and fitter Platt might well have featured more but the central triangle of Vieira, Petit and Bergkamp would pick itself at most clubs around the world.

Ian Wright had moved on to West Ham. His goals kept us afloat for a number of years prior to Wenger coming but Wenger's preference for Wreh over Wright during the run-in sent him a clear message and Anelka had already overtaken him in Wenger's plans. Despite being less of a street hustler than Wright, Anelka's directness was the perfect foil for Overmars and Bergkamp.

We also signed a diminutive Argentine, Nelson Vivas. He did a reasonable job; he was the utility man every squad needs. Perhaps the most interesting acquisition was the signing of the young Swedish prospect Freddie Ljungberg. He had been scouted by Arsenal for some time but Wenger had concerns about whether he would be able to handle the more aggressive English game. Wenger decided to make a move after, unusually, not having ever seen him play live. He was convinced of Ljungberg's suitability after watching on television as he played for Sweden against England in a European Championship qualifier, a match the Swedes won 2-1, and Ljungberg was signed for

£3m. Initially, the signing had me slightly worried. I thought Wenger might have signed him to replace Parlour. Ray had been a really big performer under Wenger; he had come on technically in leaps and bounds while losing none of his ruggedness. He had developed into a much more fully rounded midfielder than we ever really expected when he first came into the team. We knew about his engine and competitiveness but he was now a decent footballer, too.

The signings of Upson, Grimandi, Vivas and highly rated French youngster David Grondin suggested that, like Graham in 1994, Wenger was beginning to anticipate a defensive rebuild. All the members of that famous back four have spoken about how Wenger's ideas on health and fitness, diet and training methods extended their careers by two or three seasons at the top level. I think, in a very simplistic way, they had all just fallen back in love with football again and it was that pure joy of playing that kept them going. Adams said he learnt to defend 'properly', that his mastery of the positional side of the game evolved as he grew under Wenger and that if he had had to continue throwing himself around, sliding in here and there, he would have had to finish playing much earlier.

After beating United 3-0 in the Charity Shield, there was an indifferent start to the league season, which saw us draw four consecutive matches in our first five games (three of them 0-0). Wenger reacted sensitively to some fairly muted criticism of us: 'Perhaps we gave our fans too much by winning the Double. Once you've eaten caviar, it is difficult to go back to sausages.'

A repeat of the Charity Shield saw us hammer United 3-0 in the league at Highbury and late autumn would see us back in European football's elite club competition. The board had decided to stage our Champions League home games at Wembley and not Highbury. When interviewed, Marc Overmars had said that he was looking forward to playing the games at Wembley: 'It is a big pitch ... we are happy.' From my viewpoint, and I think this was largely shared amongst supporters, it looked a terrible decision from the outset. Highbury had become a fortress and it seemed as if we were sacrificing a home advantage just for more cash.

We actually made a reasonable start to our European group. But for a last-minute equaliser, we would have begun with a win away in northern France at Lens. We followed that with a 2-1 win at Wembley against Panathinaikos. A series of near misses suggested it might not be our night until Adams and then Keown scored very English goals from set pieces. That saw us go top of our group.

When Ukrainian thoroughbreds Dynamo Kyiv came to London, a win would have put us in a very strong position in our group. Over the next few years, however, teams from Ukraine would become our worst nightmare.

Arsenal played without either Vieira or Petit. Hughes and Garde came in and it was a cracking game. Dynamo, supercharged with Shevchenko and Rebrov up front, were always a handful. Not the typical forward line that Adams and Keown were used to week in week out in England. Both were technicians, as well as goalscorers; they enjoyed the space that Wembley afforded them and, perhaps as well, the effect that a big pitch had on older Arsenal legs in the dying minutes. However, it looked as if a rarity – a Bergkamp header – had won the game for us. But, with the clock ticking a minute into injury time, we failed to clear a free kick and Rebrov was ideally positioned at the far post to shoot across Seaman and level it up – the second time in three European games that a very late equaliser had pulled us back. We still hung on to top spot in our group but Rebrov's strike was a telling moment. Next up, we went to Kyiv and, with a team missing Adams, Anelka, Bergkamp and Overmars, we were turned over 3-1 in temperatures which could drop as low as minus 20 degrees. With that, we moved from top to bottom in what was a tight group.

When Lens came to Wembley, we were still missing Bergkamp, Vieira and Petit and, in an ill-tempered match, we were eliminated 1-0. Their goal was a good couple of feet offside (and not one, but two Lens players were offside). Vairelles was sent off for Lens for taking a swipe at Dixon off the ball. With one game to go, we couldn't finish in the top two due to the head-to-head results. An academic game in Greece saw us register a 3-1 victory.

Out of Europe, we went to Villa Park on 13 December. A first-half double from Bergkamp put us two up at half-time but a second-half revival from Villa saw them come back to win 3-2. However, just like with the Blackburn defeat at the same stage the previous year, there was a positive response and we promptly went on a 20-game unbeaten league run.

In February, we signed Kanu from Inter Milan. The laconic Nigerian, who never seemed in a hurry, was a revelation. His acquisition signalled, perhaps more than any other Wenger signing, the direction the boss wanted to go in. Capable of the most dreamy and casual football, he was very off-the-cuff and was given licence by Wenger to do his own thing. Bergkamp *and* Kanu in the same side felt like a luxury and, as Wenger seemed obstinately to prefer Kanu over Bergkamp, I think the cohesion of the team suffered. He provided some wonderful moments, no doubt, but you never quite knew what you would get from him and it all felt a bit too *ad hoc*.

Kanu made his debut at home to Sheffield United in an infamous cup tie. With the scores level at 1-1, United put the ball out of play for one of their injured players to receive treatment. The game restarted with an Arsenal throw-in and Parlour, respecting the conventions, threw the ball down the line into space in order to surrender possession. Kanu, in his first game in England, apparently was unaware of any such convention and, with Sheffield United dawdling, he whipped in a cross for Overmars to knock into an unguarded net. Kanu and Overmars did a little dance while the visitors went ballistic. At one stage, Steve Bruce, their manager, appeared to call his players off the pitch.

In fairness to Parlour, the Sheffield players accepted he bore no culpability and was trying to give them the ball back. The game was seen out and Arsenal won 2-1. However, within minutes of the end of the game, Arsenal had offered to replay the tie and the offer was accepted by the visitors. Given that I suspect we felt uncomfortable about the situation almost immediately it had happened, then I don't know why we couldn't have just let the Blades score direct from the restart. Anyway, the game was replayed and, with goals from Bergkamp and Overmars, we made it through to the sixth round legitimately.

On the Wednesday following that fractious game with Sheffield United, we journeyed to Old Trafford and, digging in, we brought a valuable point home to Highbury. They missed a penalty before Anelka put us ahead, only for Andy Cole to square things up.

I remember feeling that we seemed to have the measure of United and that, at that stage, we had footballers who weren't intimidated by them. The beauty of that Arsenal team, and perhaps why it should have achieved more than it did, was that it could play *and* look after itself. Vieira, Petit and Bergkamp could all look after themselves and the English backbone of the side – guys like Adams, Keown, Bold, Dixon, Winterburn and Parlour – were never going to take a backward step.

After drawing at United, we played Leicester City at Highbury and produced one of our most brutal 45 minutes of football that season. We were 4-0 up by half-time and, without scoring himself, it was Bergkamp who again gave an absolute masterclass. For a while, it was like a training session as he kept playing in Anelka and then Parlour. Anelka's first-half hat-trick was his first in Arsenal's colours. After the game, our Dutch genius speculated that it had been the best we'd played that season and, ominously for the rest, he felt we had found the same kind of momentum as the previous season.

It was to Villa Park next, for a much-hyped cup semi-final against Manchester United. The first attempt to settle it ended 0-0: a tense affair which was made more arduous for us once Vivas had been sent off early in extra-time. It was in the replay back at Villa Park three days later that the contest truly ignited. Beckham caught Seaman off guard to whip in an effort from 25 yards but, with 20 minutes remaining, Bergkamp, from the same distance, scored with a deflected effort to make it all square.

When Keane was sent off for his second yellow, the momentum swung Arsenal's way. We were playing the better football by then, having weathered the storm. As the game entered injury time, Anelka played it wide for the ever industrious Parlour, who advanced to the edge of the box and, driving past Phil Neville, panicked the full-back into a rash challenge and the ref pointed to the spot.

The following morning, Rob Smyth in *The Guardian* would describe the match as 'the greatest game in the modern era of English football'. Bergkamp, the ice man, put the ball on the spot. Arsenal's greatest technician, their coolest head versus Peter Schmeichel, probably the very last goalkeeper you would want to face in such a situation. Score a penalty and you have won the match, you're in the cup final, you wind your rivals, you go on to win the league and you change the course of history. As Bergkamp waited to take the kick, it was like being in the coliseum as you waited for Caesar to point his thumb up or down. Dennis looked really nervous as he prepared himself.

I sensed something was wrong and turned to Dean, my son, and said: 'He's going to miss this.' Was it my fault? Did I curse the great Dennis Bergkamp? In the space of time it takes a keeper to save a penalty, everything changed. If that ball goes in, I say, here and now, we win the cup and the league and United win nothing that season; their famous Treble never happens.

Bergkamp hit it cleanly but at a good height for a keeper; it was, in truth, a poor penalty and Schmeichel guessed correctly and turned it away.

Ever since that night, I have avoided seeing Giggs's goal. I'll turn the TV over or switch it off rather than watch it again. That night will be with me always, literally until my last moments. It dominated my thoughts for days, weeks afterwards. I'd wake up thinking about it, find myself driving and my thoughts would drift off towards it. No Arsenal match has ever affected me more; it was my worst experience as an Arsenal fan. I think United drew such strength from surviving that night. It helped define a new relationship between the two teams. We lost more than a cup semi-final that night.

We rallied for a while, beating Wimbledon 5-1 and then going one better, beating Middlesbrough 6-1 away, the game when Kanu scored with a backheeled flick. That result put us top but I knew, I knew ... even when we beat Derby and then went to White Hart Lane and thrashed the neighbours 3-1, I knew!

That night at Tottenham saw Bergkamp back to doing what he did best, two wonderfully weighted passes putting it on a plate for Petit and then Anelka to score. Kanu wrapped it up with five minutes to go; receiving it on the edge of the box with his back to goal, he flicked it over Young's head and, running round the hapless defender, hit it on the volley beyond Walker.

By then, George Graham had moved to Tottenham as manager, with Stewart Houston as his assistant and, if I am honest, for a time I was really quite worried about what George might achieve at Tottenham; I think a lot of Arsenal fans were. I know he wanted to get back to London, having returned to football management at Leeds after his ban, but his choice of club begs a few questions. Was it just a football decision? I can't help but think that his decision was motivated by a desire to get back at us. I don't know if he was ever happy at Spurs; it felt like a mistake but it took George a while to get over his bitterness at how he believed Arsenal got it wrong over him and how they treated him. I think that bitterness was part of what motivated him to go there.

David O'Leary had picked up the reins at Elland Road after George left the club early in the season in somewhat acrimonious circumstances and it was to Elland Road that we now headed for our penultimate fixture. The same night as we beat Tottenham, United surrendered a two-goal lead at Anfield to draw 2-2, which left us three points ahead, with a narrow advantage in terms of goal difference, but having played a game more. On 9 May, United would win 1-0 at Middlesbrough and draw level on points and goal difference.

David offered me tickets for the directors' box for the game but I wanted to be with our supporters for this one. It was one of those difficult stick or twist nights. We obviously wanted to win to keep the pressure on United but they were away at Blackburn the following evening and a draw at Leeds might prove sufficient to add more pressure ahead of their already difficult game at Ewood Park.

Leeds opened strongly, while we looked hesitant and a bit subdued. Batty was turning the clock back and driving his young team-mates on. It looked like they were going to get some reward when Keown gave a penalty away with a rather rash challenge but Harte hit the bar and his follow-up effort was saved on the line by Seaman.

It was inevitable that Hasselbaink would score and, five minutes from time, the killer blow was struck. There was a suggestion that Vivas, at the back post, let Hasselbaink get ahead of him too easily but, in reality, it was probably just a poacher's goal. At the final whistle, it felt like the title was gone; United now had a game in hand, leaving us with just one to play.

The end of the game has since become rather notorious for the celebrations of Arsenal's all-time appearance record holder, David O'Leary. He looked mightily pleased with himself and his side at the end, high-fiving all his players on the pitch – it didn't go down terribly well with the Arsenal supporters at the game or since. It was interpreted at the time as some kind of anti-Arsenal gesture but, not influenced by my friendship with him, I would say that is wide of the mark. David loved Arsenal and still does. I have never spoken to him about it but I suspect that, as a bright young manager, he was delighted to have beaten a very good football team and outwitted a very smart manager. I don't think it was anything more than that. It might have annoyed me at the time, with emotions running high, but, with the passage of time, I can see it for what it was.

Knowing a draw would give them a great advantage, United set up shop for a 0-0 at Blackburn the following night and got it. Which meant we had to beat Villa at Highbury in our last match and hope that Tottenham could stop United winning at Old Trafford – and, of course, George would be dying to do us a favour!

Spurs raised our hopes by going a goal up through Les Ferdinand but George then took off his best player, Ginola. United got two in about five minutes either side of half-time and that was that. We kept going, just in case of a slip-up, but I certainly never expected United to be pegged back once they had gone in front.

In a season when we vied between 'caviar and sausages', eventually we came up short. One statistic from that season rarely referenced is the fact that in 1991 we conceded just 18 goals and that was hailed as magnificent; in 1998/99 we conceded just 17 and I bet a lot of people aren't aware of it.

In modern football, small margins are incessantly referenced. That season, we lost in the cup because of a fantastic penalty save (half a foot higher and the ball goes in) and we surrendered the title by one point over the course of a season.

At the end of the season, Anelka handed in a transfer request, citing the English media as the reason for his wish to move, though, in truth, he was very badly advised by his brothers and would later admit it had been a serious mistake to leave Arsenal. The saga would drag on for most of the summer until Real Madrid agreed to pay the £23m Arsenal demanded for him. The profit on him of £22.5m was no compensation, really. This was still before Anelka morphed into the serial club leaver and became ubiquitously known as 'Le Sulk'; back then, he was just a young, world-class footballer who would only get better and better. He felt massively central to the whole Arsenal project under Wenger.

We plugged the gap left by Anelka with Davor Šuker. He was an odd one: a scorer of majestic goals but there was nothing bread and butter about him. Unlike Anelka, he had no pace and we already seemed well equipped for agents of the unexpected – we wanted someone to just bang them in. We also signed a Juventus misfit. His name? Thierry Henry.

In 1998/99, we were close. I still believe we were better than United that season but, though we would come close to winning things over the next two seasons, we could barely cling on to United's coat tails.

## *1999/2000*

While finishing second to United in both the seasons which followed, in 1999/00 we finished a massive 18 points behind them and, while closer in 2000/01, we still fell ten points short. The loss of Anelka was compounded a year later when both Overmars and Petit moved to Barcelona. It left Wenger and his Arsenal project at a crossroads. We were entering a period of transition from a side built purely on pace to one that looked to keep possession.

Wenger began the difficult job of rebuilding the defence by releasing veteran centre-half Steve Bould, who joined newly promoted Sunderland. Bould did a good job at the Stadium of Light; being made captain not long after arriving, he steadied the ship and helped guide them to a seventh-place finish in their first season back in the top flight.

One notable game that season was the one which featured Kanu's famous 15-minute hat-trick to win us an unlikely three points at Stamford Bridge, where Chelsea had not even conceded a goal that season (this was late October) and last time out had thumped Manchester United 5-0. Chelsea took a 2-0 lead and then, with just 15 minutes remaining, Kanu pulled one back. He scored another with a brisk turn and shot in the box. Then, with the clock ticking over into injury time, he absolutely pulled the rabbit out of the hat; after taking De Goey, the Chelsea keeper out of the game, he audaciously curled an effort from near the corner flag, which somehow evaded two Chelsea defenders on the line and hit the top corner of the net. It was a goal to take your breath away, capping a remarkable burst of football which perhaps only Kanu was capable of but one which left you wishing he could do it a bit more consistently. It takes some player to be picked over Bergkamp but such examples give an insight into why Wenger did, I suppose. At times, he was unplayable but at others he seemed unable to get into the contest; for me, Bergkamp was always the more consistently effective.

We had another miserable experience in the Champions League. We made a good start (again) with creditable draws away at Fiorentina and Barcelona and a victory at home against AIK Solna but it was the key middle games in the group at Wembley when we came up short. Barcelona were a cut above and then Fiorentina, with an outstanding strike from Batistuta, sealed our fate.

Failing to get out of the first group phase, we did at least enjoy the dubious privilege of entering the UEFA Cup as compensation. As a traditionalist, I can't say I took easily to the idea. It had nothing to do with football, just a cynical move by big Italian and Spanish clubs who wanted the safety net of another revenue stream as a back-up if they were knocked out of the 'big one' early.

Our progress in the UEFA Cup, though, was assured. We saw off Nantes, Deportivo La Coruna, Werder Bremen and Lens during an impressive journey to the final.

Our opponents, Galatasaray, had already completed a domestic Double of their own and they brought with them a reputation for making it uncomfortable – their 'welcome to hell' sentiments extended from club officials, to players and to the supporters. In their semi-final, they had beaten Leeds United and two Leeds supporters had died, stabbed, in trouble before the match in Istanbul. Consequently, the final, staged in Copenhagen, where we had triumphed in 1994, had a very tense build-up to it. Fighting broke out in several areas of the city and, while I accept you tend to think better of your own supporters, it seems the catalyst for the fighting was Galatasaray supporters storming a pub intended for Arsenal followers only and, thereafter, a cycle of retribution developed.

It gave the game an edge and the atmosphere inside the stadium felt a bit like the old days. On the pitch, we started slowly and the half chances all seemed to fall to the Turks. They were really up for it and it showed as they roared into challenges. At 90 minutes, it was 0-0 and, as the game went into extra-time, with the golden goal rule becoming active – meaning the next goal would win the game – Arsenal began, at last, to impose themselves on the game. An advantage came our way when Hagi decided to wrestle with Tony Adams and was sent off. With that, Galatasaray began to look to penalties as their best chance of winning. But the penalties really ought not to have ever happened. Parlour, who had another great game (it was his sort of match), burst to the byline before hanging a cross to the far post and, from 8ft out, Henry met the ball perfectly, heading it downwards with power and precision. I was directly in line with that header and, from the moment it left his forehead, I thought it was in but the keeper, the Brazilian Taffarel, made a fantastic reaction save. Kanu then made a chance for himself, cutting in from the right and forcing one great stop from the keeper and then another from the rebound.

The penalties were a disaster. Galatasaray scored their first four and when Suker and Vieira missed for us, with only Parlour converting, the game was over and the trophy lost.

That was the last time Marc Overmars and Manu Petit played for us – Davor Šuker, too. Šuker, at best a bit-part player, had not exactly endeared himself to us when he casually mentioned in an interview that he had purchased some shares in Manchester United. As a member of that politically charged Croatian national team in the turbulent 90s, Suker maybe garnered a reputation which he never quite lived up to. In the summer, he would move on to West Ham alongside another departure – Nigel Winterburn.

What can we say about nutty Nigel? I'd seen some brilliant left-backs over the years – Bob McNab, Sammy Nelson and a world-class Kenny Sansom – but I would still pick Winterburn in front of them all. You always got 100 per cent from Winterburn and while he didn't score many goals, those he did were beauties, always important and always from about 30 yards. He conducted a one-man feud with Manchester United for most of the 80s and 90s; the smallest guy on the pitch but the one you'd most want beside you in a punch-up. I sometimes wonder what Wenger must have thought of him; he was so uniquely an English footballing product – half footballer, half soldier.

## *2000/2001*

On 9 February 2001, a young man's life ended in a motor accident. He was just 17 years old. Wenger said he would have one day been our captain and also the captain of Italy. Liam Brady, who was the head of youth development and academy director, said this of the young prospect: 'He stood out, he had that stature and that confidence in himself ... he could also play, he was intelligent, he could read the game – he really had everything. I have no doubt he would have gone on to play in our first team and be an Italian full international.' He was Niccolo Galli.

The young Galli had starred in the Arsenal youth team which won the FA Youth Cup in 2000 and was about to be fast-tracked into Arsenal's first-team squad when, following some homesickness, a loan deal was arranged with Bologna, for whom Galli made his Serie A debut. His team-mate at Arsenal, Ben Chorley, commented on just how far in advance Niccolo was of the English boys. Ben drew attention to Galli's dedication to his life's vocation. Niccolo trained three times daily, worked out and did nothing which would harm his ability to play or train the next day.

After training one day at Bologna, he was going home – like most young Italian men, riding his scooter – when he was killed in an accident. Arsenal lost a potential great that day but the Galli family lost a son and a brother.

The following day, we played at home to Ipswich Town. A minute's silence prior to the game marked the formal acknowledgement of Niccolo's death and it was a subdued day, the match settled by a single goal from Henry.

The season marked a reasonably good showing following significant player departures and the arrivals of Pires, Lauren, Edu and Wiltord. Robert Pires would take the season to find his feet but when he did, what feet they proved to be.

While United had continued to dominate in the league, as far as results between the two of us had gone, we had maintained a bit of a hoodoo over them. In early October, we beat them again at Highbury, the game won by one of the first of Henry's wonder goals. Receiving the ball with his back to goal, around 25 yards out, in one movement he flicked the ball up, swivelled and volleyed it over Barthez in the United goal; a mesmerising effort, the coming together of a level of technical precision and creative thinking which is rarely witnessed.

On 25 February, that stranglehold over United would end spectacularly, though, and we would return to north London after a mauling that even by half-time saw us 5-1 down; a final score of 6-1 on a day when our reserve central defensive pairing of Stepanovs and Grimandi simply couldn't live with the movement from United.

It had already been well documented in the media that Vieira was becoming unhappy at the quality of player leaving the club and the United debacle must have strengthened his doubts. Not for the first time, the club's ambition would be questioned.

Another failed European campaign would have done little to convince Vieira. Progress through two group phases saw us pitched against Valencia in the quarter-finals. A late John Carew goal in the second leg was enough to see us eliminated on the away goals rule. Worse was to come.

A highlight of the season had been beating Tottenham in the FA Cup semi-final and booking a place in the final, where we would meet Liverpool. The final was switched from the building site at Wembley to Cardiff's Millennium Stadium. It made for an interesting contest: the élan of Wenger's Arsenal against the greater pragmatism of Houllier's Liverpool.

By the time we finally scored, Ljungberg putting us 1-0 up on 72 minutes, we really should have been out of sight. In the first half, Henry had a goal-bound effort pushed around the post by Liverpool centre-back Henchoz on the line, a clear handball for which we didn't even get a corner! Then, as we mounted attack upon attack in the second half, Cole had a goal-bound effort blocked and then Ljungberg's chipped effort was cleared off the line.

Liverpool hit back and equalised through Owen with seven minutes remaining and won the cup in the last minute when Owen, again, first held off Dixon and then Adams to steer it beyond Seaman.

To lose so late on from a winning position was sickening and after the game, Vieira didn't hold back. His festering frustration at, amongst other things, the size of Arsenal's squad, the quality of some recruits, the ambition of the club and the still open wounds from the sales of Anelka, Overmars and Petit gave rise to serious doubts over whether he would be around to see out the remaining years on his contract.

## Chapter 31

# 2001/02

BY THE spring of 2002, there was absolutely nothing artisan about our football diet; it was caviar all the way again, with crates of champagne thrown in. It was, perhaps, the richest diet of football I have ever consumed with Arsenal. By the end of the season, I was convinced I had seen the best Arsenal side and the best football that I was ever likely to see.

Back in the summer of 2001, a second Double under Wenger felt a long way off. We were becoming a team that was making a habit of falling short. Since 1998, we had finished second three times, lost a UEFA Cup Final on penalties and an FA Cup Final to a last-minute goal.

Then everything changed: Sulzeer Jeremiah Campbell signed for Arsenal!

I was doing some business admin at home, with Sky Sports on in the background. An announcement was imminent by Arsenal, presumed to be the confirmation that Ipswich Town's goalkeeper Richard Wright had signed for us. Hardly anyone bothered to turn up – and what a story they missed. When Sol Campbell calmly walked on to the platform and took a seat alongside Wenger and David Dein, I was a bit bewildered. Sol looked relaxed as he fielded questions and Dein just grinned. It was a major coup for us. So much hard work had gone into that deal, most of it carried out clandestinely late at night at Dein's house, so preoccupied were both parties that no one should find out. It still feels remarkable to this day that no one *did* know anything about it until that moment when Sol appeared.

Campbell was a fine player, a great addition to the club – there would have been very few elite clubs in Europe who wouldn't have wanted him – but the crowning glory was that he was Tottenham's icon, captain and folk hero. I'd always been chuffed that we took Pat Jennings off their hands for a measly few quid back in 1977 and now here we were, signing Campbell on a free.

While I thought it possible he might be a bit overhyped by the press, I'd have to admit that I had never seen him have a poor game. I think what he most obviously brought was a phenomenal sense of focus. It is often the case that the tone of a team is set by the centre-backs. Adams and Bould had done it for years. Wenger had begun to dabble with continental central defenders, footballing defenders, but I wasn't massively comfortable about it. I've always thought a centre-back's job, first and foremost, is to defend; it's a bonus if they can play. Campbell wasn't a great footballer with the ball at his feet but he could defend and was probably the pre-eminent English centre-back by some distance at the time. Built like a heavyweight boxer, but with the athleticism of an Olympic sprinter, he was the real deal.

His signing would have been a tremendous fillip to Vieira and I think we got a bit extra from Vieira that season as a result of Campbell's arrival at the club.

The other signings weren't as headline grabbing but the arrival of Giovanni van Bronckhorst from Glasgow Rangers was a shrewd bit of business. He was a tidy, intelligent player; he didn't catch the eye but he kept things moving. He suffered a bad cruciate ligament injury halfway through his first season and by the time he was fit to return, Edu and Gilberto Silva had supplanted him in the pecking order. He was probably a better player than he had the chance to show us.

One of the criticisms levelled at us was that we couldn't score routine goals; that everything had to be a contender for goal of the season. What we had lacked since Anelka left was someone who came to life in the penalty box. The signings that summer suggest that Wenger was looking for people who could make an immediate impact, players who knew the English game. Campbell and Richard Wright were both English and even van Bronckhorst had had a couple of highly successful seasons with Rangers in the Scottish Premier League. When we signed Francis Jeffers, Wenger's 'fox in the box', it seemed, at a superficial level, as if it could be a reasonable punt on a young kid who looked as if he had goals in him. At Goodison Park, he had a good goals-to-appearances ratio, scoring 18 in 49 starts, but just look a little deeper. Those 49 starts were spread over three seasons, which suggests an inclination to pick up injuries. In fact, he had spent most of the previous season on the treatment table and, crucially, he was coming to the end of his contract and had told Everton he wouldn't be signing a new one.

Jeffers agent was Jerome Anderson and he was, by then, a sort of unofficial in-house Arsenal agent. He had the ear of Dein and Wenger and I know that he really pushed Jeffers to the club and I think Anderson genuinely thought Jeffers was a great prospect. I think Wenger might have been talked into it a bit, though, and apart from anything else, it was a lot of money – £8m plus a possible £2m in appearance-related add-ons for a youngster who seemed to always be injured and only had a year left on his contract. I doubt there were clubs queueing up round the block to buy him and I think we massively overpaid for him. To put it in perspective, we only paid £2m more for Thierry Henry. I think that, in view of the fee we paid for Jeffers, he must be just about the worst signing Wenger made. He played for 11 different clubs and only for Everton did his goals tally get into double figures. For a career constantly interrupted by injuries, he deserves a bit of sympathy but I didn't really think he was much of a footballer; so, from a business and footballing perspective, his signing was a huge mistake.

Richard Wright had looked a good prospect for his hometown club Ipswich after making his debut at only 17. We also had young Stuart Taylor, who was highly thought of, coming through. Wright had been signed as Dave Seaman's long-term replacement but he struggled after getting a run of games sooner than anyone had anticipated. I don't think he ever really recovered from making a mess of things in injury time at Tottenham, turning a victory into a 1-1 draw; this was despite making a brilliant save only minutes earlier. Thereafter, poor Wright looked ill at ease and a nervy keeper's game can become brittle very quickly.

That game at Tottenham has now become infamous for so much more than Wright's error. 'A reception fit for a criminal rather than for a returning favourite son,' said Jeff Stelling on Sky. It was all in honour of Sol Campbell. It had begun with Spurs fans attacking the Arsenal coach on its arrival at the ground. Banners with the single word 'Judas' on them, thousands of balloons featuring the same word, too, and a wall of boos and whistles greeted him when he came out to warm up. This only intensified tenfold when the players came out for the game. Words like 'vitriolic', 'unsavoury' and 'disgraceful' really didn't come close to capturing the atmosphere. The crowd had even planned a 'minute of contempt' for their one-time club captain.

Campbell had a great game, never put a foot wrong and, despite what must have been going on inside his head, he looked unflappably calm. In all my 74 years supporting the Gunners, Campbell's performance that day was the bravest I ever saw; he dealt with everything.

Pires scored a blinder with just under ten minutes remaining but Wright's injury-time howler stopped Campbell getting the three points his performance and bravery deserved.

We were a bit in and out until late December but then we started to motor. We lost 3-1 at home to Newcastle on 18 December (all three of our defeats that season came at Highbury, so we remained unbeaten on our travels for the season) and then went undefeated for the rest of the season – 21 matches winning an incredible 18 and drawing the remaining three. We took 57 points from a possible 63 – magnificent. That unbeaten run includes a sequence of 13 straight victories.

It was a brilliant season, with some magnificent football. The shape of the season mirrored our Double campaign in 1998, with an unstoppable run that gathered pace and power. Campbell was immense and deserves a lot of credit; Bergkamp was back to his best; Pires had a golden touch that season; and Ray Parlour was outstanding. Ray gave absolutely everything, an engine that purred from the first to the last minute, and, by 2002, he had become one of the most effective all-round midfielders in England. I'd been watching him in an Arsenal shirt since he was 14 and it sounds like faint praise just to say I admired his effort but even as a kid he got stuck in – he worked at his game and eventually there wasn't much between Parlour and Ljungberg for what they brought to the team.

In the February, I finally blotted my copybook regarding 'jibbing'. We were up at Leicester for a midweek game at the old Filbert Street stadium. I hadn't got a ticket but some friends were going, so I was talked into it, thinking I would get in anyway. It all went to plan to begin with and I got into the ground but at half-time, the turnstile operator appeared in the Arsenal section with two police officers and, once he spotted me, began excitedly shouting: 'That's him! That's him!' With my silver hair, I did rather stand out. I managed to get back in when they opened the gates with ten minutes to go, just in time to see Wiltord seal a 3-1 victory but it was a disappointing end to my long run of 'jibbing' successes.

After trailing in United's wake for what felt like too long, it was highly satisfying to eventually clinch the title at Old Trafford. I had to watch the game sat amongst the home fans; Jerome Anderson had provided Dean and me with tickets. So, while we were wary of being too conspicuous in our support for Arsenal, all attempts at disguise were dropped when Wiltord scored. We had outplayed United that night, despite their efforts to kick us off the park *again*, and I think everyone sat around us knew that. United should have had three sent off. At the final whistle, Dean and I wanted to celebrate with our travelling London supporters and, in a state of high excitement, we rushed out and into the Arsenal section, where I bumped straight into Johnny Hoy and his lad. It was the first time I had seen John in many years and we enjoyed a big celebration hug. John lived up in Newcastle now but followed the Gunners still when he could. His lad was another Arsenal fanatic but with a broad Geordie accent.

We'd clinched the FA Cup at the Millennium Stadium a few days before the United game, with a thoroughly commanding show against Chelsea; we won 2-0 with two cracking goals from Parlour and Ljungberg to banish any lingering frustrations from 12 months earlier. We had to weather an early storm, as Chelsea settled quicker than us, but we stood firm and gradually turned the tide of the game. Once we had taken the lead, Wenger withdrew Bergkamp to shore things up, with the more defensive Edu. Parlour's 'it's only Ray Parlour' moment was the icing on the cake.

A final league outing against Everton at home, a 4-3 victory, saw Richard Wright start the game and Stuart Taylor come on at half-time so that both could claim their tenth appearance and, therefore, be eligible for a medal. Arsenal in 2002 remain unique in that they had three goalkeepers who all played enough games to receive a medal.

It was a season for individual awards, too: Wenger was Barclaycard Manager of the Year, Ljungberg was Barclaycard Player of the Year, Pires was named the Football Writers' Association Footballer of the Year, Henry won the Golden Boot and Dennis Bergkamp won the BBC's goal of the season (again) for his sublime flick-shimmy-shoot manoeuvre at Newcastle. It was an outstanding season and, alongside 1970/71, probably my favourite following Arsenal.

With the season complete, there was one remaining rite to complete – a fond and heartfelt farewell to big Tony Adams. Calling time on an outstanding and inspiring one-club career (four league titles, three FA Cups, two League Cups and one European Cup Winners' Cup), he bowed out in a game against Celtic played in front of a full house. There is nothing more that really needs to be said about Adams's career but one record especially captures his longevity in the game – he captained Arsenal teams to the league title in three different decades; not bad for a lad written off as a 'donkey', who was derided up and down the land and who very publicly fought and won a battle against addiction. Even in teams full of creative and technical brilliance, Adams's heart, nous and bravery stood out. I doubt we'll ever see another centre-back like him.

## Chapter 32

# 2002/03

IN 1998, we hailed Wenger as the future of football. By 2002, he had achieved what we thought was impossible: neutrals now began to openly admire and enjoy Arsenal's football. It was at this stage that Wenger became a prophet, too.

> 'It's not impossible to go through the season unbeaten and I can't see why it's shocking to say that ... every manager thinks that but they don't say it because they're scared it would be ridiculous.'

With a mocking reference to the Iraqi military commander of the time 'Chemical Ali', Wenger became 'Comical Arsène' in the media. It was ludicrous, they said. Has he taken leave of his senses? Is it his Gallic arrogance? No, not really. It was an assessment based on evidence. Having gone the previous season unbeaten away from home, perhaps the most difficult part of the trick to pull off, he believed it to be possible – not probable, but possible.

It remained a possibility until the tenth game of the season when, sitting in top spot, we travelled to Goodison Park, went one up, were pegged back before half-time and then, in injury-time, a 16-year-old Wayne Rooney announced himself on the scene with an admittedly brilliant strike. 'Remember the name,' they said.

A slight wobble was soon steadied with a decent run, including a 3-0 victory at Highbury against Tottenham which included another of Henry's wonder goals as he carried the ball three-quarters of the length of the pitch, took it through or around eight spinning opponents, stopped, feinted, accelerated and curled the ball low into the corner of the net before running the entire length of the pitch in celebration.

Making good progress in the FA Cup, including a 2-0 fifth-round victory at United and a quarter-final replay success at Stamford Bridge, we looked at one stage in early spring a solid bet for a second successive Double: top of the table and in the cup semi-finals, where we'd play Second Division Sheffield United.

We were getting closer in the Champions League, too. After coming top in the first phase, we began our second-stage games brilliantly, winning 3-1 in Rome, but then we could only draw our next four group games, which left us with nasty trip to Valencia, where we needed a draw to advance to the knockout stages. A double from John Carew was enough to beat us 2-1 and knock us out, although it must be recorded that Henry hit the bar and, in the dying moments, Pires was booked for a dive when replays (not at the ref's disposal, obviously) showed a clear trip on the Arsenal man inside the penalty area.

A place in the cup final was secured with a 1-0 victory over Sheffield United at Old Trafford. Astonishingly, the game was David Seaman's 1,000th professional appearance and, in the 84th minute, he became the star of the show with a clawing save, falling backwards to keep out a Peschisolido header, literally as the ball hung over the goalline.

The following midweek, United came to Highbury for a showdown that seemed likely to settle who would claim the title. After we fought back to take a 2-1 lead, Giggs scored only moments later and the pendulum swung United's way, the game ending 2-2. The ramifications weren't felt immediately but when Ferguson's mate and henchman, Sam Allardyce, revved up his Bolton team to come back from two down against us a couple of weeks later, I think everyone knew that, with just three games remaining, those two dropped points would be crucial.

It was an ever-present narrative back then; the further north we travelled, the more fun it seemed to be to boot Arsenal off the pitch. I respected that teams had the right to compete and not just sit back and admire our football but, without any doubt, when we went to some places, not all, their ideas began and ended with kicking us off the park. Bolton away was usually a prime example of this but Old Trafford was probably the worst. In the end, you had to take it as a compliment but let's not forget that Abou Diaby, Eduardo and Aaron Ramsey were on the receiving end of tackles befitting of Sunday morning park football. I think we had every right to be unhappy about it and I am glad Wenger made such an issue of it; perhaps he could have said more.

When we lost 3-2 at home to Leeds a week after the Bolton game, that was it. At that stage, an odd thing happened; some commentators in the media began to say they hoped we won the FA Cup, as our football that season warranted some silverware. Our cup final opponents were Southampton, who, as things would have it, still had to visit Highbury in the league. Ten days before we were to meet at the Millennium Stadium, we warmed up for the big day by beating them 6-1 with a young debutant, Jermaine Pennant, getting a hat-trick and Pires getting the other three. A 4-0 romp at the Stadium of Light completed the league season.

Preparations for the big day were slightly derailed, with injuries to Vieira and Campbell meaning Wenger had to draft in Ukrainian right-back Oleg Luzhnyi to play alongside Keown in the middle while Parlour moved into a more central position at the side of Gilberto for the absent Vieira. With the skipper missing, Wenger bestowed one last honour on David Seaman, for whom this was to be his final appearance for the club, in asking him to lead out the team and wear the captain's armband in what was our third successive FA Cup Final.

Following a frenetic opening, when we could have been two up after eight minutes, the contest settled down. Pires got the only goal of the game shortly before half-time following a cross from Bergkamp. After a second half of chances for both sides, good goalkeeping and a goalline clearance by Ashley Cole in injury time, we managed to hang on and retain the cup.

I still think that a double Double might have more accurately reflected the quality of Arsenal's football. We were far superior to any other English team at the time. We played football you could only dream about but I think the accusation that followed us around that to win we had to play well was a fair one. A lot of it was built around Bergkamp, Pires and Henry and if, for some reason, that didn't click, then we could struggle. There wasn't really a Plan B. We won a lot but I think we should have won more; Arsenal's football excellence and superiority was just not reflected in the silverware accrued.

## Chapter 33

# 2003/04

I GREW up with the tags 'Lucky Arsenal' and 'Boring Arsenal' and, in time, largely because of Wenger, we reclaimed both and, with irony, threw them back at the rest of the football world. However, in 2004, another epithet came along, one which takes no nonsense, closes down arguments and silences dissent: It is ... 'Invincible'!

It was a special trophy for a special season, a campaign which the Premier League recognised by presenting to Arsenal a solid gold replica of the Premier League trophy. It was a season which proved sensational by any known measure of success. Yet, oddly, it was one that, even at this distance, can still leave room for a lingering regret.

As we went into the new season, David Seaman left Arsenal for Manchester City at the right moment after 13 years and his replacement, the German, Jens Lehmann, proved an inspired choice. If ever a goalkeeper was cut out to play for Arsenal, then it was the tall, rangy character from the Ruhr Valley. He was a great character, technically sound in his keeping and psychologically as tough as old boots. Whereas Seaman had been largely respected by opposition supporters, Lehmann seemed to think it a wasted afternoon if he'd not managed to wind up the opposition – players and supporters – with his antics. His calculated madness masked a calmness and cool-headed precision of thought that, in its own way, was as deadly as Dennis Bergkamp's. Although he could appear distracted and eccentric, I never had any doubts he was completely in charge of himself. He was a fabulous signing and a fascinating footballer; one well-liked by the supporters.

Wenger produced a surprise at centre-back, too, when he moved the all-action wildcard that was Kolo Toure from midfield to play alongside Sol Campbell at the back. Toure had all the credentials to be a fine centre-back: he was an athlete, physically strong yet highly mobile, brave and excellent with the ball at his feet. I think the extra focus and discipline that playing in the centre of defence demanded was the making of him.

For an extremely modest outlay, Wenger also looked to the future with the signings of Van Persie, Fàbregas, Clichy, Senderos and Djourou and, in the New Year, for considerably more money, we brought in a young man from Sevilla whose smile was as bright as his football – Jose Antonio Reyes.

Jose Antonio quickly became a fans' favourite, a very likeable young man. He lived close to one of my shops in Barnet and I saw him occasionally when he would come in with his family. A good two or three years after he had signed for us, his English was still quite limited and I don't think he ever really settled in London; a superstar with a very homely, family oriented and low-key outlook. I think his popularity may have pricked Henry's ego a little. Jose Antonio was taken to the supporters' hearts really quickly; he scored two goals against Chelsea in the FA Cup on debut, including a searing drive from 20 yards which flew like an arrow into the top corner and announced him to English football.

Before the season started, there had been a significant turn of events across London at Stamford Bridge. After a number of clubs, ourselves included, had shut the door in his face, Abramovich eventually found a seller. 'Roman Abramovich has parked his Russian tank in our front garden and is firing £50 notes at us,' was David Dein's comment. An audacious PR stunt to try to prize Henry away from Highbury was Abramovich's response. Dein's displeasure at developments at Stamford Bridge is easy to understand. Initially, he had thought a permanent move to Wembley suited the club best but Danny Fiszman was championing the Emirates project. The Wembley idea was a truly terrible one; it would have resulted in us losing our heart and soul in one fell swoop. Eventually, Dein dropped it and he fell out with Fiszman. However, with the appearance of Abramovich at Chelsea, the club, overnight, had largely lost any financial clout the move would have given us before we had even played our first match there.

Vieira and Pires both signed new contracts in the summer. Vieira was now approaching the prime of his career and Pires must have been towards the top of every leading club's wanted list. By 2003, Pires had proved himself a peerless talent, which was all the more amazing when you watched him shuffling about the pitch. Pires had all the casual insouciance of a French playboy, long hair and beardy thing, but what a massive talent he was. He was one of the last of a type of footballer you rarely see these days, with the contemporary game's emphasis on athleticism and physical build. Pires was an artist to the tips of his toes and found a receptive home at Highbury under Wenger.

That season, we looked like a team whose business was winning the title. Perhaps there is no better example of that than the game at Old Trafford. For a 0-0, it had everything. What it demonstrated was Arsenal's character and togetherness and the perception that, in Keown and Lehmann, we had two of the strongest personalities in football.

If Van Nistelrooy had hit that penalty four inches lower, there would have been no unbeaten season but, as Keown said, he got our captain sent off, so he got what was coming. The scenes after the penalty miss, where Van Nistelrooy was surrounded by Arsenal players baiting him, were highly cathartic; Keown screaming at him and smacking him round the head might not have been quite the beautiful game but it spoke volumes for what we were all about. In a season of some wonderfully aesthetic football, some genuinely beautiful stuff, the image that survives is of Keown snarling in Van Nistelrooy's face.

After being humiliated 3-0 at Highbury by Inter Milan in the first Champions League game of the season, we desperately needed something when we travelled to Italy. We returned home with a mouth-watering 5-1 victory: a success achieved without Lauren, Silva, Vieira or Bergkamp.

From then on, the season gathered pace. One game, in particular, showcased Arsenal's resolve as we moved into early spring – Chelsea away. The early kick-off was only 27 seconds old when Chelsea took the lead following a rare mistake from Vieira but the skipper soon made amends, tucking home after Bergkamp had literally carved open the Chelsea defence with one immaculately weighted curling pass with the outside of his foot which left Vieira with an opportunity he wasn't going to miss. When Edu turned home a loose ball from a corner, the turnaround was complete.

Early April saw us scheduled to play four games in an eight-day period: an FA Cup semi-final, a Champions League quarter-final second leg and two league games. For me, in selecting his team to face Manchester United at Villa Park in the FA Cup, Wenger made a really bad error of judgment. We had Chelsea just three days later in arguably a more important game but to rest Henry for a cup semi-final struck me as madness. I am convinced that if Henry played, then we would have beaten United. What bothered me was the question of momentum. Going into that week, we were cruising and I think we genuinely could have won all three that season. I think, by resting Henry, Wenger risked that momentum and gave United a chance to peg us back.

The day of the game and the occasion felt anaemic; it was overcast and the ground was not full, by any means. The early start had taken its toll of the atmosphere once again – one of the traditionally great days of the season reduced to being a mere viewing package for television. And when I learned that Aliadiere was starting in place of Henry, I thought it was a mistake – although, by then, we had learned to trust Wenger's judgment implicitly. United won by a single goal to keep their season alive; Henry came on with half an hour left but, by then, the mood of the game had been set. Why not start with him and take him off if we got ahead?

He returned for the next game, Chelsea at Highbury in the Champions League. This was starting to look like the year we might make the breakthrough in Europe's premier competition. Having drawn the first leg 1-1 at Stamford Bridge, it was advantage Arsenal and when Reyes scored a poacher's goal on the stroke of half-time, it put us in a great position.

But early in the second half, Lehmann spilled a powerful shot from distance and Lampard was on hand to hit home the rebound. It took the wind out of our sails for a while and the goal seemed to make us cautious. In truth, Chelsea's winner was coming – Cole had already made a great goal line clearance – but the timing was cruel. With only three minutes left, Bridge played a great one-two and tucked home the goal which knocked us out of a second cup in four days. Henry had a quiet game against Chelsea; Wenger's decision, I think, backfired.

It was a huge disappointment made worse when you consider the teams left in the competition. Had we survived the Chelsea tie, then we would have joined Porto, Monaco and Deportivo in the last four and we would have been on very short odds to win it. Ranieri tinkered and blew Chelsea's chance in the semi-final. Porto would go on to lift the trophy and I've sometimes wondered if we had won our first

Champions League that season whether Mourinho would ever have gone to Chelsea and become that constant thorn in the side of Wenger?

When, three days later, Liverpool came to Highbury for a Good Friday game and took a 2-1 lead into half-time, things looked bleak. We were staring down the barrel of a third straight defeat – a run of games which could have utterly destroyed our season.

A neat finish from Pires squared things up early after the restart and then came arguably Henry's most important goal of his Arsenal career. He collected the ball close to the halfway line, as was his habit when things weren't going well, dropping deeper to exert his influence. He tentatively began his approach, weighing up the field and, with sudden burst of speed, he first eliminated Hamann, leaving him floundering on his back; then, moving the ball from one foot to the other, at great speed and with hypnotic menace, he left poor Carragher spinning to the ground; the defence opened up and the unimpeded Henry strolled into the box and passed the ball into the net. The time taken from the moment he received the ball until it hit the back of the net was no longer than six or seven seconds. It was a goal of the rarest quality, matched only by the rawest of emotional outpourings as he ran around the pitch in celebration; we all knew what that goal meant and, after two horror games, we were ourselves again. Henry added a fourth for good measure but Liverpool were already beaten by that third goal; for there was no way *that* goal wasn't winning this crucial game of football.

A draw at St James' Park followed and then, back in north London, Henry scored a second successive Highbury hat-trick, bagging four in all as Leeds were routed 5-0. And with Chelsea dropping points, we moved to within touching distance of the title as we headed to White Hart Lane.

My son, Dean, was with me as we went two up, needing only a point to clinch the title. The first goal was pure Arsenal. Henry's goals could sometimes be all about him – being conceived, built and executed by him alone – but our first that afternoon at Tottenham was a collaboration of genius. Henry carried the ball out of defence, while Vieira made ground galloping forward; Henry passed the ball inside the full-back for Bergkamp to cross it first time into the path of Vieira, who passed it into the back of the net – two passes, one shot, one-nil. The second was almost as good: Bergkamp played it once more inside the hapless right-back and this time Henry passed it first time for Pires to convert. It was brilliant but no surprise; we had played like this all season.

Spurs pulled one back and then, deep in injury time, Lehmann jostled with Keane on the line as they waited for a corner and a penalty was given. That penalty was a disgrace; I believe that in every 100 incidents like this, perhaps one *might* be given. Spurs equalised but nothing was lost; the whistle blew and Arsenal were crowned champions.

I know Wenger was very annoyed about that penalty and blamed Lehmann for it – he wanted the title clinched with a victory – but we had played some wonderful stuff that afternoon, a performance befitting of champions and, White Hart Lane or not, we were going to celebrate. The Tottenham hierarchy had requested that the Arsenal players not celebrate on the pitch in the event of them title being secured. The players were told before the game and Henry said later that he reluctantly understood the request and would respect it. However, the response to Tottenham's equaliser persuaded him otherwise. Their little left-back, Mauricio Taricco, was the problem. Henry claimed that, when Keane converted the penalty, Taricco had goaded him, jumping in front of him to the extent the little Argentine gave himself cramp. Henry just smiled and said: 'Are you kidding me? You celebrate a draw?' Taricco, it seemed, had not understood that a draw still gave us the title.

At the final whistle, Henry decided to show the locals what they were missing and led the celebrations. A steward tried to stop Lauren – good luck with that! How blessed was I to *twice* see Arsenal win the title at White Hart Lane.

With the title in the bag, there were four games left to play and Wenger now honed in on what would eventually set this season apart from just any title-winning season. It all went back to when he was ridiculed for suggesting he thought it might be possible to go through an entire season unbeaten. Four games stood between us and invincibility. I've seen some great teams, some era-dominating teams, but none had played an entire season and remained undefeated since 1888/89 when Preston North End completed their 22-match season without a loss – ours amounted to 38.

The record was duly achieved on 15 May when, after an unscripted goal by ex-Arsenal man Paul Dickov for Leicester City, Henry from the penalty spot and Vieira, following yet another sublime Bergkamp pass, claimed the goals which saw us home. Arsenal had done exactly what Wenger had suggested was possible. He had never said we *would* go unbeaten, only that it was *possible*.

It had been an outstanding team effort, but Henry's return of 30 goals from 37 starts was remarkable. His efforts earned him both the PFA and Football Writers' Player of the Year awards; is there a player as good as Henry who never won the Ballon d'Or? It is sometimes wrong to single out players from team achievements but, even against such a stellar backdrop of footballers, Henry stood out. It is testament to him that he never stood still in terms of his development; for such a talent to appear to get better year on year is, perhaps, the reason why, for a season or two, he was probably the best striker in the world. There is no doubt that his being rested against United at Villa Park almost precipitated a crisis or that his goal against Liverpool a few days later refocused the team. That is what great players do; they take control, seize the moment and dictate outcomes.

Looking back, I don't think we ever got remotely enough recognition for our achievements that season. Sir Alex Ferguson, though, was fulsome in his praise and gave us credit. For me, the league title has always been the big test; while there is glamour in the Champions League, I would always put the title above everything. If sporting success is about momentum, then had we beaten United in the FA Cup semi-final, I think we would have beaten Chelsea, too, in the Champions League. If you also recognise that we lost in the League Cup semi-finals with a mainly second string XI, then something simply unbelievable was within our grasp that season – an era-defining season of complete domination. I get rather annoyed when our achievement in 2004 is compared with Preston's in 1888/89; after all, that wasn't so long after they used their coats as goalposts!

I think it's commensurate with what he gave the game in England that Wenger's achievements included something unique like the 'Invincibles' season. Without 2004, there would be no thoroughly original success. Wenger's legacy alone deserves that. The magnitude of the achievement is matched by the level of gratitude I feel towards him.

## Chapter 34

# 2004/05

MARTIN KEOWN and Ray Parlour both moved on. By 2003/04, Keown had been on a pay-as-you-play deal and, perhaps, wanted some greater security. With the wisdom of hindsight, Martin might have been worth another 12 months at Highbury. Campbell was troubled with injuries in 2004/05 and a player of Keown's experience would have helped settle a defence which looked ill at ease at times. I think there might have been ten games still in Keown that season.

Parlour was very much one of our own. A very costly divorce had made a move something of a necessity and the deal Middlesbrough offered him was really too good to turn down. He had lost none of his drive, his pugnacious battling spirit or his cheeky grin over the years and he had blossomed, morphing from an ultra-George Graham midfielder into a footballer of genuine technical ability under Wenger. I was pleased he had his moment in the 2002 FA Cup Final, his 'it's only Ray Parlour' moment when he burst through and scored a terrific goal to cap a man-of-the-match performance. Surrounded by the talents of Bergkamp, Henry, Pires and Vieira, Parlour never looked out of place; a smashing character to have in your dressing room and a top player. I was sorry to see him leave; he was the type of player who often didn't stand out but he always gave an eight out of ten performance and, like Rocastle and Merson before him, when he left, a bit of Arsenal went with him.

Sylvain Wiltord left, too, moving back to France to join Lyon on a free transfer. Wiltord was a difficult player to categorise. In 2008, he was voted the 33rd greatest player in the club's history, which was most likely due more to the tyranny of short-term memory than any actual contribution meriting such a place in our history. Wiltord scored the goal to clinch the title and the Double in 2002 and was always around and seemingly involved but was he really one of the first names on the teamsheet? Perhaps he was always more of a nuts and bolts type player and I might be being unfair. When he signed, I think we were all so confident about Wenger's judgment that we could have signed Sacha Distel and we'd have been licking our lips.

Two summer signings looked to the future: Robin van Persie and Cesc Fàbregas. From the moment he arrived as a young kid, Fàbregas had everyone talking and not just about how good he would be but how good he already was. At 16, he looked ready for the first team and made his debut aged just 16 years and 177 days. Even at that age, he demanded the ball from more senior team-mates and demonstrated a range of passing and a temperament far in excess of what was expected at his age; over the years, he would stand out as supremely committed, a 110 per cent man, a model of consistency and a player who, at times, seemed to be pulling the team along on his own.

Robin van Persie arrived in north London a couple years older than the Spaniard, with a reputation for being somewhat truculent and with a spikiness that, in time as he settled at Highbury, he would learn to channel into his football. He played on the edge, physically and temperamentally, but in doing so he became one of the most effective strikers in world football – another Wenger conversion from the wing to the centre, too.

The portents were good at the start of the season: league champions and with a strong tailwind in the form of a 40-game unbeaten run. Perhaps, though, there comes a time when a long unbeaten sequence can become something of a hindrance. By the start of the new season, our run was something we were very proud of, something very much to defend and keep going.

Nottingham Forest's 42-match unbeaten run was the record to beat and it so nearly didn't happen. After opening the season with a comprehensive 4-1 win at Everton, we faced Middlesbrough at home, able to equal Forest's record. Yet, only moments into the second half, we found ourselves 3-1 down. A horrible opening to the half had seen Cygan make a hash of a routine through ball for one goal and then Lehmann was yards out of position expecting a cross when a disguised shot from distance sailed into an unguarded net. But we then proceeded to blow away Middlesbrough with an unstoppable four-goal riposte. For 20-odd minutes, Reyes, Bergkamp, Fàbregas, Pires and Henry played football that was almost telepathic and of such high quality that it felt like even the artistry of the 'Invincibles' had been momentarily surpassed.

Despite the fact there remained a creative irresistibility about Arsenal's football, there was no escaping, either, that a certain frailty had crept into our defensive play. Perhaps the loss of Campbell through injury could more effectively have been met by the now departed Keown rather than either Cygan or a young Senderos? Toure fought on valiantly but I felt he needed that purely defensive presence of a rock like Campbell or Keown alongside him. That aspect of our football was becoming increasingly problematic and one game, in particular, illustrated the difference between our effectiveness with and without the ball.

That game was the north London derby at White Hart Lane in mid-November. The occasion produced a nine-goal thriller which simultaneously showcased Arsenal's potency and irresolution. The 5-4 victory was an endless procession of attack v. defence. Arsenal prevailed but the victory brought with it as much misgiving as it did celebration. As we left the ground, I voiced the opinion that we would not be capable of winning the title that season with that defence and the view found little opposition amongst the other Arsenal supporters I was with. I think Mourinho said (for what it matters) that he could not view such an outcome as a victory and that Arsenal's defending had turned it into more of a symbolic defeat. While the chance to wind up Wenger may have been at the bottom of Mourinho's observation, there was, contained within his words, an uncomfortable truth.

Over the next couple of seasons, Campbell, Cole and Vieira were all allowed to walk out of the door with relatively little attempt to retain them. Had Wenger's indifference to defensive muscle now become an obstinately worn badge of honour? Was the failure to replace Keown with a like-for-like signing an oversight or illustrative of Wenger's stylistic shift to out-and-out ball-playing centre-backs above resolute defenders? Is that a small insignificant detail or where the pursuit of 'the beautiful game' became an almost obsessive absolute at the cost of all other considerations?

In a way, our football under Wenger, for all its mystery and glamour, had at its base a simplicity which was beguiling. The 4-4-2 formation, with a defensive unit who primarily knew how to defend and a protective and athletic pairing in front of them, allowed the others to choreograph freestyle. Trusting to instinct, we often made it up as we went along but the talented virtuosity of those artists meant that something outstanding often emerged from the freedom of expression Wenger allowed them. In many ways, the model was broken when Fàbregas burst on to the scene – a truly world-class footballer who could dictate for 90 minutes – and Wenger radically changed his approach to build a team around him; the price was that the 'nuts and bolts' became 'feathers and flowers'.

As we headed up to Old Trafford for the yearly 'title summit', our unbeaten run stood at 49. United would be a massive test and, as it happened, an even bigger one than we anticipated, given the exceptionally brutal approach from United and the refereeing of Mike Riley. Wenger, his players and the Arsenal supporters were left fuming by the experienced Riley's performance in a highly-charged atmosphere in which huge pressure was applied by the home crowd, the United players and the Old Trafford staff. He awarded a penalty even though Campbell failed to get within a foot of Rooney before the United man threw himself to the floor. Let's be clear, Riley didn't give a penalty believing it to be the wrong decision but he and his linesman got that horribly wrong. That said, we all make mistakes, but Arsenal hotly disputed a number of decisions and Wenger claimed after the game: 'Riley decided the game, like we know he can do at Old Trafford.'

The list of Arsenal complaints was long. Reyes was the most harshly treated; scythed and assaulted all over the park on an ongoing basis by the Neville brothers. United captain Gary Neville later admitted that he and his brother Phil's actions were premeditated and, although Riley did eventually book them both, they were fortunate to even see half-time.

Ferdinand hauled down Ljungberg with Arsenal's man clean through on goal but there was not even a booking, let alone a straight red.

Van Nistelrooy 'bravely' picked on Arsenal's smallest player, Ashley Cole, with a foul worthy of another straight red but which received no sanction from Riley – although the FA later charged the United man and gave him a three-match ban.

The physicality of United, perhaps, has to be seen in the context of the immediate history of the two clubs and the matches between them; as galling as their anti-football approach was, it remains the award of the penalty that, after all these years, still sticks in my craw.

The fouling and the premeditated assaults merely added weight to the central theme of injustice; it is the penalty which changes the course of the game. It was the equivalent of the fairground bare knuckle fighter getting lucky with a low punch against an elite boxer. The game was – and still is – a stain on the Premier League.

If the match was fractious, then what followed immediately after the sides disappeared from view has become notorious: variously described as 'the Battle of the Buffet' and 'Pizzagate'. New contracts for Parlour and Keown might easily have been justified for this moment alone. Both sides got stuck in. All that is known for certain is that Fàbregas, a latecomer to United-Arsenal escapades and eager to make up for lost time, lobbed a slice of pizza which may or may not have been deliberately thrown at United's manager, Alex Ferguson. It means the aftermath of the game is now forever captured in something approaching comedy.

The Arsenal AGM followed not long after the game and, in asking a question about how the club proposed to respond to the persistent sight of Arsenal being kicked off the pitch, I referred to United as 'having once again brutalised us'. Wenger, I noticed, gave my comments and question an ostentatious and deliberate round of applause. The following morning, the back page headline in the *Daily Express* was along the lines of 'Arsenal Accuse United of Brutal Treatment' and the article referred to me by name.

For me, the United game remains the best and most compelling argument for VAR that has ever existed. With VAR that day, Arsenal win by a couple of goals against eight men. Indeed, I'd go further. Had we had VAR under Wenger, then I think it perfectly reasonable to claim we would have won at least a couple more titles than we did. I was sick of the way certain teams acted when we visited; it is not going too far to say that some of the tackles we suffered during that era contributed to ending players' careers. It was, typically, the result of provincial small-mindedness which, perhaps, has always been directed towards us throughout our history. When it came to brutality against us at Old Trafford, though, United were on a different level most seasons.

The defeat at Old Trafford ultimately became more of distraction than it ought to have been. For a while we played in the shadow of that run-ending defeat and once more I was reminded of the notion that to win, Arsenal had to feel confident. Wenger, too, may not have been the best man to settle the ship in choppy waters. He was so overwhelmingly undone by defeat that I can't help but believe his response to losing big matches might at times have not helped the players move on. Given the dismissive and disrespectful response to his suggestion that Arsenal might one day go through the season unbeaten, I think the unbeaten run meant a lot to him. It preceded him into press conferences and, for a while, dressed him in an aura of untouchability – never again would anyone laugh or sneer at Arsène Wenger – but I suspect he reacted especially badly to the unbeaten run ending and United's antics just made it that much worse.

We stumbled from dropped points to dropped points and then, a few weeks later, just before Christmas, Wenger responded to another defeat, this time at Liverpool, by dropping Lehmann. The big German had become inconsistent and it was common knowledge he could be a thorn in the side of his managers and coaches.

We kept notionally in touch with the title race but never really looked capable of stringing together the kind of run which gets you to the top. Arsenal had never managed to defend their title under Wenger, so it was not wholly unexpected. Although it is the sort of thing 'big' teams should cope with, I think the 'Invincible' tag weighed us down slightly; certainly, the loss of the unbeaten record struck hard at the core of our confidence and self-belief for far longer than it ought to have.

The season ended in happier circumstances, lifting the FA Cup without Thierry Henry after beating United. We were outplayed but somehow took the game to penalties and ended up winning it. Vieira took the winning penalty, a moment full of symbolism and symmetry, given it was the skipper's last act in an Arsenal shirt. After what felt like a long-running series of 'will he or won't he?', he finally called time on his Arsenal career. Vieira had given the best years of his football life to us and his contribution is impossible to quantify. He was a winner in a dressing room full of winners, a man born to lead in the pursuit of honours. He was Wenger's first signing and his departure gave credence to the idea that another, different kind of Arsenal must now be built.

Arriving back at the coach after what had been a poor game, I couldn't believe what I found there – it was like a morgue. I said to everyone: 'Remember how you felt after Liverpool robbed us a few years ago? We have won the FA Cup against our bitterest of rivals and, for me, that is just great.' If you hadn't enjoyed the game, I thought, then you must have enjoyed Ferguson's face when the winning penalty hit the net? I loved it; it was the cup and it was brilliant to ram it down United's throat – the injustice of our success from their perspective that day merely enhanced it in my eyes. We did it without Campbell and Henry, too, and, given the shenanigans at Old Trafford, there was some consoling justice to be had in ensuring they finished the season empty-handed.

The next season was to be an important year; the final season of football at Highbury and one which would suggest what direction the club under Wenger was going to head in. Was it towards a land of plenty or a frustrating cul-de-sac where we would become a mere caricature of ourselves, condemned endlessly to repeat the same mistakes over and over again?

Chapter 35

# 2005/06

THE 2005/06 season was not only the last hurrah for Highbury, it was, in many ways, the last hurrah for Wenger, too. Hereafter, his project shifted inexorably towards the management of debts incurred through the move to the Emirates and, thus, Champions League qualification became the golden chalice. Paris in the springtime of 2006 can now be seen almost as Wenger's last stand, his final serious opportunity to add to his legacy of greatness, with the bauble he probably craved most of all.

There would be future skirmishes for the title, for sure, and runs to the latter stages of the Champions League but none of those efforts would have the same conviction of Wenger's early period; even while we hoped, deep down we knew. As we moved swiftly into the 'Fàbregas era' in a new ground, I think for a while we searched for something overlooked amidst the now hollowed-out emptiness of Highbury, something left behind – and, in truth, I don't think we ever found it in the years following the move.

It wasn't just the transition from the Edwardian splendour of Highbury to the modernistic Emirates; the team, too, was changing, not only its personnel but also its personality. The big skipper, in many ways the icon of Wenger's formative seasons, Patrick Vieira, finally cut the apron strings and moved back to Italy to join Juventus. The man in whom Wenger's whole ideology found its most authentic expression, Dennis Bergkamp, was embarking upon his final season; Robert Pires, Lauren and Campbell would also join the exodus as 2006 proved to be an ending for so much more than just that wonderful old ground.

The pre-season had been carried out in an air of unrest, as both Jose Antonio Reyes and Ashley Cole had come under scrutiny following ill-judged episodes. Reyes had fallen victim, in early 2005, to a hoax call live on Spanish radio from a person claiming to be Real Madrid's sporting director, Emilio Butragueño. During the call, Reyes had claimed to be delighted that Real Madrid were interested in him and that 'God willing, it can happen'. Reyes went on to claim he had not settled in London and, although this may have been an issue born of the translation process, Reyes was accused of adding that there were 'bad people at Arsenal'. To his credit, Reyes distanced himself immediately from the claims and publicly confirmed his commitment to Arsenal. I don't think there is any doubt that Reyes was unhappy in London. Jose was a proper Andalusian boy, very close to his family and roots. He was never able to learn English and away from football, I think he found the life here very alien.

Ashley Cole was reprimanded by Arsenal for having conducted unauthorised talks with Chelsea in which he allegedly discussed a potential move to Stamford Bridge. These talks took place around the same time as Reyes's radio embarrassment, which probably exacerbated Arsenal's not unreasonable pique at both stories. Cole would sign a one-year extension to his contract and claim to be happy at Arsenal. I thought that was only ever a postponement of the inevitable, though. He was injured for most of his final season, although he did regain fitness and claim a starting place in Paris. For both players, this would be their final season with the club.

To mark the final season at Highbury, the club took the decision to play in a kit based on the strip we wore in our first campaign there in 1913. I understood the rationale for the blackcurrant strip but I can't say I was ever a fan of it. As in the late 1960s, when we dropped the white sleeves, I wasn't happy. Arsenal's shirt is known the world over; it is a thing of beauty and I have never liked any of the pillars of the club's identity being messed with – and for basically financial reasons, too. We could have worn it for the final game against Wigan but not for the whole season. The club badge had changed, we were leaving Highbury and now they had us in a different kit.

Vieira's departure was a massive vote of confidence in young Fàbregas. For seasons, thereafter, Wenger would build a team around Fàbregas and, in so doing, perhaps unwittingly strike at the very cause of Arsenal's initial success under him. The emergence of Fàbregas created a new mould for the type of footballer Wenger would now pursue; namely physically small, highly technical and mobile players. Go back just six years and standing next to the Arsenal team in the tunnel before the game would have been intimidating: Adams, Keown, Vieira, Petit and Bergkamp, all big guys creating a solid spine to the team. Now, it was all about fluidity of movement, technical skill and a low centre of gravity.

The season began in inconsistent style and before too long we were well adrift in the title race – indeed all but out of it by the time Manchester City came to Highbury in late October. The game against City was won 1-0 but not without controversy. Pires converted a penalty to put us one up and when we were awarded another spot kick, he and Henry decided to be clever. As Pires ran up, he planned to tap the ball sideways for Henry to run on to but he got too slight a touch on the ball and it merely wobbled on the spot and the moment was lost. I can remember Wenger was apoplectic on the sidelines; most supporters had their heads in their hands and Danny Mills, as ever, had a lot to say for himself. It was an idiotic thing for Pires and Henry to do, not least to try it at 1-0.

Our form up to Christmas was poor and largely accounts for why we eventually finished a full 24 points behind eventual champions Chelsea. However, we did make a sound start to another Champions League adventure, going unbeaten through our group, only dropping two points.

The side was unsettled, though; Lauren, Cole and Campbell all picked up long-term injuries and the merry-go-round at the back was compounded by Wenger's policy of selecting Lehmann in goal for league games and Almunia for the cup games, including the Champions League.

Heading into the New Year, I don't think any of us expected the team to suddenly start setting defensive records. I think we had all become so totally reconciled to the view that defensive solidity was now viewed as a thing of the past. But then, for 919 continuous minutes in the Champions League, Arsenal's defence suddenly went all George Graham and didn't concede a goal between 27 September and the 76th minute of the final on 17 May – ten successive clean sheets made all the more outstanding as this was achieved with a reserve right-back, a makeshift left-back and a young, inexperienced centre-back. Eboue, Flamini and Senderos all contributed to a record that will surely stand for a long time.

The record remains a testament chiefly to them but also to Martin Keown. Our old battle horse was at Highbury studying for his coaching badges and worked with the new-look defensive unit. Indeed, our old boss, Terry Neill, went as far as to say that Arsenal's new-found resilience was down to Keown's efforts and input alone. It isn't recorded how appreciative Wenger might have been but one anecdote suggests not that much. Martin had videoed one of the players, who he believed kept making a slight positional error, and this error, left unchecked, was going to prove costly. Martin asked the manager if he could go through a video of it with the particular player but Wenger refused, saying he didn't want to adversely affect the confidence of the player in question. I suspect even at that stage there was a reluctance on Wenger's part to formally acknowledge and share any credit.

Our progress in Europe was steady, while in the Premier League we huffed and puffed rather. Before heading to the Bernabéu for the first knockout round, we had one of those domestic sequences of results which summed up our season. A defeat to Everton was followed by elimination from both the League and FA cups and then a midweek home defeat to West Ham.

The last of those matches, the defeat to West Ham, also saw Campbell withdraw himself from the game at half-time, shower and immediately leave the ground. We were 2-1 down at half-time and Sol had been culpable for both goals against us. He has spoken about how walking off the pitch at the break he noticed a figure in the crowd staring at him, his fist shaped into the shape of a gun and pointing at him; this person pulled an imaginary trigger, made the sound of a gunshot and laughed. Campbell walked straight through the dressing room into the treatment room seeking refuge – but from what? Perhaps he didn't and wouldn't ever truly know but he did know he couldn't continue.

Sol has opened up on the unrelenting abuse he still receives for his move across north London, which made him such a very public pawn in other people's tribal battles. There is an uncomfortable honesty about Sol, which means things can rarely be left unsaid or actions left untaken. The courage and single-minded manner with which he negotiated that short, yet poisonous journey from Tottenham to Arsenal speak of an intensity which, at times, is in danger of turning in on itself. There is, in all of us, a strength which can also be our weakness. That he had some issues to sort out in his private life is documented and we all have a breaking point; and rich, young, physically healthy elite sportsmen and women are no different. Sol would take a sabbatical away from the game but returned to training inside a couple of weeks. On his return to the fold, he would sit out the next couple of months and I think that once he felt mentally ready to return, he was then further aggravated by Wenger's reluctance to play him. However, along with the injured Ashley Cole, he would return in time for the final in Paris.

So, in late February, I travelled to Spain for the first leg in Madrid, more in hope than expectation; we had picked up four points from a possible 15 going into the contest. I am usually a beacon of unrealistic optimism for almost any game Arsenal play but I was fairly sure we would struggle against Real. Remember this was a side containing genuine 'galácticos': Zidane, Ramos, Ronaldo and Roberto Carlos, with a supporting cast led by David Beckham. In the first half, we had the marginally clearer-cut chances – one run and shot from Reyes was particularly uncomfortable for Casillas – and Lehmann was having one of his calmer evenings, no dramatics. Then, early in the second half, Henry conjured up one of those sequences that only he can; running from deep diagonally, he beat players, fooled players and simply surged beyond them until, at the corner of the box, he shot from a less-than-propitious position beyond Casillas and into the corner – a truly world-class goal.

Real's response was tetchy and indignant: players began to dive and Ramos was lucky a frustrated swipe with his fist on Eboue, after the Arsenal man had chased the Spaniard down and dispossessed him, was missed by the ref. Arsenal continued to prosper going forward, with Henry and Ljungberg running in behind Real's ever more anxious and stretched rearguard. In the end, Real were reduced to simply demanding free kicks and histrionically waving their arms around. A final flurry resulted in nothing more than spurious claims for penalties. The roars from the travelling Arsenal contingent at the final whistle rose into the night sky, while a visceral atmosphere of defeat amongst the Spanish was telling and authentic. They had been well beaten; the bull had fought back and slain the matador.

I stayed on in Madrid after the game and had a wonderful time visiting the club museum and getting on to the Bernabéu pitch. When we returned to London, we duly lost our next league game and, in early March, Real arrived for the second leg.

It was a very tense game, with Madrid playing with absolutely no suggestion of having the handbrake on. The first half could be characterised by last-ditch defending on both sides. It was an open game, played at pace. The best chance came our way before half-time when Reyes hit the bar. The second half became ever more end-to-end and Raul, the Spaniards' poster boy, was unlucky to see his shot rebound off the post. Arsenal held on and a famous victory against European footballing royalty felt like a nice way to mark the final season at Highbury.

Juventus, with Vieira in their midfield, might have provided more stoical opposition in the quarter-finals but the pretender to Vieira's throne, Fàbregas, checked, held and pushed his illustrious opponent back. Poor Vieira wasn't given a moment's respite. In fact, it was Vieira who was caught in possession in the move which led to our first goal by Fàbregas.

In the second half, Fàbregas set up Henry to give us a commanding two-goal lead to defend in the second leg in Turin, which was duly accomplished as we played out a goalless draw.

After seeing off Madrid and Juventus, I think we fancied our chances against the less glamorous Villarreal in the semi-final. The first leg was a hard-fought contest of few clearcut chances and we nicked it with a fairly un-Arsenal-type goal, Toure getting in at the near post to force it over the line. The second leg saved its drama until the final moments when Villarreal were awarded a penalty, giving them the chance to take the game into extra-time. But the Argentine playmaker Riquelme rather tamely and weakly placed it too close to Lehmann, who chose the right way to go, and that was that. It was Arsenal in Paris for the final which I think every neutral wanted: Arsenal v Barcelona. A battle of style and substance worthy of the competition.

Before the Champions League Final in Paris, we had one final emotional journey to make to Highbury when, after full-time, we would leave her for the last time. I, and so many tens of thousands of others, had grown up standing and sitting in that beautiful old ground, where generations of the same family made the same pilgrimage along the same roads and pavements to and from it, come rain or shine, on a Saturday afternoon. Every brick and shadowed corner of it could tell a story; it is where people lived out their lives and dreamed their dreams.

The afternoon could easily have become a funeral as we said goodbye. But when Henry scored a fitting hat-trick to win the game 4-2 and, with the news filtering through at full-time of 'lasagnagate' when West Ham had done us a favour by beating Tottenham (Arsenal had to get a better result on the day than Tottenham to clinch the final Champions League spot) there was, in truth, more an air of celebration than sombre goodbye.

That Edwardian solidity and easy-going affluence had served us well but the future was chrome and modernity and the Emirates stands as a magnificent edifice and testament to a different world to the one Highbury had been born into. I was aware that we had outgrown Highbury and the move was necessary in order to accommodate the thousands of supporters who couldn't ever get to a match. So, while it was a loss, it was exactly the right thing to do and I have grown to love the Emirates.

After the game, I headed over to the West Stand, as the club had invited everyone to help themselves to whatever keepsakes they wanted. So, always having had a fondness for the big rugs with the cannons woven into them, I duly rolled one up and, looking like a carpet fitter, walked off with it over my shoulder!

So, off to Paris for the final with Barca, a side packed with artistry and the talent of Ronaldinho, Eto'o, Iniesta and Deco, the fight and power of Van Bommel and a player we had tried hard to sign, the Brazilian centre-back Edmilson, plus the familiar face of Arsenal old boy Van Bronckhorst. A young Lionel Messi, at 19 years of age, missed out on the final through injury. For us, Campbell and Cole came back, with the plucky Flamini and Senderos making way. Pires got a start, too, after being something of a bit-part player that season.

This was to be Bergkamp's final game for us and of his career. Dennis had been on one-year contracts for a few seasons now and before he signed each new extension, there was talk of him calling it a day. The archetypal professional, he knew his physical abilities were at some stage going to fail to keep pace with his technical and intellectual attributes. He was playing fewer games by 2006 and calling it a day, sadly, felt right. If ever there was a stage for a player of Bergkamp's brilliance to complete his cycle of creativity in, then a Champions League Final was surely that setting.

The story of Paris is the eternal story of football – 'if only'. We played from the 18th minute with ten men after Lehmann had been sent off after the keeper brought down Eto'o and we had bravely defended the one-goal lead given us by Campbell's crashing 37th-minute header. We played with a spirit you could only be proud of;

there could be no recriminations. I think most neutrals would even agree that we bossed much of the game and, despite being a man short, could have been two or three up by the stage we tired. Both sides had chances but the better ones generally fell to us. By the 70th minute, we were out on our feet; Barca's remorseless passing and movement just wore us down.

I immediately felt Henry's miss would cost us the game – a one-on-one with the keeper which could have settled the game. Barca were, inevitably, going to get on top of our ten men and a two-goal cushion would have given us something really substantial to defend.

Their equaliser was the killer and once that went in, the second goal felt inevitable. It was as brutal a few minutes as I have ever experienced following Arsenal. I think it has since been shown that the winning goal should have been disallowed for offside, too – come in VAR!

I have always held that the domestic league title is the ultimate target each season, superior even to the Champions League. But we needed that European scalp more than ever that night. Ours is a footballing CV missing the ultimate arbiter of distinction – one little Champions League star above the badge. Paris remains our only appearance in the final of the pre-eminent club tournament. Winning would have been the perfect way to bring down the curtain on the Highbury era; instead, defeat in Paris left a feeling of incompleteness. We were embarking on a new future and winning the Champions League would have signed off history and allowed it to rest in peace with no misgivings or regrets.

## Chapter 36

# 2006–2009

### *2006/07*

That tangible sense of loss at leaving Highbury had been compounded by the defeat in Paris but this negativity, I hoped, would be balanced out by the move to the Emirates. Although Ashburton Grove represented hope and the future, the story for the next few seasons was largely to become tediously familiar: one of hope unfulfilled.

During those early years at the Emirates, it began to feel that, even if the quality of the football remained high, with every passing season there was less and less hope of us achieving anything of consequence.

The mood around the club wasn't helped by there being a number of diverse ambitions. On the one hand, the supporters wanted to see us winning trophies and if that meant spending, then so be it; that, after all, was the whole point of the move to the Emirates. But, for the board, the objective was Champions League qualification and, if possible, the knockout stages; that was their bottom line – their trophy – to enable the repayment of debts. It was this clear difference which lay at the heart of the decade-long disconnect between those in the boardroom and those in the stands. In 2006, that battleground was beginning to open up.

We haemorrhaged established players, too. Half a team would depart in the summer of 2006, adding to the previous year-on-year loss of players like Adams, Seaman, Keown and Vieira. Now, Bergkamp, Lauren, Pires, Campbell, Reyes and, a few games into the season, Ashley Cole would all leave.

Of these moves, I think Cole was the hardest to take and it was also the most tellingly illustrative of the new order taking shape in English football. Cole had a career ahead of him. He had grown up an Arsenal supporter and we were all he had ever known but he was friendly with a number of the England players at Chelsea and I think they turned his head. Cole was the best left-back I'd ever seen representing Arsenal, absolutely world-class. I might be going out on a limb here, and I know he is widely held to be a greedy so and so who was 'left trembling with anger' at only being offered £55k a week, but I genuinely think that, along with his desire for a better contract, his ambition took over: the prospect of linking up with his England team-mates, Terry and Lampard, and joining a club who were becoming serial winners contrasted favourably with Arsenal, who were starting to regress. Cole would get his wish but for us to only get £5m cash for him plus a makeweight who was 29 was poor business to say the least – as if the loss of Cole wasn't bad enough, we also struck an incredibly bad deal.

One high point of the season was beating Tottenham in the League Cup semi-finals. After coming back from two down in the first leg at White Hart Lane to draw 2-2, a compelling second leg at the Emirates saw us triumph 3-1, with Adebayor finishing a ravishing move for the first before Aliadiere showed all too briefly the predatory instinct of the finisher we all hoped he might have become to hit the second in extra-time. Rosicky got the third to conclude a first memorable cup night at our new home.

For the final, in Cardiff, Wenger decided to continue with his policy of giving youth an opportunity. So, whereas Chelsea were at full strength (Terry, Makelele, Lampard, Ballack, Essien, Shevchenko and Drogba all played), Arsenal started, for a variety of reasons, without Henry, Gilberto, Eboue, Clichy, Flamini, Gallas, Adebayor, Hleb, Van Persie and Rosicky.

Arsenal flew out of the traps, though, and it was no surprise when 17-year-old Theo Walcott was put through by a perfectly weighted pass from Diaby and curled the opening goal around Cech in Henryesque style. We looked really lively, full of ideas and running, and well worth the lead.

Chelsea began to get a foothold in the game, while an intriguing battle between Senderos and Drogba emerged. Arsenal's young Swiss defender could never be faulted for his attitude and spirit but, as the game progressed, Drogba began to get on top of him. Senderos gamely stuck at it but after Drogba had levelled with a first-half strike, late in the second half he beat the battered Senderos to the ball and glanced a winning header beyond Almunia.

There was still time for three red cards and a bit of a melee, which saw both Wenger and Mourinho on the pitch, thus establishing a pattern for subsequent encounters between the two clubs over the ensuing years.

Then, in April 2007, a bombshell: David Dein was forced off the board and out of the club. 'Irreconcilable differences' between Dein and the rest of the board, chiefly over the attractiveness of American investment, lay at the bottom of this very brutal falling-out. Once Abramovich had set up shop across London, Dein was quite clear in recognising that we needed the same level of investment in order to compete; the move to the Emirates alone was not going to be enough for us to keep up and without investment, the whole move to the Emirates appeared much less advantageous.

There was a danger concerning Wenger, too, as a result of Dein's exit. The manager only had one year remaining on his contract and Dein was the Frenchman's chief reason for coming to Arsenal; he was Wenger's main ally in the boardroom and the man who got Wenger's transfer business done. It is not especially original to say it but Wenger and Dein were two sides of a very special coin; they both saw and embraced the future of football, the one on the pitch and the other off it, and shaped it to Arsenal's benefit. Dein was a major force for good at Arsenal.

There were certainly tensions between Dein and the more conservative members of the board but also, in time, between Dein and Danny Fiszman, too. Initially, Dein and Fiszman had been allies. They were the twin modernisers on the board. But once the need for the club to move from Highbury had been established, Fiszman very strongly opposed Dein's suggestion that the club should consider moving to Wembley permanently and this may have been the catalyst for a cooling between the two of them. Fiszman, a private man, was very well trusted and liked by everyone who knew him. I suspect that, over time, Dein, unlike the more boardroom savvy Fiszman, may have been just too challenging. It is a shame that Dein and Fiszman fell out, though: two friends who did so much to further the cause of Arsenal in the modern age.

The greatest irony of Dein's departure was that it was over American money buying into Arsenal. Hill-Wood, in airing his own views on the subject, famously left no room for doubt. The chairman indicated that a rift between Dein and the board had been growing for some time, with Hill-Wood and his colleagues believing that Dein was much closer to Kroenke than he was admitting.

> 'Call me old-fashioned but we don't need Kroenke's money and we don't want his sort. Our objective is to keep Arsenal English ... I don't know for certain if Kroenke will mount a hostile takeover for our club but we shall resist it with all our might.
>
> 'We are all being seduced that the Americans will ride into town with pots of cash for new players. It simply isn't the case. They only see an opportunity to make money. They know absolutely nothing about our football and we don't want these types involved.'

Dein had apparently approached Kroenke directly without first informing the board, which gave them their opportunity to oust him. There lingers, though, a charge of hypocrisy which can be levelled at the board, too. Given their robust opposition to Kroenke, they did eventually sell out to him.

I think Dein was correct in his assessment of what was needed financially but wrong in the way he went about trying to achieve it. There had been gently simmering tensions between Dein and the board for some time and Kroenke simply brought it to the boil.

Wenger apparently offered his resignation, which the board swiftly declined. Rather than weakening Wenger, I think the departure of Dein actually strengthened his position and gave him considerably more power and authority as a result; and to know his offer to leave had been quickly refused did him no harm at all.

Dein had been the link between Wenger and the rest of the board. He was the only board member who actually worked at the club every day, the football man amongst bankers and landed gentry. In Dein's absence, Fiszman became the moderniser-in-chief. It had largely been Fiszman who had driven through the move to the Emirates, something for which I don't think he has ever received quite the plaudits he deserves.

In the midst of all this, Thierry Henry, after a disappointing final injury-hit season, called time on his Arsenal career, citing the departure of Dein and concerns over Wenger's future as his reasons for leaving. I believe what Henry has always said about his being an Arsenal supporter and that the turbulence in the boardroom and uncertainty around Wenger played on his mind but I suspect he recognised, also, that he just needed a change. Barcelona was a dream destination and, deep down, no one could really begrudge him that; he owed us nothing.

Henry was very close to David Dein; indeed, Thierry's agent was Dein's son, Darren Dein. I had always thought it inappropriate for Dein's son to represent a player that Dein himself might have to negotiate with over a contract. At the very least, the situation must have been seen as potentially risking a very real conflict of interests. In my opinion, the rest of the board should have stamped down on it hard from the moment Darren got involved with the players and Dein should have been clearly told that it was inappropriate for him to remain a director if his son was going to represent our players. Darren learnt his trade working for Jerome Anderson and eventually went on to represent a number of our players. Ultimately, it remains another illustration, in my opinion, of how weak the board could be at times and how they lacked a real intuitive understanding of certain situations.

Arriving at that year's AGM, shareholders were invited to pen a tribute to Wenger in a presentation book to mark the tenth anniversary of his appointment as our manager. I remember my own contribution clearly: 'Thank you Arsène – you have made all my dreams come true.' I had always wanted Arsenal to win things and to do so playing a style of football that everyone else admired; under Wenger, that was exactly what had happened.

## *2007/08*

The 2007/08 season saw William Gallas appointed club captain and for a while that season, we flirted with a title challenge. For a time, in fact, it looked as if it was ours to lose. The season, though, hinged on 90 minutes in the West Midlands in early spring.

After just three minutes of the game at Birmingham, our popular centre-forward Eduardo received a sickening leg break from a tackle by Martin Taylor, for which he received a red card. It really shook the players, especially Fàbregas, who looked bereft. That heartbreak was compounded by a mistake by Clichy in injury time, leading to a penalty from which the Blues rescued a point.

Worse was to come: upon the final whistle, Gallas stayed sitting on the pitch long after his team-mates had departed and refused to budge. I think he badly let down his club, his manager, his team-mates and especially young Clichy that day. The only possible mitigation is that he was so disappointed that he simply took leave of his senses but, given *all* the events on that tumultuous day, I think that is very weak. I am convinced an Adams or a McLintock would have handled it – and themselves – very differently.

Wenger could be a ditherer in the face of confrontation and that it took him until the following November for Gallas to be relieved of the captaincy can't be easily overlooked or forgiven. I'd never felt that Gallas looked captain material.

## 2008/09

It was another year of occasionally scintillating football, with semi-final appearances in the Champions League and the FA Cup. I think we punched according to our weight that season. It did still feel as if we were marking time, though, and while Wenger was successfully picking up some little gems – Nasri and Arshavin spring to mind – there was no great feeling that we were building a team for the future.

Two eight-goal thrillers, a 4-4 draw at home to Tottenham and a 4-4 draw at Liverpool, succinctly captured the team's character: chaotic and spontaneous mayhem. It could feel like 11 footballers *ad libbing*; park football played by elite technicians. For me, it flattered to deceive; it was always a flimsy embellishment, which hid an uncomfortable truth at its core. The draw with Spurs had seen us outplay them; we were 4-2 up with only minutes left and it remains a game I just can't get out of my head.

In the background, disconnect between many supporters and the club was growing noisier and a hostile atmosphere was developing in the crowd – unthinkable two or three years earlier. At that stage, my voice was most assuredly with the pro-Wenger camp.

It still felt as if he hadn't quite nailed his legacy. I still felt he had one more team in him, one more Premier League title and a Champions League, too, and I clung to that narrative for as long as I could.

## Chapter 37

# 2009–2012

### *2009/10*

One of Wenger's guiding principles was that, as a coach, he must be a facilitator and supporter of youth and, indeed, under his leadership, the name of Arsenal had become respected across the globe for its commitment to youth. In 2009, he had a host of talented youngsters coming through, especially in midfield: Diaby, who was for a time flourishing in a rare injury-free spell, Aaron Ramsey, Song and a precocious homegrown talent – Jack Wilshere. With Fàbregas playing like a veteran, though still only 21, the future looked bright and safe in the hands of these youngsters.

One of the practical implications of Wenger's commitment to youth was his desire to make sure older players didn't stand in the way of up-and-coming talents, blocking their development, and it was just such a commitment which, for me, stands as the only plausible explanation for possibly the worst transfer blunder in his whole time at Arsenal.

Xabi Alonso, Liverpool's Basque midfield general, was so keen to partner Cesc Fàbregas at Arsenal that he just told everyone: 'Get the deal done – I am going to Arsenal.' Fàbregas had been a go-between and put a lot of effort into securing Alonso's signing. The deal wasn't that expensive, either. Liverpool wanted £18m, while we opened with a £15m offer. A difference of a mere £3m feels implausibly insignificant to have stood in the way of creating a Fàbregas-Alonso axis in midfield. Fàbregas chased developments daily; he was as keen as Alonso to get the deal done.

But the days and weeks dragged on, reminiscent of the bad old days in the 1950s and 60s of our flawed chases for Blanchflower and Banks, as hesitation turned slowly into indecision.

Eventually, the deal fell through, at a later date, Alonso signed for Real Madrid and we would miss out on a player whom I believe might easily have turned us overnight into genuine title contenders. I felt instinctively that Wenger was to blame. One thing I do believe is that with Dein still at the club overseeing transfers, there would be no way that Alonso would have slipped through the net. The signing of Alonso may very well have been evidence of sufficient ambition from Arsenal to convince Fàbregas in a couple of years' time that his footballing future lay still in north London and not back in Spain with Barcelona. His disappointment with the transfer not happening, especially considering the spadework he had contributed to getting it done, may well have been the catalyst for him to realise that Arsenal's lack of ambition was not for him.

The team was screaming out for some nous and leadership; Alonso knew the Premier League, had proved what a talent he was. Whatever the reason, missing out on Alonso was desperate and remains one of the biggest failures for the club during the Wenger years.

Adebayor, and Toure who by all accounts didn't enjoy a good relationship with Gallas both moved to Manchester City for a combined fee of approximately £40m, while Wenger spent £10m on Belgian centre-half Thomas Vermaelen from Ajax – which suggests we'd have still turned a nice little surplus, even with the purchase of Alonso. I was disappointed to see Toure go; a whole-hearted player with the courage and strength of a lion, he had never let us down. Adebayor, though, would quickly turn any lingering regrets at his departure into feelings of out-and-out bile.

We made a good start to the season, scoring ten goals in our first two league games and 36 in all in our first 11 league matches: a flying start which prompted some optimism. A 2-1 defeat at Old Trafford didn't rock us unduly; we had been the better team and lost to a penalty and an own goal after taking the lead. Wenger famously got sent to the stands after kicking a water bottle after an apparent late Arsenal equaliser was ruled offside.

We returned to Manchester for our next game, away at Maine Road. A 4-2 defeat was largely remembered for Adebayor's extravagant celebration after scoring for his new club – running the whole length of the pitch to celebrate provocatively in front of our travelling fans. It had the look of a premeditated act, for which he was fined and given a three-match suspension. Adebayor was far from being a hero at the Emirates. His comments about his excitement at the prospect of joining Barcelona when a moved looked likely were never forgiven or forgotten by supporters who were probably beginning to tire of feeling as if we had become something of a feeder club for Europe's elite teams.

On his day, especially at the start of his Arsenal career, he looked an inspired signing, another Wenger rough diamond on the cheap, but in the end, I don't think anyone, quite possibly including Wenger himself, were unhappy at his leaving.

Despite the free-scoring football, the two games in Manchester demonstrated that nothing had really changed and that nothing had been done to address the soft underbelly that seemed to be a part of each new Wenger XI. I admired the football still but it felt like we were just elegantly marking time and hoping no one would notice.

We went top in late March after a spell which included a run of 18 points from a possible 18 but then, following a defeat at Barca in the Champions League, we took just one from a possible 12; in one of those games, leading 2-0 at Wigan with ten minutes to go, we contrived to lose 3-2.

The season contained a rarity, too; Wenger admitted that he totally lost his temper on one occasion in the dressing room. Losing 1-0 at Anfield at half-time, he threw the ultimate accusation at his players – that some of them were not fit to wear the shirt. We rallied and went on to win the game 2-1. I can't help but think it might have been better if he had shown that level of passion more often. He would be cerebral, considered and insightful but sometimes you just need to remind a team that there are times when you have to be prepared to go to war.

One game which didn't, as a rule, require the players to be reminded that football could be war was Stoke City away. It has always been a tough place to go down the years; Stoke have had some really hard teams. This particular encounter would be remembered for an horrendous tackle on Aaron Ramsey.

Going a goal down, we equalised through a good Bendtner header. Then, with 20 minutes left, Stoke centre-back Shawcross took a heavy touch and, stretching in an attempt to keep possession, he caught Ramsey on the ankle and broke his leg. It was almost exactly two years to the day since Eduardo had suffered a similar fate at Birmingham. Throw Diaby's leg break into the mix, too, and you begin to understand why Wenger was so sensitive to the excessive physicality shown to Arsenal over the years. Some games were brutal; some teams little more than pub sides in their approach and, yet, if we complained, it felt as if they had won, that they had reduced us down to the moaning 'southern softies' they wanted to pigeonhole us as. I think we were thought of as a team who didn't relish a battle; we had technicians when, at times, we needed some bruisers.

Poor old Ramsey though; right from the off, he looked a wonderful player at Arsenal. Considering his age and the fact his only football experience was at Championship level, he took to the Premier League and European football like someone to the manor born. As Wenger said, for such an injury to strike a young footballer on the threshold of their career was heartbreaking. Although it might have felt like an irrelevance, we somehow found the wherewithal to score twice in injury time to win 3-1 at Stoke.

There was one final European evening to enjoy that season, a 5-0 demolition of Porto, which secured a quarter-final spot. It was probably the season's high point and all the more commendable given that it was achieved without the injured Fàbregas. In his absence, Arshavin and Nasri stepped up and conducted something of a masterclass. Our third goal, scored by Nasri, was reminiscent of Maradona: twisting and turning with a low centre of gravity, he took out four defenders before hammering it home.

The quarter-final saw the return to the Emirates of Henry after we drew Barcelona. Two open games resulted in us going down 6-3 on aggregate. After the second leg, Wenger commented: 'We lost against a team that is better than us and that has [Messi] the best player in the world.'

## *2010/11*

By 2010/11, each new season felt like the previous campaign. There was a spell of three weeks in February in which every facet of Arsenal was on show; the good, the bad and the ugly. Three matches stand out which describe in clear and damning clarity what we amounted to back then; three matches which capture a period of six or seven years.

On 5 February, we travelled north to take on a Newcastle team rocked by the sudden and unexpected sale of their talisman, Andy Carroll. In a vitriolic atmosphere, Arsenal helped ramp up the locals' disquiet by scoring after just 40 seconds and then made it two inside the opening three minutes. More was to follow, with a third on ten minutes and when a fourth was added before even the half-hour, Newcastle fans began to leave. Arsenal's first-half performance had been brilliant, which renders the second half showing even more inexplicable.

Just after the break, the momentum changed and it was wholly a self-inflicted wound. Diaby was severely provoked and left in a crumpled heap from a tackle from Joey Barton; clearly angry at the challenge, he fronted Barton and pushed his assailant to the floor and received a straight red card for his reaction. We were four goals to the good but within those few foolish seconds, the tone of the game changed completely.

Though they pulled one back from a dubious penalty, we seemed to have weathered the storm and, with just 15 minutes left, still had a three-goal cushion. That was quickly cut to two and when an even softer second penalty was awarded, Newcastle trailed by just one goal with seven minutes remaining. They only needed four of those seven minutes to level up the score with their best goal of the lot, a shot from distance that dipped and swerved into the corner of the bewildered Szczęsny's net; the look of numb despair on Wenger's face was absolute and complete.

The Newcastle collapse was desperate and was one of those games which leaves a mark on a team. I think for a while after it, we doubted ourselves: like an aspiring heavyweight contender with a glass chin, we were always just one blow from a knockout.

Earlier in the season, we had experienced something of a rehearsal for the Newcastle game – leading Tottenham 2-0 at half-time at the Emirates, we proceeded to lose the match 3-2. It takes a while to get these things out of your system. The Newcastle result beggared belief but the Tottenham defeat was worse.

When talking with other Arsenal fans, I still openly defended Wenger and was quick to challenge any critical opinions of him, which were starting to become more strident. I was in awe of him still, I understood the constraints he was working within and I recognised everything was directed towards making us a stronger club financially at some point in the future. However, because we didn't know when that point in the future would be reached, it became an increasingly difficult proposition to sell to success-hungry supporters.

With the illogical logic of the football supporter, the fact we could play so well just made it all worse and harder to take. In essence, we were just unpredictable and to prove it, less than two weeks after our embarrassing capitulation at St James' Park, we achieved one of our most impressive results under Wenger.

By 2011, we were at the stage when either Barcelona or Bayern Munich routinely knocked us out of the Champions League. The season before, it had been Barca and it was against them again that we were drawn in the round of 16. Barcelona back then were a phenomenal team and it is easy to see why Wenger chose to model each new Arsenal side on them; they were easy on the eye, stylistically *avant garde*, hugely successful and they did it with the chutzpah and ebullience of the 1970 Brazilian World Cup-winning side. On top of that, they had Messi – a player I consider the greatest of all-time.

The game at the Emirates turned out to be a classic. The noise and the mood that evening proved just how galvanising and atmospheric the ground could be when the occasion prompted it. It felt like something special was in the air and even when David Villa's goal nearly half an hour in put Barca one up, it didn't puncture that spirit; the crowd stuck by the team and the XI in red and white responded with a courage we hadn't seen for a while.

Fàbregas prompted, Nasri teased, Arshavin conjured, while Van Persie hunted and pressurised. To their immense credit, Arsenal never stopped giving it a go, increasingly leaving their defence wide open to the mercies of the most predatory of counter-attacking sides.

There was little more than ten minutes remaining when, from the acutest of angles, Van Persie manufactured an opening out of nothing and, shooting early, hard and low, he surprised Valdes and beat the goalkeeper at his near post. The place erupted and Van Persie ran to Wenger – a very public show of support for his manager.

Five minutes later and a move of swift, precise and incisive football cut through Barcelona, the ball moving from our penalty box to the back of Barca's net in what felt like no more than a few seconds. Cutting in from the right, Nasri seemed to have crossed behind the men in the box but running in unseen off his wing was the little Russian wizard Arshavin, who calmly sidefooted a curling shot beyond the stranded Valdes to give Arsenal the victory their bravery deserved.

The heroic late turnaround had secured a victory that guaranteed nothing, though; a second leg in Catalonia still awaited us. However, I think the victory meant a lot to Wenger; it was a vindication, an emphatic response to the small, yet growing mood of discontent that was becoming part of the culture around the club. You could hardly imagine the side that gave away a four-goal lead at Newcastle could come from behind to defeat Barcelona but this kind of performance was always there lurking behind every clutch of disappointments. That night, the best possible Arsenal had shown up and it gave us all hope.

For a while, there was a jauntiness in our step and before we journeyed to Spain for the second leg, there was the matter of Wembley and the League Cup Final against Birmingham City, who would be relegated come the end of the season, and the chance to end a wait for a trophy that stretched back to 2005. In the grand scheme of things, six years is hardly forever but it felt much longer at the time.

Birmingham scored early but when Arshavin did some great work down the right flank, shortly after Wilshere had hit the bar with a long-range effort, Van Persie was on hand to turn in a half chance and level the scores. Although Van Persie had to go off with an injury, we pressed and strove but, in the 89th minute, the ball fell tamely in the Arsenal penalty box and a glorious cock-up between Koscielny and Szczęsny – the ball bouncing of the keeper's knee – gave Martins the chance to win it for Birmingham. In recent seasons, we had found new and imaginative ways of throwing away games but nothing compared to this.

I don't think the Birmingham defeat was that influential in terms of the growing 'Wenger out' agenda but it gave it a bit of a push; from what I could see, it was the case that once people had turned against him there seemed no chance they would reconsider. I think, for some, the frustration they felt with Wenger was really a frustration with the circumstances the club were mired in: selling their best players year after year, still competing with the best and sometimes getting tantalisingly close, but ultimately failing, always just coming up short. Wenger was the very visible lightning conductor for much of that angst, disappointment and frustration.

Thereafter, the season petered out. Barcelona did, indeed, overturn our victory by beating us 3-1 in the return leg – but not without more hand-wringing controversy. With the score still at 1-1, Van Persie went clean through, unaware amid the noise of an 80,000 crowd that he had been flagged offside, and was sent off for continuing to play on. It was, without doubt, one of the most ludicrous and crass refereeing decisions I have witnessed in all my years. It had been a spirited performance in Spain but one where, in all honesty, we were hanging on. No complaints – there are times you just have to admit you are beaten by a better team.

This was Jack Wilshere's breakout season: he would start 44 games and become the only bright spark of the season. Jack had everything. He was technically gifted, had vision, confidence and drive and, with a low centre of gravity, he looked as strong as an ox. He was cocksure with it, too. He was, perhaps, overplayed for an 18-year-old but it was understandable – if not forgivable – given that, at times, he carried the team single-handedly. He was as brave as a lion – too brave, in fact, for his own good – and was a big positive to emerge from the season.

It was a boardroom now without its one remaining Arsenal 'supporter', too. With Dein gone, that left Danny Fiszman as the sole real supporter and when he sold his remaining shareholding to Kroenke just two days before he passed away, the club lost its last guiding hand that intuitively understood the football side of the boardroom's affairs and, though he necessarily viewed the game from a rarer perspective than the rest of us because of his immense wealth, his aspirations and ambitions for Arsenal were the same as yours and mine.

Although each season we paid off some more of the stadium debt and made the promised land of unfettered spending feel that little bit closer, we all knew we were fooling ourselves: football is about the next match, not the pragmatic, methodical journey to solvency. The board might have considered fourth spot a trophy but no one was tying red and white ribbons around a shrinking corporate debt and taking it on an open-top bus parade through Islington. Football has only ever talked in the language of passion – hopes, dreams and glory remain the only items on the balance sheet for supporters.

## *2011/12*

The 2011/12 season hadn't even kicked off and we were beset with problems. In a pre-season game against New York Bulls, Jack Wilshere suffered a stress fracture of his ankle. The prognosis was that he would be out until February but Wilshere wouldn't play a competitive game the whole season – sadly, a sign of things to come.

The sale of club captain Cesc Fàbregas to Barcelona came as no real surprise to anyone. We all knew Barca were all over him. We were probably surprised he hadn't moved 12 months earlier but, perhaps out of loyalty to Wenger, he had resisted the lure of his home city. Like Vieira's much-touted move to Real Madrid, the 'Fàbregas to Barca' story might have run every summer but while Vieira was winning things with Arsenal and could be persuaded to stay, Fàbregas wasn't and could only look on wistfully at Barca's successes. The only aspect of the deal that didn't really stack up for me was the fee: Fàbregas was world-class and had his career still largely ahead of him but he moved for a mere, in relative terms, £35m – that has always surprised me. I thought at the time and, still do, that £50m would have been more the figure Arsenal should have got for him. It was greeted as a great PR success for Barca, on a par with a return of Gibraltar to the Spanish.

Nine days later, Samir Nasri became the latest Gunner to sign for Manchester City, moving for a fee of £25m not long after left-back Clichy had made the same move. It felt as if the club was in chaos, a feeling confirmed when we made four signings on the very last day of the transfer window. It was an unholy mess. The timing of the signings suggested a degree of panic.

With Clichy departed, Wenger had put his trust in rising star Kieran Gibbs but Gibbs had picked up a hamstring injury, which had left us without a left-back. Andre Santos was signed for more than £6m, only £1m less than we sold Clichy for. Clichy apparently didn't want to move but was effectively told he had no option because we wanted to make space for Gibbs to develop – and then we ended up with Santos. He had played for Brazil but there must have been a lot of injured Brazilian left-backs at the time for that to happen!

The opening to the season was horrific. Losing our first home game 2-0 to Liverpool, we followed that with a chastening 8-2 defeat at Old Trafford. By early October, after losing at Tottenham, we were in the lower reaches of the table. And though we climbed to respectability, eventually finishing as high as third, it was a season defined by defeats. It was getting harder and harder to see any progress.

Thierry Henry returned in the New Year for a loan spell which lifted our spirits; it was maybe the highlight of the season. The script was written as he came on to score the winning goal in front of a rapturous stadium against Leeds in the cup.

I wondered what he must have thought of the state of the club on his return – we were a million miles from those great early Wenger teams for which he had been so central. Both on and off the pitch, he must have been taken aback by what he saw. It would have felt like a very different club to the one he had left.

However, the Arsenal of old flickered briefly one evening in early March. After a 4-0 drubbing in the San Siro against AC Milan in the first leg of our Champions League second-round tie, back in north London for the second leg, we rallied and though we left the field at full time defeated, it had been a performance that did us credit. By half-time, we were 3-0 up. Milan, though, dug in after the break and saw out a 4-3 aggregate victory. The tie frustratingly had been lost amidst the avoidably sloppy defending three weeks earlier. It felt like this was all we were going to be, that the promises founded on the move to the Emirates were hollow offerings. We had become soulless.

We did qualify for the Champions League again, following a dramatic last game of the season, winning 3-2 at West Brom in a game we had to do better in than Spurs did in theirs. Three magnificent goalkeeper clangers from West Brom's ex-Tottenham debutant keeper Márton Fülöp contributed to the cause; as did an outstanding last-minute block from Gibbs, which I was directly in line with.

It was around this time that I started to hear the chant 'We want our Arsenal back'. It felt as if the Arsenal we all cherished had been mislaid on the short journey from Highbury to the Emirates.

## Chapter 38

# 2012–2014

*2012/13*

Pat Rice, Arsenal's assistant-manager retired. Pat gave Arsenal 44 years of loyal, committed and proud service as player, captain, coach and assistant manager. His calm authority was what set him apart as both a player and a coach and a simple desire to serve Arsenal in whatever capacity the club wanted was always pursued with modesty and an unassuming air. After playing more than 500 games for us, he returned to Highbury in 1984 as a youth team coach from Watford after captaining them to a promotion and, after a brief spell as a caretaker manager, he was there to support and guide Arsène Wenger as the Frenchman negotiated his choppy introduction to English football at the hands of the notorious British tabloid media. I had known Pat since his earliest days at the club and held him in the highest esteem; a decent family man who has never lost his passionate love for the club. If ever we need another idea for a statue, then they could do a lot worse than consider Patrick James Rice.

For the new season, Steve Bould would replace him: a position that Bould, another respected and well liked ex-player, never looked comfortable in. Over time, Steve would be sidelined and perhaps too often denied the credit his work deserved. Unquestionably, Bould seemed initially to have brought some defensive expertise to bear on the team; after the chaos and mayhem of some recent seasons, there appeared, at last, to be some organisation and order. The first 13 games saw us concede a mere eight goals. I recall the press responding very positively to our defence that season and I don't think Wenger was happy about credit being given so fulsomely to his No.2. There was a post-match Sky interview with Wenger, quite early in the season, when it was suggested that Bould had already made a difference to our defence and Wenger didn't look happy at all. The mood around the club, even as the season opened, had been negative and quarrelsome and there was certainly by then real momentum in the case against Wenger. Despite the signing of some very good players that summer – Cazorla, Podolski and Giroud – the close season's business had been dominated by yet another painful departure, this time of probably our last remaining truly world-class player, Robin van Persie, to Manchester United. Everything about that transfer felt toxic.

In his final season with us, Van Persie, by now our club captain, scored 34 goals and was so outstanding he became only the fourth ever player to be voted both the PFA Player of the Year and the Football Writers' Association Player of the Year in the same season.

At first, a move to Juventus looked on the cards and you could speculate that the fallout from his eventual move to Old Trafford could have largely been avoided had he moved to Italy. I was fed up with players leaving us for the blue side of Manchester but United were a mortal enemy and to feel that a player who, in his own words, had 'become a man at Arsenal' could leave us for them really stung.

In order to manage the media narrative, Van Persie put out a public letter to supporters. Along with most people, I thought this was a huge mistake; it was never going to be read in the way Van Persie hoped it would. Reading the letter calmly now, there isn't much in it that I can disagree with but he was badly advised to do it. At that stage, he still had 12 months left on his contract and he said in his open letter that he would not be extending his deal. According to Van Persie, no formal new contract offer was ever made to him by Arsenal.

I am not sure if this was the first, second or third summer we had been strongly linked with the signing of the Argentinian centre-forward Gonzalo Higuaín but that summer, like never before, we needed him or a signing of that magnitude. We did sign Cazorla, who immediately, despite a slightly stocky frame, looked at home in the hustle and bustle of the Premier League. Podolski became a firm fan favourite, although I was never completely convinced he was quite as good a player as his reputation led you to believe, and Giroud was a comparative slow burner to begin with, despite coming here with an excellent goalscoring record. Over the course of his career, he would prove himself adept at the spectacular and the unexpected but less reliable when it came to the more mundane aspects of the game. You felt you'd get half a dozen cracking goals from him every season but none of the stock-in-trade of your top centre-forward. He was a player equally as flamboyant as he could be frustrating.

Elsewhere on the pitch, we bought another left back, this time Nacho Monreal from Malaga during the January transfer window. An uncomplicated player who resolutely went about his very efficient business, he would never let us down, even during a spell of games when, in the midst of an injury crisis, he played in central defence. I don't think he ever got the recognition he deserved for his resolute defending – one of the more successful of Wenger's later signings.

We hovered around the fringes of the Champions League places all season and put an excellent run together towards the end of the campaign of just one defeat in 18 games, winning 12, to clinch fourth spot on the final day – our Holy Grail. Similar to the previous season, we came agonisingly close to turning round an almost impossible position in Europe. Again, we lost it in the first leg, going down 3-1 at the Emirates to Bayern Munich, only to go to Bavaria and win 2-0. Once, I might have been proud of such a gallant fightback but now it merely underlined the sheer inconsistencies of Arsenal.

Wenger's reluctance to take domestic cups seriously was also beginning to backfire on him. How many times were we knocked out by lower division teams? That season, we lost a League Cup quarter-final at League Two Bradford City on penalties and lost at home to Championship side Blackburn Rovers, who only avoided relegation by four points, in the FA Cup. I understood the importance to the club's long-term finances of achieving fourth spot and the consequent Champions League place but Wenger was now under some pressure – even from quarters that had been staunchly loyal to him – and a cup might have helped.

We did put seven past Reading in a wonderful League Cup tie which ended 7-5 after Arsenal came back from four goals down and also put five past Tottenham and seven past Newcastle in the league but most days we could just as easily concede that number of goals. It was exciting, cavalier football but it no longer added up to anything; it was the proverbial 'lipstick on a pig'.

## *2013/14*

When the trophy drought finally ended, it was inevitable that it would follow some nerve-shredding drama, not to mention possibly the best build-up to a goal that an FA Cup Final has ever witnessed. The highs and lows of the cup final were pure Arsène Wenger. The contest swung from the defensively ridiculous to the attacking sublime: it was Wenger's Arsenal in a nutshell.

The season which ended so famously began with less of a bang and more of a whimper. There had been talk that we were in the market for a forward and were prepared to pay big to get someone to provide some potency. For the umpteenth time, Higuaín was strongly linked but the rumours were quickly silenced with the news that we had picked up Yaya Sanogo on a free transfer from Auxerre. Yaya, we felt, wasn't quite what we had been promised. However, if the pulse wasn't sent racing with the signing of the young Frenchman, a couple of months later the club would pull off a seemingly audacious signing, breaking their record transfer fee by £27m to secure Mesut Özil for £42m.

He was an artist and, perhaps, the finest technician since Bergkamp to play for us. But he would prove over the next few seasons to be a bit of a flat track bully who never really did it against the better teams when it mattered: ultimately, a rare talent but simply not one designed for the Premier League. Although his was an exciting signing, even back in 2013 it was clear he wasn't *really* the player we needed. Midfield wasn't a problem for us: Wilshere, Ramsey, Cazorla, Rosicky and Arteta, plus the emerging Oxlade-Chamberlain and Gnabry, gave a sufficiency of options; it was patently up front where we were short.

For a while, though, we were all bowled over by Özil. Apart from acquiring a player of his obvious talent, I think we were all hoping the signing signalled our emergence from the tight, self-imposed austerity that had held us back on the pitch but simultaneously put us on the sort of surer financial footing whereby we *could* now buy players like Özil for that amount of money.

In the boardroom, there was an ending of an era, with Sir Chips Keswick taking over as chair of the club. Just like predecessor Peter Hill-Wood, Sir Chips was a merchant banker and an Old Etonian. Hill-Wood had stepped down following a heart attack the previous year and it brought to a close a period when it felt like a Hill-Wood had always been at the helm; his grandfather, Sir Samuel Hill-Wood, had become chairman 84 years earlier.

At times, it can seem that the only useful function the board of a football club serves is to be a convenient target for criticism but the

Hill-Woods had served Arsenal impeccably, that much is beyond dispute. I might have had my own irritations with Peter Hill-Wood but there was never any doubt about his decency; he was, like his father and grandfather before him, full to the brim with a notion of service and he represented a sense of continuity which was both welcome and reassuring.

After two honourable failures, the season's Champions League elimination was more routine: a 2-0 defeat against Bayern at the Emirates in the first leg – a game of missed penalties for both sides and a sending-off for Szczęsny – was followed by a brave but insufficient 1-1 draw in Bavaria to see us knocked out in the last 16 for the fourth year running.

Domestically, we had a good run in the league. We were top in February and had been for a while until we travelled to the north-west and lost 5-1 at Liverpool. The effect of that mauling was predictable: a poor result derailed us long enough to see us drop off the pace. One especially poor run of results later in the season included a disaster which coincided with Wenger's 1,000th game in charge of Arsenal.

I have never liked Mourinho. In fact, I would go as far as to say he remains the football figure I dislike the most and I have always referred to him as the enemy of football. It was galling that it was Chelsea away which was to mark Wenger's milestone: we knew what would happen and we knew it would be ugly. The game was set up for an entirely different story. Chelsea and Arsenal were top and second in the league and it was the game of the day on a fine spring afternoon. Chelsea led us in the race for the title by four points but had, crucially, played a game more; if we could do what no one else had done at Stamford Bridge that season and take three points away with us, then who knew what might happen.

Sadly, any pride Wenger might have felt on the occasion barely lasted the opening skirmishes. By seven minutes, Chelsea were two up. It became three after 17 and four by half-time, with a painful afternoon ending with Chelsea six goals to the good. It had been an afternoon which illustrated tactically just how exposed Wenger was happy for his rearguard to be. Twice in the opening flurry of goals, Cazorla, the deepest midfielder, got either caught on the ball or gave it away with a risky pass – errors which led to goals. Apart from one penalty, all the goals against us that afternoon were from counter-attacks after we had over-committed numbers forward. The result was a personal disaster for Wenger. His players hardly gave performances that suggested that they wanted to help him celebrate this auspicious occasion and, ultimately, it was an utter humiliation for him.

A month before the game, Mourinho had stoked the fires by claiming Wenger was a 'specialist in failure' due to his having missed out on silverware since 2005. Mourinho added, perhaps not without justification given the volatile regime under Abramovich, that if he had a similar run without a trophy, he would be leaving London and not coming back.

Between mid-December and mid-March, we conceded six at Manchester City, five at Liverpool and six again at Chelsea. Teams who harbour realistic hopes of chasing the title just don't do that and those results allowed the momentum against Wenger to build.

One of his oddest moves – the sort of thing which now stood out, whereas a decade earlier it would never have been challenged – was the loan signing of Kim Källström. The Swedish midfielder, who possessed a languid style, was discovered to have a back injury during his medical; Wenger decided to persist with the deal despite this injury keeping Källström out of action for nearly half of his four-month loan period. However, once back to fitness, Källström was to have what he later described as his 'best 15 minutes in football'.

Playing the FA Cup holders Wigan Athletic in the semi-final, Källström famously emerged from the bench to score his penalty in the shoot-out following a 1-1 draw and, after much huffing and puffing, we were back at Wembley for an FA Cup Final against Hull City, a team we had systematically dismantled away from home 3-0 barely three weeks earlier.

It felt a bit like the League Cup Final against Birmingham City, a golden opportunity against a theoretically weaker team to end a painful trophy drought. Nine minutes into the final, though, the game had taken on the proportions of a full-scale crisis. Two goals from set pieces, which we dealt with poorly, did the damage and without a goalline clearance from Gibbs a few minutes later, the situation might have already been irretrievable.

It was the quality of Cazorla's strike for our first goal that gave us hope. His pinpoint long-range free kick was like a defiant gesture. With that goal, Hull retreated and Arsenal grew. The drama and significance of the game seemed to begin to wear Hull down. Arsenal turned the screw and eventually, with less than a quarter of the game remaining, Koscielny swivelled and shot home from close range to bring the sides level. By then, the momentum had swung in Arsenal's favour and efforts from Gibbs and several from Giroud almost won it for us in normal time.

The first 15 minutes of extra-time were all Arsenal, with efforts from Ramsey and Cazorla coming close while Giroud, a constant threat, hit the woodwork. Hull were defending with their lives, deeper and deeper, but when it came, the goal Arsenal constructed was as pure a piece of Wenger football as ever graced his Double teams or his 'Invincibles'. Wilshere, a replacement for the flagging Özil, played an incisive, diagonal ball to Giroud; the big Frenchman was running away from the goal at an angle but managed to backheel into the path of Ramsey who, having no time to alter his position or stride, managed to strike the ball first time with the outside of his boot and, from around 18 yards, beat the keeper at his near post to win the cup for Arsenal. At the whistle, you had no doubt what the success meant to the club – and especially Wenger. A cup success – this was our 11th – was never more cherished.

Had we gone down against Hull, I think Wenger's position would have been untenable. Had we have lost then, it would have been ten years without a trophy, with two golden opportunities to win something squandered, and I don't think he could have survived that.

As it was, Wenger got a three-year extension to his contract. For a time, the negativity around the club quietened. We'd won a trophy at last. The signing of Özil clearly signalled a willingness to spend – the period of austerity was coming to a close. There was a bit of optimism around the place as we paraded the cup through the streets of Islington.

## Chapter 39

# 2014/15

WENGER'S NEW contract was signed and sealed but, rather than quietening the debate around his future, it seemed to increase the vehemence with which supporters spoke out about him.

Much of the transfer business was with an eye to filling out a squad with either experience or promise. Mathieu Debuchy, a redoubtable full-back and, indeed, a surprisingly good defender, arrived to replace another Manchester City-bound Gunner, Bacary Sagna (Sagna was, in my view, a world-class defender and certainly one of Wenger's better buys in this period). Danny Welbeck would offer cover across all the forward positions. The signing of 19-year-old Callum Chambers from Southampton, a player with a mere 22 games under his belt, for a substantial fee of £16m represented the gamble of the summer. With Fabianski's contract lapsing, David Ospina became the latest less-than-convincing goalkeeper to sign for us.

Chambers was a gamble but to Wenger's credit, he never shrank from the chance to develop young talent. I do doubt that Arsenal at that time was the best place for a guy like Chambers to be learning his trade, or for that matter the promising Rob Holding, who signed a bit later. Soon, both of them would be added to a growing list of hot young defensive prospects that just never kicked on: Senderos, Clichy, Djourou, Gibbs, to name a few.

When Debuchy picked up an injury, young Spanish full-back Hector Bellerin burst on to the scene and almost immediately looked the part; a dashing Musketeer of a player, galloping down the wing, looking like a young Salvador Dali, he played as if he enjoyed his football. Injuries and outside interests would derail his development but in 2014/15, he was still a bright young thing at the Emirates.

Vermaelen moved to Barcelona for £15m. The big Belgian defender had been a steady performer to begin with but a run of poor form over the past couple of seasons, together with the success of the Mertesacker-Koscielny partnership, limited his outings. Despite being a Barca player for five seasons, he only ever played a handful of matches for them; he was good enough to play 85 times for Belgium but his career, despite taking in stints at clubs like Ajax, Arsenal, and Barcelona, probably didn't do him justice.

Going in the opposite direction from Barca to Arsenal was the key bit of business that summer and this deal was, indeed, more proof positive that, financially, the club seemed to have turned a corner. To the delicate elegance of Mesut Özil, we now added the raw power, non-stop engine and technical excellence of the Chilean Alexis Sánchez for a fee of £31.7m which, relative to the £42m we paid for Özil, represented something of a bargain.

Nicknamed 'the Wonder Child', he was playing senior football in Chile at the age of just 15 and moved to Italian football at 18. Barca signed him in 2011 and he excelled, scoring 39 goals in 88 starts, but there was talk of his face not fitting at the Camp Nou and he allegedly jumped at the chance to sign for us, turning down an offer from Liverpool to come to London. I thought he was close to being world-class. In two summers, Wenger had invested upwards of £70m on an attacking midfielder and a forward: if he was going to go down, it was to be in a blaze of glory.

We began the season at Wembley in the Community Shield, soundly defeating Manchester City 3-0. Alexis immediately showed his potential and just how much his direct style of play would suit the Premier League. An attacking unit which could boast Ramsey, Cazorla, Wilshere, Walcott, Özil, Alexis and Giroud was mouth-watering, for sure, but the perennial defensive concerns remained. The mythic 'rainy January night at Bolton' might have felt a million miles away from the sunshine at Wembley but it was there waiting in the wings to ambush us once again.

We drew four of our first six games, then went down at Stamford Bridge and, thereafter, the hopes and dreams that had seemed so vibrant in the Community Shield faded amid a rash of unconvincing displays. Defeats at Swansea City, Stoke City and Southampton demonstrated that, no matter how much potential firepower we had at our disposal, nothing had changed in terms of defence and organisation for ten years. The defeat at Stoke even provoked Wenger into lamenting how 'soft' Arsenal had been. If we couldn't get the ball down and play, there was still no Plan B; we were at the mercy of the opposition, especially an opposition who wanted to see if we 'fancied it'.

Wenger had the reputation of being a 'light touch' coach tactically and intelligent enough to give players like Bergkamp, Henry, Pires, Fàbregas and Vieira the freedom to express themselves. He was also fortunate to initially inherit a world-class defence. But he would go on to assemble the Lauren-Toure-Campbell-Cole backline; the 'Invincible' defensive unit was his. Now, though, he seemed to have no patience for building a defence worthy of the name. He was like a kid in a sweetshop with no taste for the healthy options, going straight for the sugar rush of Özil and Alexis. As good as they were, neither of those signings were really what we needed. We needed centre-backs and midfield spoilers – what we got was more creativity.

The Champions League had a familiar ring to it. For once, we avoided either Barcelona or Bayern Munich and drew the decent but definitely beatable Monaco in the first knockout round. However, our performance in the first leg at the Emirates was described variously in the media as 'naïve' and 'incompetent' as we went down 3-1. The first goal followed an unlucky deflection to wrong-foot Ospina but the second and third goals were simple counter-attacks against a team who had massively over-committed players to attack: the second was a two-against-one and the third goal was one player breaking from the halfway line.

When we travelled to the south of France, we did give it a go but a 2-0 victory left us high and dry once more, with Monaco progressing on the away goals rule.

With a level of consistency that was starting to grate, our final 14 league games included a run of eight consecutive victories; ten wins in all alongside three draws and just the one defeat. The run helped cement a respectable third-place finish after briefly flirting with a title shot, only for this to falter when Chelsea, the eventual champions, came to the Emirates and held us to a 0-0 draw. While all this was going on, we progressed with uncharacteristic calm through the early rounds of the FA Cup. We had beaten Manchester United 2-1 at Old Trafford in the quarter-finals, with Welbeck enjoying a goal on his return. In the semi-finals, Alexis chipped in with a couple as we overcame Championship side Reading 2-1 after extra-time.

The final at Wembley against Aston Villa was one of the most enjoyable cup finals I have ever witnessed with Arsenal. We hit our stride early on. We kept opening up Villa and the only surprise was that it took until just before half-time to take the lead, a walloping effort from Walcott, who had been given the nod over Giroud for a central striking role following Theo's hat-trick in the final league game of the season. Walcott's movement was predatory and unsettling; that afternoon, harrying Villa's backline from right-back to left-back, he was the Theo Walcott we had all hoped he would one day become.

After the break, the best individual goal was struck by Alexis, a curling, dipping brute of an effort which simply confounded Given in the Villa goal, every inch a companion piece for Cazorla's great strike 12 months earlier. Mertesacker nodded the third from a corner and, in injury time, Giroud scored his customary elegant contribution.

It was a record-breaking 12th time that Arsenal had lifted the FA Cup. Poor Villa must have been glad to see the back of us as they trudged off the pitch; the 4-0 hammering followed 3-0 and 5-0 victories against them in the league.

Alexis was duly voted the PFA Fans' Player of the Year following his extraordinary debut season in English football. You got more than you bargained for with Alexis. One thing that took us all by surprise was his workrate; it's rare that a player with that level of technical ability has the same levels of physical hunger and power. He was brilliant at leading the press but was frequently let down by his team-mates not showing anything like the same level of intensity.

It had been a very similar season to the previous one – an inconsistent league campaign, an FA Cup win and a disheartening European failure – but there was some evidence of a revival; if not buds, then green shoots at least. Wenger remained a man who divided opinion: the doubters continued to doubt and the lovers continued to love. For some, probably still most at that stage, the two FA Cups were a vindication of the club's decision to extend his contract while, to the rest, they were flimsy bits of wallpaper stuck over yawning great cracks. For myself, I was still supportive of Wenger but beginning to have my doubts going forward.

## Chapter 40

# 2015–2017

### *2015/16*

The transfer window was keenly anticipated. There was a half decent team there and the missing ingredients were *so* well documented that we looked forward to a posse of defenders and midfield destroyers joining the club. It came as a huge disappointment, therefore, when absolutely no outfield players were signed. Wenger did seem to have picked up a decent keeper, though. There was some satisfaction with the signing of Petr Čech; 'he'll win us ten points a season' was the general consensus and I didn't doubt it. He'd been a top keeper at Chelsea.

The midfield anchor role remained in the possession of Francis Coquelin and, given Wenger's laudable commitment to youth, he still clearly preferred to be patient with the young Frenchman and let him grow into the role. Coquelin formed, at times, an effective midfield base alongside Cazorla. I don't think anyone will forget a game at Manchester City a couple of seasons earlier when the Coquelin-Cazorla axis nullified City, contributing significantly to a spirited 2-0 victory. Coquelin, though, had never really progressed. He was one of a number of bright talents that slowly faded as they reached their early to mid-20s. In the January window, Wenger would sign Mohamed El-Neny. I think every time Wenger signed a 'prospect', we all hoped we'd found the new Vieira; El-Neny certainly wasn't that but he was a decent enough player, just not quite top drawer.

We made a slow start but, in late September, we put an end to Leicester City's positive opening to the season, going to the Walker's Stadium and winning 5-2. Leicester would famously only lose one more game before they visited the Emirates in February for what felt like an early title showdown. Everything had clicked for us in the East

Midlands; we looked solid and had turned around early momentum against us. Leicester away was the kind of game we traditionally struggled with but we had comfortably beaten a very effective team in their own backyard.

We built on that result by beating Manchester United 3-0, with all the goals coming in an explosive first-half performance, and then went on a run of three wins in four which saw us go top. Away from the league, though, we were wildly inconsistent; beating Bayern at the Emirates 2-0 in the Champions League group phase, we were then beaten at Hillsborough by championship team Sheffield Wednesday 3-0 in the League Cup before going down 5-1 in Munich. The defeat in Bavaria wasn't the usual catalyst for a run of defeats, however. After a surprise 4-0 defeat at Southampton on Boxing Day, we were soon back on top of the league. A home defeat to Chelsea seemed to have finished off any outside hopes of the title but those hopes were rekindled when the leaders Leicester came to the Emirates and were defeated with a very late goal from Welbeck. There was a real conviction to the celebrations at the final whistle and somehow it felt different. But, just as soon as we got going, the wheels fell off. A 3-2 defeat at Old Trafford against a really struggling United team was followed by home and away defeats to Barcelona in the Champions League and then a meek surrender to Watford at home in the cup saw the last glimmer of silverware disappear. Despite a ten-game unbeaten run up to the very end of the season, we were never contenders for a title which ended up going to Leicester City. We had the pleasure of finishing second and above Tottenham again, who thus became known as the only team who could manage to finish third in what was, for some weeks, an exclusively two-horse race between them and Leicester.

A top three that didn't include either Chelsea or Manchester City would not have been a popular bet when the season kicked off. Leicester's recipe for success was a solid, unglamorous defence, with attack dogs in midfield, and then they would hit you on the counter – there was something reassuringly familiar about that to some of us.

Leicester only lost three games all season, and two of those were against us, but defeats on our travels at places like Southampton, Swansea and West Brom were always likely to scupper a title bid; a poor Chelsea team did the double over us, too.

There was a year left on Wenger's contract; a cup win had previously convinced the board that an extension was the right thing to do, not merely the sentimental thing to do. Five or six years earlier, I felt Wenger still had a title in him. Now, I was pretty sure that idea was fanciful. We were lucky we had Alexis but you could sense his frustrations, too. These were his best years; he had scored 17 goals, contributed to more, and led the press like a tiger that only ever got half-hearted buy-in from team-mates. Take him out of Wenger's starting XI and we looked a very tame proposition.

As far as I was concerned, Wenger now stood in danger of seriously tarnishing his reputation. By 2016, aspects of his 'method' were becoming old hat; all the things he had introduced into English football that had given him an advantage were now part and parcel of the game and others had taken some of those ideas further or younger, more innovative coaches had introduced other, better ideas. His unique selling point was no longer so especially unique.

I couldn't see any circumstances that would lead the club to offer him an extension. By this stage, my frustrations with the situation frequently boiled over into anger. It was the age old dilemma for me – here was someone, no matter how legendary, who was now beginning to regress the club. My sincere wish was that he now walked away with dignity; all due homage paid to him and he would go with his head held high. In my anger towards him, I had to wrestle with the knowledge that Wenger was a man who had made all my football dreams come true and, for that, he will remain a pivotal reference point in the club's history forever, but everything comes to an end and, in my heart of hearts, it felt as if that point had probably been reached some time ago.

## *2016/17*

Wenger's future became an all-consuming distraction for the club and wasted so much energy, including my own. By then, opinions about Wenger were rarely neutral or measured and this had the effect of escalating an atmosphere of unrest: Wenger had exclusively become the story.

As far as the transfer window was concerned, most of us would have said we needed a centre-forward, a defensive midfield enforcer and a physically dominant centre-back. What we got appeared to go partway towards meeting these requirements.

Granit Xhaka was signed for a reported £35m. We did our business with Xhaka early that year, which meant he had already signed for us when we watched him play for Switzerland in the Euros. I was worried when I saw him, as he had no great pace; he was great on the ball but he didn't look like someone suited to the demands of English football, especially in a deeper role. In time, I would grow to love him but, initially, I had big doubts that he was quite at the level we required.

We then signed what we thought was the answer to our defensive problems. Shkodran Mustafi, a big lad costing £35m, was a World Cup winner. I also watched him in the Euros playing for Germany and I think we all thought we had signed a proper centre-half when he joined us.

Rob Holding arrived from Bolton, a speculative buy for a mere £2m – a young man who probably made Chambers look overpriced at £16m. Over time, like Chambers, he proved to be good but just not good enough; neither of these likeable young players were quite at the level.

The summer's inward business was completed with the signing of Lucas Pérez. A real journeyman who seemed never to have found a home, he arrived in north London following a standout season in Spain. We paid £17m for him but then never really gave him much of a chance. When Lacazette later signed, the Frenchman was given Pérez's squad number without Pérez being told first and that was largely the end; Pérez said he felt 'cheated' by Arsenal and made clear his wish to leave.

A disappointing sale was that of Gnabry. I'd seen a lot of Gnabry while he grew up. I am friends with the grandparents of young Arsenal prospect Austin Lipman, a contemporary of Gnabry's, and I watched all the youth team games, matches in which Gnabry stood out. I'd thought it odd when Wenger sent him on loan to West Brom, to Tony Pulis of all people, a guy Wenger had a stormy relationship with. He made one appearance at The Hawthorns and was duly sent back to his parent club with Pulis stating that Gnabry 'was not of the required level to play for West Brom'. I think Wenger wanted to extend Gnabry's contract but left it too late and, besides, the German was keen for first-team football and moved to Werder Bremen for £5m. Perhaps Wenger had some doubts about him; I know I certainly didn't. He has, of course, gone on to play for Bayern Munich and be a regular in his national side.

Elsewhere, Arteta retired – the first chapter in his Arsenal story completed. Rosicky left on a free with the admiration of us all; a fantastic talent who had had his career limited by injuries. Flamini left, too, for the second time. The French midfielder had never let us down nor did he get the credit his unobtrusive teamwork deserved.

One peculiarity of the season was Wenger's decision to play Čech in the Premier League and Ospina in the Champions League. Personally, I didn't think there was any doubt that Čech was, by some distance, the superior keeper and, in my increasingly negative frame of mind towards Wenger, I saw it as a weak and unnecessary disruption – this decision just seemed as if Wenger was avoiding conflict.

New Year was ushered in with a goal which, even by Giroud's standards of showmanship, was exceptional. Midway through the first half against Crystal Palace, he 'scorpion' kicked the ball from behind him to put us one up. The goal won the FIFA Puskas Award for goal of the season. What a trail of memorable goals Giroud left behind him and what an amazing career he has had since leaving Arsenal.

If that individual strike was illustrative of Wenger's Arsenal, then so was the next performance – a 3-3 draw on the south coast against Bournemouth. Eighty minutes of being bullied and outpaced saw us three goals behind but then Alexis kickstarted a memorable fightback. The second goal was a great strike from Perez and then Giroud nodded in an equaliser in injury time. It felt like a point salvaged but to Alexis, as he made clear, it was two points tossed away through 80 minutes of carelessness: the first real public airing of a level of frustration which would not take long to escalate.

Alexis's frustrations were mirrored all around the Emirates. Regular altercations in the ground were happening between 'Wenger in' and 'Wenger out' supporters. Feelings ran high and the mood around the ground on matchday was becoming toxic; towards the end of the season, social media was full of videos of fights and arguments between opposing groups of Arsenal supporters. None of it showed us in a great light; it was a bit like the supressed desire for a revolution that finally breaks its banks and spills out on to the streets. Once the anger against Wenger had been expressed, it was never going to go away; while another season seemingly careered towards more fruitless capitulation, it was only going to get worse.

A final straw for some had been the abject humiliation inflicted upon us by Bayern Munich. We weren't even close to Bayern but to have our inferiority so comprehensively exposed was soul destroying. Another 5-1 defeat in Bavaria was compounded by a second 5-1 defeat back at the Emirates – a level of humiliation that the 10-2 aggregate scoreline only hinted at.

If the initial reaction had been one of numbness, it quickly morphed into a visceral anger. The Emirates became a furious bowl wherein two opposing armies stood in total opposition. 'Forever In Your Debt' read one flag at the Emirates but these were now becoming fewer and further between; the mood for most was captured in one banner reading 'Arsène: Thanks for the Memories But Time to Say Goodbye'. It had been first seen nearly a year earlier and when it first appeared, Wenger had been asked about it; he chose to dismiss it as 'boring'. Calmer voices would still point to the early successes and the efforts he had put in to reduce the debt; but, by now, our fans were looking beyond that. It was more a case of whether he was the man to take us forward and it felt as if, by 2017, he had fallen behind the leading coaches. He had revolutionised football but now, as a club, we laboured beneath the sheer weight of his reputation; he was becoming a figure that it was almost impossible to sack and I suspect the board were deeply concerned by the thought they *might* actually have to sack him. At the time, the Kroenkes tended to look more at the balance sheet than at what was happening on the pitch and we were regularly turning a decent profit, so perhaps it is that alone which kept Wenger in his job.

I had always thought that if he'd employed a younger coach, he might have been able to ride out some of the unrest. His way was increasingly looking blunt in the face of contemporary tactical ideas. A younger, more enlightened view, marrying different ideas to his own philosophy, might have rejuvenated him and given him a second coming but perhaps his ego wouldn't have allowed it.

When even his most loyal backer would have been hard pressed to argue against his stubbornness and the feeling that his ideas had become obsolete, Wenger hit back in the best possible way – on the pitch. A season which was sliding towards a catastrophic first failure to qualify for the Champions League since 1997 was saved in just two games at Wembley when, for a short time, we all fell in love again with 'Wengerball'.

Against Manchester City in the FA Cup semi-final and then against Chelsea in the final, Arsenal produced two tactically astute performances which defeated not only those two sides, but two coaches both perceived to be in advance of Arsenal and Wenger.

In both games, we returned to Wenger's first year at the club and employed a three centre-back system with high wing-backs and a deep-laying central midfielder – the idea being to flood the midfield – and, through an uncharacteristic commitment to the press, we stopped both teams from playing through us. Also, in both games, Özil delivered something close to a masterclass playing between the lines.

Against City, we rode our luck; coming from behind to win 2-1, it felt a million miles away from the capitulation against Bayern just a few weeks earlier.

Five straight wins leading into the final saw us taking a degree of confidence into a game which two months earlier we would have been watching from behind the sofa. Wenger employed the same system as against City in the semi-final but this time, crucially, selected Mertesacker for his first start of the season. It is arguable that had Koscielny not been given a straight red in the final league game, then Mertesacker may never have played. It seemed a huge gamble to play Mertesacker, who was missing any kind of match sharpness, and who had no pace or great mobility, up against the mean and uncompromising Diego Costa but it turned out to be a masterstroke. The big German had the assassin-like Costa in his pocket as he produced the classic centre-back performance, using every last bit of his experience to blot out a man who scored 59 times in just 120 appearances for Chelsea. It was the high point of Mertesacker's playing career with us and his performance was outstanding, especially considering it was his first game of the season.

The team from Stamford Bridge had already secured the title and were most people's favourites to clinch a Double. But Arsenal excelled on the day; at times, we were well on top and Chelsea didn't quite know how to play against us, when to press and when to drop, and again Özil responded with one of his last great Arsenal performances. As with the final against Hull, it was Ramsey who scored the winner.

Ramsey was a real credit to the club; in my opinion, it was only his injuries which held him back from being truly world-class. He left a real mark on the club and his two cup final-winning goals are there in the record books.

In many ways, you had to acknowledge that to select Mertesacker was not only a big and brave call but also very astute – for he neutralised Chelsea's matchwinner. Arsenal had won the cup for a record 13th time and no other manager had won more FA Cups than Wenger (seven).

He had twice sent his team out at Wembley against better opponents and had confounded expectations; both performances went a long way towards potentially vindicating the decision to have renewed his contract two years earlier.

Three FA Cups in four years went some way towards re-establishing Wenger's relevance to the modern game, especially in the manner of this, his latest triumph. When he put his mind to stopping the opposition, Arsenal looked an infinitely better team.

Before the cup final, a parting of the ways had seemed much more likely than at any other stage of his time with the club. Did the cup win complicate things for the board or allow Wenger an honourable way out? I vehemently hoped it would be the latter. I just couldn't see him wanting to get to grips with things over the course of a season as he had in those two one-off cup ties and now that we had failed to qualify for the Champions League, he was looking more vulnerable than ever before. He had gone some way towards answering a number of his critics; but, in reality, he would probably only ever be one defeat away from the same kind of anger being directed towards him when the new season kicked off. The toxicity around Wenger should have been enough for Wenger to meet up with the Kroenkes, come to a financial agreement and step down. He should have done this for the health of the club, which was tearing itself apart.

As far as I was concerned, the cup win changed nothing: thanks for everything you have done for us Arsène, but the future of the club is for someone else to shape.

## Chapter 41

# 2017/18

ON THE back of three FA Cups in four years, the board probably felt they had no option but to offer Wenger a new two-year deal. As far as I was concerned, it was the worst thing they could have done. It felt like the board had retreated a little from the levels of leadership they owed the club, no matter what personal loyalty they may have individually and collectively felt they owed to Wenger.

It was a dismal, unhappy season: we lost 13 league games, conceded in excess of 50 goals in the league alone and tamely surrendered our FA Cup at the first hurdle, losing 4-2 at Nottingham Forest. We did get to the League Cup Final but were outmuscled by Manchester City, going down 3-0. City's first goal summed up everything that was wrong with us at the time: a simple ball over the top for Aguero to run on to after too easily pushing Mustafi aside, while the big German defender lamely appealed for a foul while sat on his backside. You could almost hear Tony Adams snarling: 'Take the ball and the man.'

There was also a run to the semi-finals of the Europa League but, just days before the first leg of the semi-final, Wenger announced his intention to leave the club at the end of the season.

Finally, the long, unhappy saga could be put behind us. Once it was announced, I suspect there was some hand-wringing and a bit of 'Oh, what have we done?' in some quarters but the whole season had been played under a cloud; the optimism the cup win generated dissipated quickly and I was as relieved as I was pleased to know he was going.

Alexis cleared off to Manchester United and I think Wenger made a massive blunder of the whole saga. In the summer of 2017, only six months before Alexis walked out of the door, Arsenal had received a bid of £50m from Manchester City and the player desperately wanted to go. Crucially, he had only one year left on his contract but, incredibly, Wenger turned down the offer. I couldn't believe it; it was almost as if he was being disrespectful or even spiteful towards the Kroenkes. To this day, I remain really unhappy about his actions. It was £50m down the drain. And to rub salt into the wound, when Alexis moved to United we got Mkhitaryan – a player I would have thought expensive if he was free. I don't think United could believe their luck that they could unload Mkhitaryan so easily.

In January, the board had informed Wenger that he was being released from the final year of his contract, which would be paid up in full; the timing of the announcement was left to Wenger's discretion. The board's decision coincided with one particularly gruesome run of results which culminated in one of our most pale and bootless performances, losing 2-1 at Brighton; the side that day were unrecognisable as an Arsenal team.

Wenger chose to announce his departure on 20 April in a statesmanlike manner. There was no public ill feeling and the parting was as civil and respectful as possible. What the statement didn't say, and this will be no surprise, is that Wenger really did not want to go.

Despite spending over £100m on Alexandre Lacazette and Pierre-Emerick Aubameyang, we had fallen well off the pace. These two deals begged more questions than they answered. For one thing, what did they say about sensible team planning?

Wenger had been linked with Lacazette for quite some time but a deal never materialised because, despite Lacazette's fine goalscoring record in France, Wenger clearly had reservations. These may have centred on concerns around Lacazette's stamina levels for English football. So, this was a massive panic buy for a huge fee, with Aubameyang following him into the club for an even bigger fee not long afterwards. I'm still not sure what the board or owners were thinking by authorising Aubameyang's transfer; considering they had already decided, or were close to deciding, that Wenger was leaving at the end of the season, the £56m they sanctioned to be spent on Aubameyang seems to suggest they had taken leave of their senses.

A final personal gripe against Wenger was the sale of Giroud to Chelsea. He was still a great asset to our squad but Wenger felt he owed it to the player to let him leave for a club where he would be a starter and, therefore, have a better chance of selection for the French squad for the forthcoming World Cup; very decent but, as

I see it, Wenger was looking after the player's interests in front of the club's.

Considering how bad things were, I think the club did well to give an impression of holding it all together until the Europa League semi-final and when the night of the game came along, we put all thoughts of Wenger behind us. Appropriately enough, it was one of those typical Arsenal European nights. Atlético had a player sent off very, very early and we played them off the park. We could have been three or four up within 15 minutes but we didn't take our opportunities. A single goal was all we had to show for the chances that added up well into double figures; and then the sucker punch – a late Antoine Griezmann equaliser. We really had played well but the football gods had fallen well and truly out of love with Wenger by then.

The second leg was a noisy and passionate night in Madrid and it was perhaps inevitable that one of Wenger's tormentors from the past would come back to haunt him in his last chance to sign off with silverware – Diego Costa. He scored a typically clinical goal and, though we huffed and puffed and never gave in, there was just too much stacked against us. Our Achilles' heel for so long had been streetwise teams and here again a possibly inferior football team had outsmarted us.

Everything around the club was demoralising at this time, nothing more so than the attendances at the Emirates. It was humiliating: there were great swathes of empty seats. And most of those seats were owned by season ticket holders who had paid big money for their tickets and now couldn't be arsed to attend. Then, to cap it all, the PA announcement of the attendance would be given as 59,600! It had been like this going back over a number of seasons, too.

The season careered into the slow lane and, devoid of passion, came to a rest. Wenger's final game at the Emirates had an air of thanksgiving about it with an emphatic 5-0 victory in the sunshine. Afterwards, watched by the playing staff, coaching staff and some ex-players, he spoke to the crowd. It was a ceremony heavy with reminders of Wenger's glory days. '49, 49 undefeated ... playing football the Arsenal way', sang the crowd as Wenger received, as a leaving gift, the golden Premier League trophy awarded to us in recognition of the 'Invincibles' season – two outstanding achievements, amongst many others, that now only emphasised the decline of later years.

It was, perhaps, apt that Wenger's final game in charge should have been at Huddersfield Town. We once lured the great Herbert Chapman away from Huddersfield. Chapman, the great moderniser, had been responsible for redefining the club's place in the world; Wenger did that, too, but for the modern age. Chapman and Wenger were separated by nearly 70 years, yet their projects had been so similar: to create a new Arsenal like no one could ever have imagined possible and, in so doing, proscribe what the future of the game would look like. Some events become so profoundly significant that they mark the beginning or end of a passage of time. For many, and not just those sentimentally disposed towards Arsenal, Arsène Wenger is just such a reference point for contemporary football: Wenger is where modern football began.

Away from the limelight, though, Wenger was unquestionably bitter about how things had worked out. David O'Leary suggested to me that Wenger was still unable to accept what had happened and felt badly let down by the club and I think that is still the feeling which prevails in Wenger's heart today.

We are still too close to properly assess Wenger in a way that doesn't allow the disappointments of the latter years to obscure the glories of the former.

# Part Seven: Unai Emery

## Chapter 42

# 2018–2019

ON REFLECTION, Unai Emery never stood a chance. A poisonous dressing room, appalling player recruitment, which I suspect Emery had little influence over, some confused tactical thinking and problems expressing himself in English did for him. Did any of us really know what we wanted after Wenger? So much energy had been put into voicing a wish for him to leave that I don't think anyone had a clear idea of what we wanted the future to look like.

Emery felt like a reasonable choice: he had a proven track record and, crucially, the experience that Arteta lacked but a two-year contract didn't feel like a massive vote of confidence in him from the club. Initially, Emery set out a plan which, after several years of *laissez-faire* thinking, seemed promising, at least. We were to be 'protagonists', according to Emery, on the front foot, being assertive. I liked this. Sokratis and Torreira fitted this profile. Sokratis was maybe past his best but he instinctively felt like the sort of centre-back we had been missing and I thought him a good stop-gap signing. Torreira came to us with an outstanding reputation.

I think that when he signed, he was the second most effective defensive midfielder in Europe. Under Emery, though, Torreira's role would quickly change. Emery, for some reason, decided that, for a player who had very little goal threat in him, he was better suited to playing further forward and we never really saw anything from the Uruguayan after that.

Initially, things looked good; a 22-game unbeaten run, including 11 straight victories, suggested that even if the corner hadn't been turned, it was at least in sight. The high spot was a vibrant victory against Tottenham, with Guendouzi outstanding, early in his reign and it felt like such a breath of fresh air that you sensed a little of the immediate past being blown away. The Emirates felt brighter and less cluttered with unhelpful memories after that victory.

At some stage we morphed, again according to Emery, into a 'pragmatic' team; the boss had shifted to a tactical approach which would be based on the opposition and how to nullify them. This approach seemed suited to when we played against better teams; against sides we ought to be beating, however, it could make us look cumbersome and flat-footed, without any real idea.

True to Emery's previous success in Europe, there was a Europa League Final. By the time the game against Chelsea came around, in Baku, things had started to fall apart and I don't think any of us took much hope into the game. Ultimately, it produced a 4-1 defeat, an awful performance and a truly dispiriting experience. Only UEFA could get two teams who played in the same city to travel halfway round the world for a game. If ever you wanted an example of how far football has drifted, in the hands of corporate interests, from being the 'people's game', this was it. The season ended in turmoil, which felt like nothing more than a continuation of what had gone before.

The summer's recruitment did little to lighten my mood. We signed Pépé for a club record fee of £72m and, in doing so, went explicitly against Emery's wishes to recruit Zaha instead – a player desperate to sign for us. Tierney, with his kit in a plastic Tesco bag, appeared a great character, a bit of a throwback to an earlier age … but £25m for someone who was never fit?

After all the recent years of angst and unrest around the club, it was inconceivable to think that by the time Wenger had gone, the bottom had still not quite been struck. That happened in late October 2019. The playing out in public of this painful episode signalled a new low. Responding to the boos which greeted him as he left the pitch, throwing his shirt to the ground and walking straight down the tunnel resulted in Xhaka losing the captaincy of the club. In a nutshell, it seemed to capture the disconnect between club and supporter, a distance that felt as if it was widening once again as Emery's honeymoon period came to an end.

In a considered response, Xhaka apologised but, importantly, outlined the background to the flashpoint which had at that moment come to a head and caused him to respond as he did. He set out the kind of abuse he had been receiving on social media from supporters, targeting his family as much as at him. In wishing 'cancer on his daughter', the perpetrators of such unforgiveable behaviour said much more about themselves than their supposed support for our club. Under Arteta, he would go on to enjoy a rehabilitation which would see him re-emerge as an important cog in the new machine. Through his commitment to the cause, his leadership qualities and human decency, he totally won me round. For season after season, he was played out of position and when finally given a role commensurate with his ability, he became the player he was always capable of becoming with us. But at the time, the incident felt bad and suggested Emery was beginning to lose the run of things; I think this and a run of seven winless games precipitated the end for him.

A two-year contract eventually proved optimistic and in the autumn of his second season, Emery was sacked. Perhaps the club needed those 18 months of implosion, a short burst of blood-letting, before the future could begin.

Emery's subsequent successes with Villarreal and Aston Villa have done much to restore his reputation. He weathered the storm at the Emirates with dignity and I tend to view that period in our history as him being the right man but at the wrong time.

# Part Eight: Mikel Arteta

## Chapter 43

# 2019–2024

MIKEL ARTETA'S first press conference set an immaculate, pitch perfect tone. He seemed to instinctively understand Arsenal. When he applied for the job, he would have been fully aware of our bloated, substandard, overpaid squad, some of whom were potentially going to be troublemakers, too. He would have explained to the owners that the task of revamping this squad was not going to be quick, would need patience and financial support so that he could, piece by piece, put together his team, which would once again have Arsenal challenging for major honours. For Arteta, it was always going to be about camaraderie, too, a tight dressing room, with every player trusting one another and pulling in the same direction: the team above all else.

    He galvanised the entire club: everyone had a role to play in creating that key aspect of the successful modern football club – the 'winning culture'. From top to bottom, we won or lost as one. He talked of humility and accountability and essentially of the need for those two beating hearts of the club, the team and the supporters, to reconnect – if they did, we would be unstoppable. It was his idea to have Louis Dunford's 'The Angel', better known as 'North London Forever', played in the moments leading up to kick-off at the Emirates. A choreographed but totally authentic few moments which I think help connect everyone and centres the players on the fact that they represent a physical place, the streets and alleyways where people live their lives.

    I think we all knew Arteta would be starting from scratch when he arrived but all we asked for at that stage was a team we could believe in; a team that looked like it cared. Prowling on the touchline, he looked like nothing we had ever seen before but his newness brought us back to our roots; he clearly understood what Arsenal stood for and quickly gave us an authenticity we had lacked for some time.

Not long before he succeeded Emery, he had visited the Emirates with Manchester City and triumphed 3-0. The mood that day around the ground was a spiky mixture of frustration crossed with anger and a defeated resignation; a heavy and toxic atmosphere. A clear illustration of that toxicity was the relationship, such as it was, which existed between the supporters and Granit Xhaka. After the unpleasantness of the Crystal Palace game, Xhaka's heart and head were already on a plane out of London but Arteta calmly convinced him he needed him and that he had a role for him. Over the next four years, Xhaka would re-emerge as a footballer transformed: it was the first example of Arteta's almost militant positivity, which left no room for doubt, uncertainty or distrust.

He had COVID-19 and the eerie, echoey emptiness of grounds to contend with in his first season, which oddly might have helped him a bit, as he began to get to grips with the task away from the immediate glare and emotional response of supporters now almost programmed to suffer and complain. Over the first couple of years, the performances and, indeed, some of Arteta's decisions were questioned on occasion by a fanbase which could be impatient and unable to understand Arteta's 'process'.

Winning the FA Cup in his first season was an early vindication of the decision to appoint him. Even at that stage, he was considered an immensely talented young coach with a big future: Pochettino made overtures to Arteta in trying to bring him to Tottenham, which he rejected, recognising his destiny lay at the other end of the Seven Sisters Road.

The record-breaking 14th FA Cup triumph was as welcome as it had been unexpected. I think the fact that Arteta was able to organise the team he inherited, especially the defence, to beat two top teams – Manchester City in the semi-final and Chelsea in the final – immediately marked him out as a coach who was going places. Going a goal down in the surreal atmosphere of an empty stadium, we rallied and were well worth our eventual 2-1 victory but, in truth, it felt as if the process Arteta was asking us to trust in had really barely begun.

There were high profile casualties – Özil and Aubameyang the most prominent. I think the arguments around Özil had persisted for just too long; a disruptive sideshow which ran alongside the real business of forging a new Arsenal team. It was a sideshow that had likely inconvenienced Wenger and Emery before him but, while Wenger didn't want to act and Emery possibly felt as if he didn't yet have the authority to act, Arteta pressed ahead with what he believed was the right thing to do for the team, squad and club. With Aubameyang, I think we were left with a bad taste in our mouth once Arteta offloaded him but it is only fair to acknowledge his form had been outstanding, his winning goal in the cup final a case in point. Ultimately, his contract wasn't his fault; it was Arteta and the board who sanctioned it in trying to mitigate the risk of losing him on a free.

When the European Super League was announced, with Arsenal a part of it, the Kroenkes came in for some stick. If I am honest, I was never a critic of our American owners, other than in connection with the proposed European breakaway league and that I thought they shouldn't have persevered with Wenger for so long. To my mind, they have backed every one of their managers in a big way financially, only to see fortunes frittered away. So, to the fans, the Kroenkes must seem like fair game; but did they really deserve it? The European venture was a mistake but one that was mirrored by other greedy Premier League owners.

In the turbo-charged world of elite football, by the time Arteta's Arsenal had finished eighth for the second season running under him and then fifth after a disastrous start to the season and a weak finish which saw us pass up a Champions League spot following ragged defeats at Tottenham and Newcastle, there were some sounds of dissatisfaction; nothing like the civil war that marked Wenger's final years but audible questions nonetheless. And then, just as quickly, the clouds parted and the sun shone and we were suddenly Manchester City's only serious challenger. In fact, we were looking at one stage favourites to win a first title since 2004 until injuries pulled us up with a reminder that you don't win titles anymore without two high quality players for every position and a bit of know-how.

As a guide to establishing Arsenal's improvement then, take a look at the stats: under Arteta, our points tally for each season incrementally improves year on year.

In 2022, we had welcomed Jesus and Zinchenko from Arteta's old stomping ground, Manchester City, but it was the young French centre-back William Saliba, back from his loan spell in France, who made the greatest impact. Initially, I think Arteta had some reservations about him, doubts I shared when I watched his early games out on loan, but, without question, he flourished at Marseille. The season also confirmed the importance of Saka and Ødegaard to Arteta's project. We reached 50 points by the halfway stage, a figure only equalled once before. We looked on target and, until March, likely to topple City and take the title. Saliba proved again how important he was; for, as he picked up an injury in March – which would sideline him until the season's end – we fell away after being five points clear at the top. When Tomiyasu also picked up an injury, our season was totally derailed. Saliba had been operating at world-class level in almost every game and was irreplaceable.

Twice we surrendered two-goal leads in crucial games and although the setback at West Ham was the more unexpected, it may have been the draw at Anfield which psychologically did the more damage. It is odd that, while we would get closer the following season, this one strangely feels like the title which might have got away. Our football had been brilliant at times but the injuries and the pressure of City breathing down the necks of our very young team proved just a bit too much for us.

The 2023/24 season was a near perfect one. The levels of endurance, resilience and durability that Arsenal reached can rarely have been attained without a league title to show for them. It had taken six transfer windows for Arteta to start to show a sustainable improvement in performances but now each window seemed to dramatically enhance the squad, which still only really lacked depth. Raya, Havertz and Rice all arrived and showed that Arteta was prepared to ruffle feathers for improvements, trust his instincts and back his judgment with big transfer fees – all three signings would have a big season.

City were pushed to the last game and survived our run of 16 victories from the final 18 games – a brilliant run of results but one which proves that, these days, 'near perfect' isn't necessarily quite good enough. Defensively, we were at levels which would have made George Graham proud: 18 clean sheets and the lowest goals against total for the division. Saliba and the 'King of Brazil', Gabriel, must take so much credit – the best central defensive partnership at Arsenal since Campbell and Toure and close to being the foremost partnership in world football. Both would lend their presence to a development at the other end of the pitch, too, with Arsenal's 20 goals for the season from set pieces. Arteta proved that he was very good at getting the basics right: a strong, resilient defence and, with Nicolas Jover's appointment as set piece coach, we reaped a significant reward from corners and free kicks.

In open play, Ødegaard began to present a case for being the complete midfielder he had been predicted to be early in his career before he became lost amidst the clamour and noise at Real Madrid. Saka, too, would enhance his 'star boy' reputation. Two young men, dedicated to their football, who revel in being loved by supporters and manager alike.

All three new boys made contributions. We all loved Ramsdale but Raya was always a big upgrade. All credit to Arteta, he wasn't going to shirk difficult decisions, even if they were unpopular with some fans. Rice carried on being the player who had dragged West Ham to an unexpected European success and shone as England began to fulfil the promise of yet another golden generation. Rice was simply immense in his debut season for us. Havertz, though, is the one for whom Arteta rightly wins plaudits. Before signing for us, he had fallen out of favour at Chelsea and seemed destined to cut short his stay in England; his promise had fizzled out. Indeed, Havertz is a strange case: capable of the most exquisite stuff, agile and hard-working but then, in his early days at the club, he looked like someone frightened to hit the ball too hard. Once a couple of goals were notched, we got used to hearing the ironic '£60m down the drain' chant more and more often and he has toughened up under Arteta, too. He appears a clever young man and he adds so much to the team and fans can sometimes miss the hard yards he puts in.

There was a heart-warming run to the quarter-finals of the Champions League, too; just to get beyond the first knockout round felt like success. The significance of that victory over Porto was felt by every supporter. Raya's penalty save was important, too – the moment he really won over the Arsenal fans.

Arteta remains irresistibly ambitious and now Arsenal are a coming force. I believe by next summer he will finally have the last pieces of the jigsaw in place. I think the supporters are right when they sing 'We've got super Mik Arteta; he knows exactly what to do'. I don't doubt it. George Graham also won a trophy in his first season, slightly ahead of schedule, and then went on to build an Arsenal team that could look any of its predecessors in the eye. Arteta is destined to do the same.

The club is now on a different level to when he arrived. He has developed a squad which is comparable to some of the best in Europe and, most importantly, he has given our fans back their pride. It wasn't only matters on the field which needed his attention, either. Fortunately, he was blessed with the energy to see his masterplan implemented.

The club is unrecognisable from the angry, unsettled, apathetic place it once was in recent history. The Kroenkes now receive the respect they deserve, for they have backed their managers with signings and contracts. I think a greater level of understanding and trust has now grown between the owners and the supporters and this has been helped by the success the team are once again enjoying.

You get a feeling about a manager. When a banner was produced bearing the Spanish word 'vamos', it was well chosen – 'let's go' and 'come on' are its nearest English translations. Arteta has signalled that call to arms that, in my lifetime, has been sounded before: I heard it under Mee, under Graham and under Wenger and the team and the supporters responded.

So, be proud of our heritage and everything that Arsenal represents; but also do the same as I have done for 75 years and follow Arsenal through thick and thin.

# Epilogue

I'VE BEEN supporting Arsenal now for more than 70 years and, since my first game at Highbury in 1952, I have been privileged to have seen Arsenal win seven league titles, 11 FA Cups, two League Cups, one Fairs Cup, one European Cup Winners' Cup, plus ten Charity/Community Shields (plus one shared Charity Shield). I have never seen Arsenal outside of the top flight; a run of consecutive seasons which presently adds up to 108 – no other club comes close. I have witnessed in the flesh every major Arsenal success, with the exception of the COVID-hit FA Cup victory of 2020.

I have seen some fabulous world-class footballers in our famous red and white: Joe Mercer, Jack Kelsey, Joe Baker, Frank McLintock, Liam Brady, Tony Adams, Dennis Bergkamp, Thierry Henry, Cesc Fàbregas and Martin Ødegaard ... the list is as endless as it is subjective; simply so many wonderful players.

Great games shine still in the darkness of history, afternoons and evenings when my world was illuminated – Anfield 1989, Anderlecht 1970 and Copenhagen 1994 to name but three – plus those great Double seasons of 1971, 1998 and 2002. And, for good measure, I've twice seen the Gunners clinch the title at White Hart Lane – one a Double season, the other an 'Invincible' season.

After years of confusion and drift, Bertie Mee, a man carved from the rock of Arsenal past, duly returned us to the glories of earlier years. While Arsène Wenger and George Graham probably represent the two extremes of our football – one irresistible, the other immoveable – all three managers oversaw revolutions which came to define great periods in our history and, in Wenger's case, an influence which extended beyond the shores of English football.

It is apt that, as this story comes to a close, it is Mikel Arteta who leads us, a coach whose team showcases the best of all three of them:

the never-say-die of Mee, the dash and creativity of Wenger and the resilience and doggedness of Graham. Arteta feels like a man at one with Arsenal's history.

The modern game is a million miles away from the football landscape I grew up in. The football, the grounds and, not least, the players themselves are from a different world. It has been an honour to have known so many Arsenal greats but it couldn't happen now: the people's game is most certainly not 'of the people'.

As a young boy, the son of Polish refugees, I found a home at Arsenal and it quickly became my club, my life; indeed, it became my spiritual home and a lifelong obsession. I recognise that I couldn't have lived my Arsenal life without the support and understanding of my wife, Judith, to whom I would like to express my deepest love and most sincere gratitude. Judy has lived with my Arsenal obsession over so many years, fully understood and accepted my passion, never stood in my way or made me feel uncomfortable about it; even going as far as to attend games with me when the tension of it all was almost too much me. For her selfless support, I am forever grateful.

I would also like to record my pride and love for my two sons, David and Dean. David first attended Arsenal games with me in the late 70s as a boy and by the mid-80s, after a few turgid games representative of that era, it became clear that football and Arsenal were never going to be his thing. David has since gone on to be an academic pre-eminent in his fields of archaeology and anthropology and a best-selling author in his own right. It was Dean for whom the Arsenal spark caught early and over the years he has accompanied me to hundreds of games; and we've shared in some of our club's greatest moments. Dean has had a very successful career and is highly thought of in the music industry and is integral to my Arsenal life. I am delighted I have been able to share a large part of it with him.

After generations of new managers, players and teams, I remain as excited as I have ever been about the future. It is a passion which will never leave me.

After witnessing all the highs and the lows, I feel blessed to have had Arsenal in my life and I wouldn't change a single thing.

**MW & DF November 2024**